The Fascinating Girl

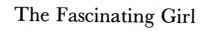

The Fascinating Girl

By HELEN B. ANDELIN

For information write:

FASCINATING WOMANHOOD
Box 3617
Santa Barbara, California 93105

Published by Pacific Press Santa Barbara
Box 3738
Santa Barbara, California 93105

9th Printing, 1977

Dedicated to every girl in the world.
Each one I revere as a potential
Fascinating Woman.

THERE IS IN THIS WORLD NO FUNCTION
MORE IMPORTANT THAN THAT OF BEING
CHARMING — TO SHED JOY AROUND —
TO CAST LIGHT UPON DARK DAYS. IS NOT
THIS TO RENDER A SERVICE?

VICTOR HUGO

A WORD OF EXPLANATION BY THE AUTHOR

Part I of this book is based upon the teachings of a former book I have written to married women, entitled *Fascinating Womanhood*. Where teachings parallel it has been necessary, for principles in winning men are essentially the same as for keeping them and making them happy. This book has its special approach, however, and much additional information has been added specifically for the single girl. It is a wholesome book written as a guide for girls approaching the marriageable age and is intended to offset some of the false and immoral teachings of our day. Many of the teachings of this book were inspired by a series of booklets published in the 1920s, entitled *The Secrets of Fascinating Womanhood*. These booklets have long been out of print and the authors unknown. Part II of this present work, "Strategy With Men," has been freely adapted from these booklets.

Contents

Introduction

The Secrets of Winning Men

We have all known women who have that "certain charm" which attracts men. Men flock around them like bees do honey, competing with one another for attention. These adorables seem to cast a spell upon almost every man they meet, while other girls who seem just as admirable and attractive go unnoticed and unappreciated.

What is this magical element of charm that wins the attention of men? Is it a pretty face? Not necessarily. Natural beauty is an advantage but it is not essential. Many girls who possess only slight physical beauty are fascinating to men, while others who are strikingly beautiful, from an artistic viewpoint, fail to interest men. Is it good grooming? Attractive clothes? To some extent it is, for a careless girl is not appealing to men. But there are girls who dress in the most stylish fashions and who are meticulous in their appearance who still fail to win the attention of men.

It is not necessarily wit, talent or intellectual gifts. These qualities are an advantage to any girl but they are not the elements of real feminine charm. No, there are girls who possess all of these qualities; they are beautiful, well groomed, becomingly dressed, and in addition are witty, intelligent and talented, yet they fail to win men's hearts. Other girls have none of these virtues to any great degree and yet captivate and fascinate men.

The girl who has this "special charm," who succeeds in winning the attention of a wide circle of men friends, unfortunately does not always win the particular man of her choice. This was the situation with Scarlett O'Hara in the novel *Gone With the Wind*. Scarlett was sought after by almost every young man in the community, but the man she thought she really wanted, she could not win. There was something missing in her, from this particular young man's viewpoint; something he felt essential and something which he found flowing freely in someone else — Melanie.

To be prepared, therefore, for the time when the right young man comes along, the one you really want, it is important that you acquire *all* of the elements of feminine charm. This book is devoted to a study of these essentials and will explain to you the principles involved in not only winning the attention and interest of many men, but in awakening the deepest feelings of love and tenderness in the particular man of your choice.

Is Sex One of the Secrets of Winning Men?

There is a mistaken idea in our modern times that "sex" is one of the secrets of winning men. Many girls have been led to believe that if they give themselves to a man in sex, they will keep his interest and eventually win him as a mate. The idea is not only erroneous, but can be one of the most disheartening experiences a woman can have. Although it may be true that a girl who yields will win a sex partner, she will not likely win a husband. Surveys show clearly that men who have sexual relations with girls, are not necessarily interested in them as mates. Of men studied in these surveys, 82% did not really care for the girls they were involved with, and only 14% were really serious.

Do not base your hopes on a false premise. If a man desires you for a sex partner it will not assure you that he desires you for a marriage partner, or that he necessarily even likes you. Sexual surrender is *not* one of the secrets of winning men into holy matrimony. It can, in fact, be a detriment, for men prefer to marry girls who are pure in character. Even more serious, pre-marital sex is a serious sin in the eyes of God. Those who indulge in it will lose the Spirit of God, the influence so greatly needed to guide them in this critical period of their lives.

Winning Men — A Justifiable Art

Do not think that there is anything wrong with the study of winning the attentions of men, or the strategy which is necessary in winning a particular man for a mate. In our Western culture a girl is left alone to find her marriage partner, without the help of parents or relatives. In other cultures, especially the Orient, and more in the past than the present, parents planned the mating of their children from early childhood. This may have had its disadvantages, but at least a girl did grow up free of the worry and responsibility of finding a suitable mate. In our society a girl has much stress placed upon her with the challenge she has before her to find a husband and father for her children, in the few short years she is considered available. I don't think we realize how some girls worry about it and many suffer because of it. Left without knowledge to guide them, some never succeed in winning the notice of men and others innocently make mistakes which drive men away. They feel "overlooked," "cast aside" and failures as women. The pain is deep and some even have had dreams about it which lasts for years, even after marriage.

The man is the pursuer, the girl the object of pursuit. This is not only custom, but basic nature of the masculine and the feminine. The girl must depend upon her charm, feminine wiles and ways and even strategy to win the man of her choice.

It is right and natural for every young girl to seek to be loved and to marry. It is not our plan, it is God's plan. She is seeking something more than just the man himself and the love that he bestows. She is seeking a life for herself, a larger and nobler life than single days offer. She wants a home of her own, a little nest to make comfortable and to warm with her love and kindness. She wants to be someone's partner and to share with him his joys and sorrows. She wants an opportunity to be a tender, loyal and devoted wife and the mother of a family. And she wants, above all, to avoid the narrow selfish life of living alone with no one to care for, to work for, to live and to die for. In fact, to want to find the man of her choice is the holiest aim a woman can entertain.

Learning the art of winning men has been rather a haphazard affair for young girls. There is little in print to guide them. The only school has been the school of experience, where lessons have been obtained at a high cost and where it is not expected that the education be complete or masterful.

Some girls, it is true, have been exceedingly fascinating and captivating, but they have relied more upon instincts to guide them than sound knowledge of basic principles. These few special charmers always do the right thing at the right time and every man they meet is more or less attracted. Other girls, though not so universally attractive, have their latent instincts for winning men aroused, when they meet a particular desirable man, who causes them to suddenly blossom out and show every evidence of real charm.

But there is a great army of girls, many of them both lovely and worthy, who cannot depend upon impulse and instinct for guidance in attracting men. Either through a lifelong habit of shyness or withdrawal from men, or through an artificial culture that has made the suppression of their natural feelings habitual, they have permitted their instincts to grow rusty. Even when nature does prompt them to do the right thing, so far as winning men is concerned, they hold back because of a typical distrust of their natural impulses or the fear of being childish. As a result, their instincts atrophy from disuse until they must depend upon something more than mere impulse for guidance in captivating men.

It is time, therefore, for a study to be made, an education offered for the most important area of a woman's life — that of winning her man and building for herself a happy home and thereby taking her proper place in society. *If you will study the subject you will find yourself capable of winning the interest of many men, where before you perhaps could interest but one or two. You will not find yourself attracting men you don't want and failing to attract the men you do. When you meet a man who is worthy of being a lifetime partner, you will not depend upon luck or instinct for success in winning him, but will depend upon sound knowledge of basic principles, upon understanding of men's characteristics and needs and upon the practical experience of thousands of women in attracting men.*

Do not think that men will mind the coming forth of this study. To find a girl who captivates him and turns his heart upside down is invigorating to a man and will give his entire life more meaning. Loving a woman is his most noble experience and marriage a part of the divine plan for him also. It is doubtful any man will mind being won by a lovable fascinating woman who would make him an ideal partner.

What This Book Can Do for You

You will learn:

What men find fascinating in women

The kind of woman a man wants

How to awaken a man's feelings of love and tenderness

How to understand men, their special needs, characteristics and vulnerable points

The way to self-confidence with men

How to be a good conversationalist

Feminine wiles and ways

The real charm that men find in women

How to be adorable when angry

How to make a man feel like a man

Strategy with men and keys to winning them

Where and how to find men

Choosing a mate — what to look for

The six stages of winning a man

How to make men notice you

Arousing his interest and love

Mistakes that drive men away

Sex and affection, the wise and the foolish aspects

Removing the obstacles to marriage

How to create romantic situations

Principles of inspiring a proposal

CHAPTER I

Celestial Love

Celestial love is a term I have used to describe the highest kind of tender love a man can feel for a woman. It is another name for true love, romantic love or story book love. This romantic love should be understood by all womankind, for it is the center of our happiness. Even in early youth, little girls have tender dreams of romance in which they are the beautiful princess who is sought after by the handsome prince. He asks for her hand in marriage and offers to give his life, if necessary, to make her happy. Cinderella and Snow White are favorites of little girls and revered by women of all ages. This tender, storybook love is what every woman has wanted since the world began. It has always been the theme of great operas, novels and songs. Romantic love, the most moving force in life, rightfully deserves our study and consideration.

The single girl must first bring her man to true love before he will have the courage to take the big step of marriage. Many fears stand in his way. Only the force of love will cause him to sacrifice his freedom, tax his usually limited resources and undertake the heavy responsibilities of marriage. After marriage, a girl must strive earnestly to maintain her husband's love if she is to make the ultimate success of her family life. Young women should take courage with the thought that they can both win and maintain a man's love by following certain established principles outlined in this book.

What is romantic love? When a man loves with all his heart he experiences an intensely thrilling sensation. It has been described as a feeling almost like pain. It can cause him to feel like biting his teeth together. He feels exuberant and light, like walking in clouds. At times he feels fascinated and enchanted with the girl. Along with all of these thrilling and consuming sensations there is a tenderness, a desire to protect and shelter

his woman from all harm, danger and difficulty. Then there
is the deeper and spiritual feelings of worship. Even this, perhaps, cannot adequately describe the "many splendored thing"
called love.

JOHN ALDEN AND PRISCILLA

There are many examples in literature of a man's deep love
for a woman. In Longfellow's account of John Alden and Priscilla, John speaks tenderly of her: "There is no land so sacred,
no air so pure and wholesome as is the air she breathes and
the soil that is pressed by her footsteps. Here for her sake will
I stay and like an invisible presence, hover around her forever,
protecting, supporting her weakness." Notice that John speaks
worshipfully of Priscilla and also with a tender desire to protect
and shelter her from all harm.

VICTOR HUGO'S LOVE — ADELE FOUCHER

Another illustration from literature, a tender protective feeling of love is found in the words of Victor Hugo, written about
the woman he loved in real life, Adel Foucher: "Do I exist for
my own happiness? No, my whole existence is devoted to her,
even in spite of her. And by what right should I have dared
to aspire to her love? What does it matter, so that it does not
injure her happiness? My duty is to keep close to her steps,
to surround her existence with mine, to serve her as a barrier
against all dangers; to offer my head as a stepping stone; to
place myself unceasingly between her and all sorrows, without
claiming reward, without expecting recompense. Alas! If she
only allow me to give my life to anticipating her every desire,
all her caprices; if she but permit me to kiss with respect her
adored footprints; if she but consent to lean upon me at times
amidst the difficulties of life." Notice here again, not only do
we find a protective feeling but one of worship, indicated by
his desire to "kiss with respect her adored footprints."

TEDDY ROOSEVELT'S LOVE — ALICE

President Teddy Roosevelt had a most devoted and tender
love for his first wife, Alice. She died after they had been married about a year and so crushed was he that he seldom talked

about her. In his diary he expressed his beautiful love for her: "Oh, how bewitchingly pretty she looked. If loving her with my whole heart and soul can make her happy, she shall be happy. The aim of my whole life shall be to make her happy and to shield and guard her from every trial. And Oh, how I shall cherish my sweet queen!" Later he writes:

"I am so happy that I hardly know what to do. My own beautiful queen is the same as ever and yet, with a certain added charm that I do not know how to describe. I cannot take my eyes off her. It seems almost profanation to touch her, no matter how gently and tenderly." And still later: "It is impossible to describe the lovely little ways of my darling. I can imagine no picture so pretty as her sweet self seated behind the tea things, in the daintiest pink and grey morning dress. She seems in beautiful health and she looks even prettier than she ever has before." Notice again the feeling is one of devotion, protection and worship.

WOODROW WILSON'S LOVE — ELLEN

Probably one of the finest examples of true and enduring love is found in the love letters of President Woodrow Wilson, written to his wife Ellen. After being married for 17 years, he writes: "All that I am, all that has come to me in life, I owe to you. . . . I could not be what I am, if I did not take such serene happiness from my union with you. You are the spring of content; and so long as I have you, and you too are happy, nothing but good and power can come to me. Ah, my incomparable little wife, may God bless and keep you." And after being married for 28 years he writes from the White House: "I adore you! No President but myself ever had exactly the right sort of wife! I am certainly the most fortunate man alive." And in another letter: "I can think of nothing, while I write, but only you. My days are not so full of anxiety and of a sense of deep responsibility as they are of you, my absent darling, who yet plays the leading part in my life, every minute of the day." These letters were taken from "The Priceless Gift," a collection of letters written by President Wilson to his wife Ellen. Each letter is a love letter, tender and devoted.

I only bring out these illustrations to show you what a tremendous feeling romantic love really is. And at this point I want to emphasize that in every case *the woman* awakens these feelings. They do not just arise spontaneously within the man, without anything on the outside to spark the feelings. The woman's actions awaken his love. And this is the kind of love she must arouse if she is to bring the man to the difficult step of marriage. Only such an overwhelming feeling of true love can cause him to face the responsibilities which will be his for a lifetime.

Some women falsely think that only a few men are romantic and adoring, that most men are more reserved, matter of fact and practical. This is simply not true. Every man has romantic feelings that can be awakened by an adorable woman. Some still argue that even though all men have the capacity to feel tender and devoted, they are hampered by their inability to express themselves. Here again the thinking is not true. Every man can and will express his love for a woman he worships, a woman who inspires these feelings. The warm tender letters of President Wilson were a surprise to many who knew his personality, that of an unemotional schoolmaster.

Is It Selfish?

A young girl's desire for devoted and tender love is not in any way selfish. In the first place she must awaken the man's love if she is to bring him to marriage, which is anything but selfish. The greatest contribution a woman can make to society is to marry, and to successfully fill her role as a wonderful wife, mother and homemaker. There is no greater aim than this. The very heart of this happy home is her marriage, which is kept together by the bonds of love.

The feeling of romantic love is also a benefit to the man. The thrilling sensation of love is a real joy to him, giving his life new meaning. He now has something to work for, to live for and if necessary to die for. Love provides him with incentive to excel and succeed in his work. He becomes a better person, and feels more like a man. The woman who awakens his love brings him fulfillment whereas the woman who fails robs him of one of his finer joys.

The aim of this philosophy is to teach you the principles of winning this romantic love, principles which have been proved in thousands of cases. This is accomplished by learning to understand men, their natures, characteristics and vulnerable points and just what it is they adore in women. We will study "the kind of woman a man wants," the kind he can treasure and cherish, and then will learn how we acquire these same fascinating traits and awaken his romantic love. Every woman can be adorable if she will only rely upon her natural instincts. Perhaps your own instincts have grown rusty, but they can be awakened and make you a more fascinating woman.

PART I

The Ideal Woman

CHAPTER II

The Kind of Woman a Man Wants

If you want to win the interest of men it is important to know just what it is men want or admire in women. It is useless to spend time, money and energy in grooming and training yourself to be appealing to men if you do not first find out just what men feel is important. This is not easy to understand since men and women differ in their opinions of feminine appeal.

DIFFERENCES IN VIEWPOINT

In considering the charms of womanhood, women are inclined to appreciate poise, talent, intellectual gifts and cleverness of personality, whereas men admire girlishness, tenderness, sweetness of character, vivacity and the girl's ability to understand men. A marked difference in viewpoint is in regard to appearance. Women are inclined to be attracted to artistic beauty such as the shape of the face, the nose, and artistic clothes. Men, however, have a different interpretation of "what makes a woman beautiful." They place more stress upon the sparkle in the eyes, smiles, freshness, radiance and the feminine manner.

If you want to be attractive to men, it is important to first understand this masculine viewpoint. Rid yourself of preconceived ideas, thoughts and standards of feminine charm so that you can understand more clearly what men want, for their standards of feminine perfection are different from our own. The things that we women admire in each other are rarely attractive to men. On the other hand, the characteristics which the average woman ignores or condemns in another woman are sometimes just the characteristics which make her fascinating to men.

Women are blind to their own charms, which is the very reason it is often difficult for them to realize what a man wants.

This difference in viewpoint is illustrated in Thackeray's novel *Vanity Fair.* For example, Amelia, one of the leading characters in the story, was not admired by the women of her acquaintance. As one woman put it, "She is facade and insipid!"; and another asks, "What could George find in that creature?" Then Thackeray adds a few observations of his own. "Has the loved reader, in his experiences of society never heard similar remarks by good natured female friends; who always wonder what you could see in Miss Smith that is so fascinating; or what could induce Major Jones to propose to that silly, insignificant, simpering Miss Thompson." But back to Amelia. What did the men in Thackeray's novel think of her? They considered her a "kind, fresh, smiling, artless, tender little domestic goddess whom men are inclined to worship."

Haven't you been puzzled at times to know what a certain man sees in a particular girl? To you she doesn't have any appeal, yet the man may be completely enamored. The fascination men feel for certain women seems to be an eternal riddle to the rest of her sex. Even when the man is asked "why," he finds himself at a loss to explain the spell cast upon him. And haven't you also known girls who appear to have all of the qualities which ought to please a man, yet they are unnoticed, neglected and unpopular with the boys. I know a girl who was very beautiful and well dressed. Her mother spent quite a lot of money on her clothes, but they still failed to attract the young men. In moments of discouragement she would look into the mirror and say woefully, "What is wrong with you?" She was blind and could not see the missing ingredients to her charm, because she was looking at herself through a woman's eyes.

This blindness on the part of women is why they spend countless hours on their appearance and may still fail to be fascinating to men. Appearance is important, but it is not all important. A woman must have a lot more to offer a man than an attractive outer shell if she is to win his heart. If you will observe, you will see many beautiful girls who dress in the finest clothes, yet who have failed to awaken the interest or attentions of men. And if you will look further, you will see others who are not particularly attractive, as we women see it, and yet they are very much sought after by men. In our study of the kind of woman a man wants, we must remember, then, that he judges with a different set of values. What are his values and what does he find appealing?

I will try to create in your minds an image of the kind of woman a man wants, the IDEAL WOMAN from a man's point of view. As you study these pages, try to build this image in your mind. Once you have this picture firmly established you will be drawn to it — you will tend to *be* this image.

You may wonder if this picture of "the ideal" does not differ in each man. Men do, of course, have different tastes. Some men want a woman who is quiet and retiring, others prefer one who is dashing and outgoing, and still others want a more dramatic or glamorous type. Some men like tall blondes; others prefer short brunettes. Some men appreciate a woman's ability to cook and sew while others insist a sense of humor is more essential. There are many different types of men in the world and they do not all want the same kind of woman. But with all their differences, men are still alike in their basic desires. There are certain qualities which have universal attraction and only certain ones will arouse their love. These are the qualities which we will analyze in our study of the kind of woman a man wants.

THE ANGELIC AND THE HUMAN

The kind of woman a man wants is divided into two parts. The one part is her spiritual qualifications. We will call this side of her the Angelic. The other part relates to her human characteristics, or her body and its expressions and motions. We will call this side of her Human.

Angelic   *Human*

Arouses a feeling   Fascinates,
near worship   Amuses

Brings a man deep   Arouses a desire
abiding happiness   to protect and
                                                     shelter

The angelic side of woman has to do with her basic character, her ability to understand men, the responsibility she assumes in her feminine role and the many virtues that she acquires. The human side refers to her appearance, manner and actions and includes the charms of radiance, bright eyes, smiles, delicate femininity and a quality of helpless dependency upon men for protection and guidance. Together these two qualities blended into one whole offer the perfect woman, from a man's viewpoint. They are both essential in winning his interest and love.

These two separate qualities arouse different feelings within a man's heart. The Angelic arouses a feeling near worship. The Human side, which is just as essential, fascinates and amuses men. The Angelic brings understanding and happiness to man, while the Human arouses in his heart a tender feeling, a desire to protect and shelter. Together the feeling is one of cherishing her.

DAVID COPPERFIELD

A perfect illustration of the Angelic and the Human in woman is in the story of David Copperfield, by Charles Dickens. Our ideal, however, is not represented by one woman, but by two, Agnes and Dora.

AGNES

Agnes represents the Angelic side of our ideal, the side which inspires worship. David Copperfield knew Agnes from childhood and worshipped her from the time he first beheld her. The following is a description of their first meeting and shows his feelings of worship.

"Mr. Wickfield (Agnes' father) tapped at a door in a corner of the paneled wall and a girl of about my age came quickly out and kissed him. On her face I saw immediately the placid and sweet expression of the lady whose picture had looked at me downstairs (her mother). It seemed to my imagination as if the portrait had grown womanly and the original remained a child. Although her face was quite bright and happy, there was a tranquility about it, and about her — a quiet good calm spirit — that I never have forgotten; that I never shall forget. 'This was his little housekeeper, his daughter, Agnes,' Mr. Wickfield said. When I heard how he said it, and saw how he held her hand, I guessed what the one motive of his life was. She had a little basket trifle, hanging at her side with keys in it, and she looked as staid and as discreet a housekeeper as the old house could have. She listened to her father as he told her about me, with a pleasant face; and when he had concluded, proposed to my aunt that we should go upstairs and see my room. We all went up together, she before us. A glorious old room it was with more oak beams and diamond panes; and the broad balustrade going all the way up.

"I cannot call to mind where or when, in my childhood, I had seen a stained-glass window in a church. Nor do I recall its subject. But I know that when I saw her turn around in the grave light of the old staircase and wait for me above, I thought of that window; and I associated something of its tranquil brightness with Agnes Wickfield ever afterwards."

David and Agnes became the closest of friends. She gave him comfort, understanding, true sympathy and comradeship. "As if," he writes, "in love, joy, sorrow, hope, or disappointment, in all emotions, my heart turned naturally there and found its refuge and best friend."

Agnes always had a sacred and peaceful influence on David. At one time, while under great stress and tension, he said, "Somehow as I wrote to Agnes on a fine evening by my open window, and the remembrance of her clear calm eyes and gentle face came stealing over me, it shed such a peaceful influence upon the hurry and agitation in which I had been living lately . . . that it soothed me into tears." But, although he had known Agnes since childhood, although he had worshipped her from the time he first beheld her, and although he senses all along that she alone is equipped to give him true sympathy and comradeship, he becomes madly infatuated not with Anges, but with Dora.

Dora

Dora represents the Human side of our ideal, the side that fascinates, captivates and inspires an overwhelming tenderness in a man's heart and a desire to protect and shelter. David describes her in the following words:

"She was a fairy and a sylph. She was more than human to me. I don't know what she was — anything that no one ever saw and everything that everybody ever wanted. She had the most delightful little voice, the gayest little laugh, the pleasantest and most fascinating little ways that ever led a lost youth into hopeless slavery. She was rather diminutive altogether . . . she was too bewildering. To see her lay the flowers against her dimpled chin was to lose all presence of mind and power of language in feeble ecstacy."

Her childlike ways, her dear little whims and caprices, her girlish trust in him, her absolute dependency upon others to provide for her, made an irresistible appeal to David's gentlemanly and chivalrous heart. She fascinated him, for he writes: "I could only sit down before the fire, biting the key of my carpet bag, and think of the captivating, girlish, bright eyed, lovely Dora. What a form she had, what a face she had, what a graceful, variable, enchanting manner."

Married to Dora, David Turns to Agnes

Yet even while such feelings toward Dora are at their highest, he misses the comfort, the understanding, the appreciation and the sacred influences of Agnes. "Dora," he tells Agnes, "is rather difficult to — I would not for the world say, to rely upon, because she is the soul of purity and truth — but rather difficult to — I hardly know how to express it. Whenever I have not had you, Agnes, to advise and approve in the beginning, I have seemed to go wild and to get into all sorts of difficulty. When I have come to you, at last, as I have always done, I have come to peace and happiness."

Dora's Homemaking

In marriage, Dora also failed as a homemaker. Their home was in constant clutter: "I could not have wished for a prettier little wife at the opposite end of the table, but I certainly could have wished when we sat down for a little more room. I did not know how it was, but although there were only two of us, we were at once always cramped for room, and yet had always enough to lose everything in. I suspect it could have been because nothing had a place of its own." Dora could not manage the household finances, nor the household help, although she tried. Nor could she cook, although David bought her an expensive cook book. But she used the book to let her little dog stand on.

The Void in His Life

While married to Dora he continued to love her. She fascinated and amused him, and he felt tenderly towards her. But it was not a complete love, nor did it bring him genuine happiness, for he said: "I loved my wife dearly, and I was happy; but the happiness I had vaguely anticipated once was not the happiness I enjoyed, and there was something wanting. An unhappy feeling pervaded my life, as a strain of sorrowful music, faintly heard in the night." And he said, "I wished my wife had had more character and purpose to sustain me; had been endowed with a power to fill up the void which somewhere seemed to be about me." Later on in the story Dora died and David turned to Agnes.

When married to Agnes, David enjoyed real peace and happiness, for she filled up the void in his life. She was a wonderful homemaker and gave him true understanding. They had children and a wonderful home life. His love for Agnes was holy, but — it was not complete. During his marriage to

Agnes he still had tender recollections of Dora that played upon his emotions. In thinking of her he writes: "This appeal of Dora's made such a strong impression on me. . . . I look back on the time I write of; I invoke the innocent figure that I dearly loved to come out of the mists and shadows of the past and turn its gentle head toward me once again."

On one occasion his little girl came running in to her father with a ring on her finger very much like the engagement ring he had given to Dora. The little ring — a band of forget-me-nots, with blue stones, so reminded him of Dora, that he said, "there was a momentary stirring in my heart, like pain!"

COMPARING THE TWO

If Agnes had had the girlishness, the adorable human and childlike manner of Dora, and her complete dependency upon man for protection and guidance, David would never have made the mistake of marrying another. His worship for Agnes would have turned into genuine love, into the desire to protect and shelter. On the other hand, if Dora had had the sympathetic understanding, the appreciation of his highest ideals and the depth of character that Agnes had, and had given his home order and peace, David's mad infatuation for her would have developed into everlasting adoration and love. Neither of the two, unfortunately for them, represents the whole of the Angelic and the Human. Each of them made mistakes, each of them won and lost David, but each of them is well worth emulating in some respects.

ANALYZING AGNES

What she had:

Agnes had four outstanding qualities that appeal to men, and they are all on the Angelic side of our ideal.

1. *She had a pure and lovely character,* for David always associated her with a "stained-glass window of a church," and said she had a sacred influence on him. Perhaps the greatest test of her character came when David married Dora. Even though Agnes herself loved David, she did not become bitter or resentful toward either of them, but continued her unselfish friendship to David, and became a friend to Dora as well. She had the courage to keep her love a secret and to live a useful

life in spite of her own disappointment. Further evidence of her character is shown in her devotion to her father and the sacrifice of many of her own pleasures for his sake.

2. *Agnes understood men.* She gave David true understanding. She knew how to rejoice with him in his triumphs and sympathize with him in his difficulties. She brought him comfort, peace and comradeship.

3. *She was a capable housekeeper.* From the time she was a child, Agnes was a "discreet little housekeeper." She took care of the meals, the house and her father, with womanly efficiency.

4. *Inner happiness.* As a result of her pure character, Agnes had a "tranquility about her, and a good calm spirit," which indicates peace, or happiness within.

What Agnes Lacked:

1. *She was too independent.* She was too hesitant to lean on David or to need him. She was too unselfish, for David said, "Agnes, ever my guide and best support — if you had been more mindful of yourself, and less of me, when we grew up together, I think my heedless fancy never would have wandered from you." Because she hesitated to lean on him for anything, this made her appear to be too independent. She did not appear to need his manly care and protection.

2. *She lacked the girlish, childlike, trusting qualities.*

3. *She lacked the gentle, tender, fascinating little ways that stir a man's heart.*

ANALYZING DORA

What she had:

1. *She had an enchanting manner.*

2. *She was childlike, girlish.* At times he would refer to her as his "child-bride." At times she would shake her curls as little girls do. Her attitude was childlike, trusting.

3. *She had tender little ways.* The way she laid the flowers against her dimpled chin, or the way she patted the horses or spanked her little dog, fascinated David.

4. *She was gay.* She had a gay little laugh, a delightful little voice, and the pleasantest little ways.

5. *She was bright eyed.*

6. *She was dependent.* She was helplessly in need of masculine protection and guidance. She had a girlish trust in David.

What Dora Lacked:

1. *She was a poor homemaker.* She could neither keep house, nor cook, nor manage her household expenses.

2. *She lacked character.* Dora was good, pure and kind, but she was very self-centered. David said, "I wished my wife had had more character and purpose to sustain me." She was too absorbed in her own little problems, cares, and whims to make a good wife.

3. *She did not understand men.* This was her greatest lack. She did not know how to offer sympathy, understanding, appreciation or intellectual comradeship, for he writes, "It would have been better if my wife could have helped me more, and shared my many thoughts in which I had no partner."

THE FEELING DAVID HAD FOR EACH OF THEM

The feeling David had for Agnes was one near worship. She had a sacred influence on him. She brought him peace and happiness, and without her he seemed to "go wild and get into difficulty." Thinking about her "soothed him into tears." He felt as though she were a part of him, "as one of the elements of my natural home."

The feeling he had for Dora was different. She fascinated and amused him; "she was more than human to me"; "she was a fairy and a sylph"; "I don't know what she was — anything that no one ever saw and everything that everybody ever wanted." All of her delicate and bright mannerisms aroused his irresistible longing to shelter and protect her.

I would like to stress that David Copperfield felt two distinctly different types of love of these two girls. David experienced a type of love for Agnes all along, but it was not strong enough to bring him to marriage. And even though this type of love brings men the greatest peace and the truest and most abiding happiness — it is not the most driving.

The kind of love David felt for Dora was forceful, consuming and intense. He felt like "biting the key of his carpet bag" when he thought of her; he was "in fairyland." He was "a captive and a slave." This type of love, however, was not complete, nor did it bring him real happiness, for he said, "I loved my wife dearly and I was happy; but the happiness I vaguely anticipated once was not the happiness I enjoyed and there was something wanting. An unhappy feeling pervaded my life, as a strain of sorrowful music, faintly heard in the night."

While married to Agnes he experienced peace and happiness and he loved her dearly, but he still had tender recollections of Dora which sent stirring feelings through his heart. David Copperfield never had the satisfaction of loving completely, for his feelings were inspired by two different women. Neither was the whole of our ideal, so neither could arouse his love in a complete sense.

There are many women such as Agnes, in this life — women with inspiring characters. They make wonderful mothers and homemakers and are good citizens. They are greatly appreciated, but if they lack the adorably human qualities that so fascinate men, they will undoubtedly fail to win the interest and love of men. A man wants more than an angel. On the other hand, there are some women such as Dora, who are tender, childlike and gay little creatures, but if they have not the depth of character and purpose, if they are too self-centered to be good homemakers and mothers, and if they lack the ability to understand men, they will only win a part of a man's love.

There is no reason why a woman cannot be both an Agnes and a Dora, for the Angelic and the Human qualities do not conflict. Both are a natural part of femininity and are essential to real feminine charm. Both the Angelic and the Human qualities are essential in winning men and in keeping them happy after marriage — thereby sustaining their love and devotion. Your complete happiness in marriage depends upon your development of both sides of our ideal.

DERUCHETTE

An example of a girl who had both the Angelic and the Human qualities is Deruchette, heroine of the novel, *Toilers of the Sea,* by Victor Hugo:

In describing Deruchette, Victor Hugo first compares her to a little bird that flits from branch to branch, as she moves about the house from room to room, coming and going, stopping to comb her hair, as a bird plumes its wings, and making all kinds of gentle noises, murmurings of unspeakable delight. She is "fresh and joyous as the lark." As one observes Deruchette, the author suggests, "one would almost be tempted to say, 'good morning, madamoselle goldfinch.' " "She has a childlike prattle" and "she who is one day to become a mother is for a long while a child."

You may think at this point, that Deruchette is a bit insipid, as the women did of Amelia in Vanity Fair. Remember, however, that Victor Hugo was a man, a rugged man who wrote challenging sea stories, speaking more the language of men than women. But here is a peek into his masculine viewpoint of true femininity.

When the young clergyman in the story proposed to Deruchette, he gave indication of her angelic qualities when he said, "There is for me but one woman on earth. It is you. I think of you as a prayer — you are a glory in my eyes. To me you are holy innocence. You alone are supreme. You are the living form of a benediction." Then Hugo goes on to describe Deruchette further:

"Her presence lights the home; her approach is like a cheerful warmth; she passes by, and we are content; she stays awhile and we are happy. Is it not a thing of divine, to have a smile which, none know how, has the power to lighten the weight of that enormous chain that all the living in common drag behind them? Deruchette possessed this smile; we may say that this smile was Deruchette herself.

"Deruchette had at times an air of bewitching languor; and certain mischief in the eye, which were altogether involuntary. Sweetness and goodness reigned throughout her person; her occupation was only to live her daily life; her accomplishments were the knowledge of a few songs; her intellectual gifts were summed up in simple innocence; she had the graceful repose of the West Indian woman, mingled at times with giddiness and vivacity, with the teasing playfulness of a child, yet with a dash of melancholy. Add to all this an open brow, a neck supple and graceful, chestnut hair, a fair skin, slightly freckled with exposure to the sun, a mouth somewhat large, but well defined, and visited from time to time with a dangerous smile. Ths was Deruchette."

There is in this world no function more important than that of being charming — to shed joy around, to cast light upon dark days, to be the golden thread of our destiny and the very spirit of grace and harmony. Is not this to render a service?

ANALYZING DERUCHETTE

Her Angelic Qualities:

1. *Her character:* "Sweetness and goodness reigned throughout her person." She had a character which was mindful of the needs of others, for she "cast light upon dark days," and had a "smile which had the power to lighten the enormous chain." Further evidence of her character is in her lover's statement that she is "holy innocence," "is like a prayer" and the "living form of a benediction."

2. *Domestic:* She was capable in her domestic duties, for her occupation is only to live her daily life," and "her presence lights the home."

3. *Inner Happiness:* Similar to Agnes, Deruchette possessed inner happiness, or she could not possibly have had such ability to radiate it to others.

Her Human Qualities:

1. *Childlikeness:* Like Dora, Deruchette had childlike ways. "She who is one day to be a mother, remains for a long while a child." She had a "childlike prattle" and "certain mischief in the eye," and at times "the giddiness and vivacity, and the teasing playfulness of a child."

2. *Changefulness:* Deruchette was not at all times the same. Sometimes she was radiantly happy and full of giddiness and vivacity; at other times she had an air of "bewitching languor." Although she was sweet and good, at times she had "a certain mischief in the eye." Sometimes she was full of teasing-playfulness, and at other times, "a dash of melancholy." Changefulness is also a childlike quality.

3. *Fresh appearance:* "She is *fresh* and joyous as the lark."

4. *Gentle:* Her gentle qualities are described in her voice; "She makes all kinds of gentle noises, murmurings of unspeakable delight."

5. *Radiates Happiness:* The most notable quality she had was her ability to radiate happiness. This was a part of her character, manner and actions.

    a. She was fresh and joyous as the lark.

    b. She shed joy around.

    c. She cast light upon dark days.

    d. Her presence lights the home.

    e. Her approach is like a cheerful warmth.

    f. She passes by and we are content.

    g. She stays awhile and we are happy.

    h. She has a smile which had the power to lighten the weight of that enormous chain which all the living in common drag behind them — a dangerous smile which was Deruchette herself.

    i. At times she had giddiness and vivacity.

6. *Grace:* Not mentioned before, but similar to gentleness and tenderness is that of grace. Deruchette was the very spirit of grace and harmony and had the "graceful repose of the West Indian woman." Her neck was supple and graceful.

AMELIA

Another example in literature of a girl who was both Angelic and Human is Amelia, from the novel *Vanity Fair,* by Thackeray.

Thackeray says that Amelia is a "kind, fresh, smiling, artless, tender little domestic goddess, whom men are inclined to worship." A few pages further he calls her "poor little tender heart." In another place he attributes to her "such a kindly, smiling, tender, generous heart of her own." He admits that others might not consider her beautiful:

"Indeed, I am afraid that her nose was rather short, than otherwise, and her cheeks a good deal too round for a heroine; but her face blushed with rosy health and her lips with the freshest of smiles, and she had a pair of eyes which sparkled with the brightest and honestest of good humor, except indeed when they filled with tears, and that was a great deal too often; for the silly thing would cry over a dead canary, or over a mouse that the cat haply had seized upon; or over the end of a novel, were it ever so stupid."

Amelia had a "sweet, fresh little voice." She was subject to "little cares, fears, tears, timid misgivings." She trembled when anyone was harsh. Altogether, she was: "Too modest, too tender, too trustful, too weak, too much woman," for any man to know without feeling called upon to protect and cherish.

ANALYZING AMELIA

Amelia had several qualities worthy of our attention.
Her Angelic Qualities:
1. *Her character:* She had a generous heart and was kindly, and since "men are inclined to worship her," she evidently had a worthy character.
2. *Her Domestic Qualities:* Thackeray calls her "a little domestic goddess."
Her Human Qualities:
1. *Her freshness:* She had the freshest of smiles, and her face blushed with rosy health. She had a pair of eyes that sparkled. She had a sweet, fresh little voice.
2. *She had childlike emotions.*
Her eyes would often fill with tears.
She would cry over a dead canary, or a mouse or a novel.
She is subject to little cares, tears, fears, timid misgivings.
She trembles when anyone is harsh.
3. *Tenderness:* She was a "tender little domestic goddess." She was "too tender, too weak, too much woman."
4. *Trustfulness:* "She was too trustful."

SUMMARY

As we come to the end of our study of these four women, we can see that there are many qualities which men admire in women. Now, I am going to blend these appealing qualities into one whole, the total woman, the kind man is inclined to worship, to protect and to cherish.

On the following page is a diagram of the total woman, with the essential qualities which men find appealing. Although she is divided, you should always think of her as one, the angelic and the human combined. Together they form the ultimate in real feminine charm.

ANGELA HUMAN

The Ideal Woman, from a Man's Point of View

Angelic Qualities	*Human Qualities*
1. Understands Men	1. Femininity
2. Has Deep Inner Happiness	2. Radiates Happiness
3. Has a Worthy Character	3. Fresh Appearance and Manner
4. Is a Domestic Goddess	4. Childlikeness

The Angelic side of woman arouses in man a feeling approaching worship. These qualities bring peace and happiness to man.

The Human side of woman fascinates, amuses, captivates and enchants man. It arouses a desire to protect and shelter.

Together He Cherishes
Both Are Essential to His Celestial Love

IS BEAUTY NECESSARY?

It is interesting to note that none of these authors placed importance upon natural beauty. Though they go into ecstacies over the girl's smile, or the similarity of her manner to that of a bird, or the glowing health that shows in her sparkling eyes and joyous manner; though they describe at length her tenderness and childlikeness and maintain the irreproachable purity and gentleness of her character, none of these authors claims that his heroine is exceptionally beautiful to the eye.

Amelia, for example, is chubby and stout, with a very imperfect nose: "Her nose was rather short than otherwise, and her cheeks a great deal too round for a heroine." Deruchette's complexion was marred by freckles and had a mouth somewhat large. So far, in fact, are the authors from claiming beauty for these young charmers that aside from pointing out the defects mentioned, they make no attempt to describe the outward appearance. To them, as well as to most other men, the most attractive and desirable thing in a woman is not her outward beauty, but her delicate feminine manner and actions and her fresh, radiant qualities. Agnes and Dora were both beautiful girls, so David's attraction was based upon their other qualities. Admitting this, we will have to rely upon man's opinions, in guiding us to what they admire in women.

You may wonder, "How do I know if these qualities are charming to men? How can I prove these things to be true?" I must warn you — if you ask the average man to define a fascinating woman, you are apt to be disappointed. He may feel at a loss to describe his feelings in words. He only knows a charming quality when he sees it in action. It takes an author, such as I have referred to in these illustrations from classic literature to skillfully describe these attributes. Can the opinions of a few authors establish these things as true, you may wonder? If you are still in doubt, try acquiring these qualities and see for yourself how men react. Then you will be convinced.

Remember, it is possible for you to become fascinating — the kind of woman a man wants, as described in this chapter. This goal is attainable, regardless of the attributes you were born with and your personality and character as they are now. You can take upon yourself finer qualities, greater charm and allurement which will aid you in winning a desirable man.

WHEN MEN MARRY GIRLS WHO SEEM UNATTRACTIVE

Now and then we will see an especially eligible and attractive man marry a girl who, to all the rest of us, appears to lack the qualities of feminine charm. They do not seem feminine, girlish, radiant, nor do they display any special merit of character. This frequently causes the question to arise, "what on earth can he see in her?" The answer is this: Just because a woman acts a certain way with all others is no reason for expecting she acts the same way for her man. Perhaps the man happened to surprise her in a moment when she had forgotten to put on her "company manner" and had acted rather childlike and gay. Or she may have portrayed a ray of angelic character that only he has detected. When he learns of this aspect of her nature, he is justified in feeling that he has discovered a woman of true charm.

An illustration of this may be of a woman who appears to everyone very businesslike and efficient, with a strong aggressive nature. She does not appear to anyone to be tender, frail, or childlike. Suddenly, however, a man comes along who appears to her a real hero. In the presence of what she thinks is his masterful strength, she feels as if her abilities, her efficiency, determination and vigor are as nothing. Much to her own surprise, she too begins to feel, in his presence, frail, weak, tender and little. At an unguarded moment she lets her manner and actions betray this feeling and the man's face lights up with interest. "What a delightful creature she really is," he thinks. "How mistaken I have been about her." And if you could peek in on them some evening you would find her acting the part of a "fluttering little bird." The only difference is that she is too proud or sensitive to act this part before others. As usual the world wonders what attracts the man to such a forbidding woman, entirely unconscious of the fact that she is not the same woman to him as she is to others.

The sad part of this situation is that women who tend to suppress their charm with an exterior of efficiency, may never have a man discover their true beauty. Many such women go through an entire life without a single man ever realizing their womanliness within. Such is the predicament of thousands of women who suppress their natural femininity and childlikeness. Unless some man comes along who calls it out and encourages it, they do not themselves know how womanly they really are and others cannot know. They think it impossible for them to act like the girls that usually attract men. You can rest assured, however, that these qualities are at the bottom of every woman's nature, placed there when she was born a woman and that they can be brought out either by her meeting with a particular man or by the exerting of her own determination to make herself an attractive woman.

Introduction to Understanding Men

The first quality of Angela Human is that of understanding men. Think of it as a definite quality, an ability to understand a man's characteristics, peculiarities and vulnerable points and to understand his special needs as a man.

Men are Different

The first thing to understand is that men are *different* from women — so different in nature and temperament that it is almost as though they came from another planet. Men do not think like women do, approach a problem in the same light, nor do they have the same sense of values or the same needs as we do. For example, the most central need a woman has is *to be loved,* whereas a man's most central need is *to be admired.* Because we fail to understand these differences we often supply men with the thing *we* need rather than the things *they* need. What are these needs of men?

Needs of Men

A man needs someone to talk freely to, someone to confide in, someone to run to in times of difficulty and in moments of achievement. He needs to have someone to rely upon, someone who will be his refuge and best friend. He needs sympathy in times of despair, and hope for the future — someone who can heal his wounds and restore his self esteem. He needs someone who will accept him for the man he is and who can perceive his truth worth. If a woman can be "all of this" to a man, she becomes indispensable to his happiness and is apt to be the "one woman in his life." Of course, it is not easy to win a man's confidence so that he will rely upon you as his refuge and best friend. But the art of knowing how to get a man to confide is also one of the keys to understanding men and one which will be taught in this book.

Agnes

Agnes had the ability to understand men. David turned to her again and again, both in difficulty and triumph, for he writes: "Whenever I have not had you, Agnes, to advise and approve in the beginning, I have seemed to go wild and to get into all sorts of difficulty. When I have come to you, at last, as I have always done, I have come to peace and happiness." And in another place, "As if, in love, joy, sorrow, hope or disappointment, in all emotions, my heart turned naturally there and found its refuge and best friend."

DORA

Dora did not have this ability to understand men, for David writes: "I did sometimes feel, for a little while, that I could have wished my wife had been my counselor . . . had been endowed with power to fill up the void which somewhere seemed to be about me." And further on: "It would have been better for me if my wife could have helped me more and shared my many thoughts in which I had no partner."

We will now devote ourselves to a study of men, their needs and feelings, their characteristics, peculiarities and their vulnerable points, so that we will be prepared to give them understanding. The following are the six characteristics of men, essential for any woman to know if she is to be able to *understand men*.

SIX CHARACTERISTICS OF MEN

1. His need to be accepted at face value
2. His need to be admired
3. His sensitive pride
4. His reserve
5. His need for sympathetic understanding
6. His need in his role as man

CHAPTER III

Accept a Man at Face Value

CHARACTERISTIC No. 1

The most basic thing to understand about a man is his need to be accepted at face value — accepted for the man he is. This means we accept his ways, his hopes and dreams, or his lack of dreams. We accept his ideas, his standards and his habits (both good and bad). We accept the little quirks in his personality, his religious views, and his political views and any traits he may have, for better or for worse. We are doing more than accepting him — we are accepting *his right to be himself*. We may not agree with his ideas, but we respect his right to his own viewpoint. We may notice his weaknesses, but we accept this as normal in human beings. We accept him for the man he is and look to his better side.

Don't make the mistake of trying to remake a man into something he is not or to offer little suggestions and hints for his self improvement. It may be all right for others to offer him constructive criticism, in the spirit of love and kindness, but not the girl he has romantic feelings for. The woman he loves must be willing to accept him at face value. In fact, to offer any indication that you are not satisfied with him just as he is may be the very thing that will discourage a man and drive him away.

It is an even greater mistake to expect to remake a man after marriage. This will only lead to trouble, for men will resist any effort on the part of their wives to make them over. It will lead to serious marriage problems that can even destroy the relationship. If you cannot accept a man as he is, it is better to face this fact and look for someone that you can accept. This makes "acceptance" an important consideration in the step of selecting a mate.

What Does Accepting a Man at Face Value Mean?

In the business world, "face value" has a specific meaning. It is the amount a bond or an insurance policy, etc., is worth today, or now. If held a number of years it would or could be worth a good deal more, but it does have a specific value now. And what does "face value" mean in reference to a man? It means what he is worth today, just as he exists now, with no changes made.

"Accepting a man at face value" means that we recognize him as a human being who, like ourselves and all other humans, is part virtue and part fault. It is a very honest approach. We realize that the faults are there, but we are not concerned about them, for we accept the total man. If he wants to change on his own, that is his business. We are satisfied with him as he is.

Acceptance does not mean tolerance, or "putting up with faults." Nor does it mean dishonesty — that we must convince ourselves that he is perfect, when he is not. Nor does it mean resignation. When you accept a man you see him as a total man and are content with what you see and prove your contentment by not *trying to change him*. Realize fully then, girls, that you will have to accept your man as he is and not expect to change him after marriage. With this thought in mind, use the utmost caution in selecting a mate — a man that you *can* accept as he is, with no changes.

His Need for Freedom

A man has a strong masculine nature of wanting to hold on to his freedom, even to the point of rebellion. He wants to be the kind of man he wants to be and do the things he wants to do and think the way he wants to think, etc. This does not mean that he does not respect the viewpoints of others, but it does mean that he does not like being "pushed." Especially does he not like being pushed by a woman.

His Need for Religious Liberty

When considering the serious step of marriage, it is wise to recognize the importance of *religious* freedom. Each individual has a right to his own religious views; it is our God-given right. Our nation was founded upon the principle of religious liberty.

The pilgrims left Europe because of it, and it is still just as important to each one of us today.

We do not have a right to expect another individual to adopt our viewpoint, or to make him feel obligated to do so. We can teach and inspire by example or instruction, but pushing our religious views onto someone else is a mistake, one which denies the individual the right to believe as he wishes and one which will surely lead to trouble in a relationship. When we do extend to another his right to religious liberty, his mind will function without barriers and he will be much more apt to be "open to religious viewpoints." Let me illustrate by the following experience.

SOME WISE COUNSEL

A girl was engaged to marry a man of a different religion than her own. Her religion was very important to her and she hoped that if she married him he would eventually join her church.

She sought counsel from a wise man who told her, "If you do marry this man, make nothing of his religious differences to him openly. Do not attempt to change his views, but rather recognize his religious freedom. If he wants to go to his church, go with him. Give him complete freedom but hold to your ideals and be the living example of what your religion teaches."

She did marry the man and she followed the wise man's advice. He did ask her to attend his church with him which she did willingly. In return, he was willing to attend hers. By comparing the two he soon became convinced that his wife's church was superior to his own and he became a member of it.

The way to acceptance is this. Respect a man's freedom to be himself and do the things he wants to do and think the way he wants to think. Accept him for the man he is, overlook his weaknesses, failures and faults and *look to his better side.*

A single girl in love may not feel this is a problem. When romance is in bloom, love is most often blind. She may feel he has no faults; at least she cannot see them. The young man may add to this blindness by "putting his best foot forward" and hiding his faults, which is only human nature for him to do. If such a blind state could continue after marriage, no problems in regards to "faults" would arise, but unfortunately we "wake up" after marriage and our husbands "relax" their better side and tend to be themselves.

The best way to avoid such a rude awakening is to take a good look at him before marriage and know just what it is you are going to have to accept. Get to know him by long hours of conversation. Ask questions on important topics. Find out his religious views, his views about family life and his standards and ideals. Talk to him about the future so that you will know his goals — his aspirations. Take a lot of time to get to know him. There is nothing like a period of time to reveal a person's "true self." Eventually those little faults which may have been obscure will become evident. This does not mean that you will not continue to respect him and to love him, but it does mean that you will be aware of what he is and what you will have to accept. You may have to force yourself to "open your eyes" and take a good look, but it will pay. You will then be able to judge for yourself if he is a man that you can accept.

Is There Ever a Time When I Should Not Accept a Man?

In answer, "No," there is never a time that you should not accept the man you love, but there are several occasions when you should *respond* to his faults in a certain way. Let me explain:
1. *When he is blind to his own mistakes:* Sometimes a man is blind to his own mistakes and such blindness causes him to get into difficulty with his associates or friends and even fail to reach success. On these occasions it is only right for the woman he loves to open his eyes. Take for example the salesman who uses a poor approach, or the department supervisor who is too dictatorial, or the student who is losing out because he offends the teacher, or even a man who is losing his friends because he has body odors. In these instances a woman should at least try to alert a man. Often others who observe his mistakes are not interested enough to awaken him, or may feel it is not their business to do so. She may be the only one who cares enough about him to help.

The way to do it is this: Keep in mind that *you do accept him.* It is the world that does not! Others are offended, not you. Tell him that you have a few ideas that might prove helpful. Let him know that you are not close to the situation as he is and that you could be wrong, but "could this be the cause of his trouble." Assure him that you admire him and isn't it regrettable that others do not esteem him for his true worth. Once you have opened his eyes, do not persist in the matter. Drop it completely. If he continues to make mistakes, fully aware of them, you will have to allow him this freedom.

2. *When he mistreats you.* Must you accept a man at face value when he mistreats you, and just overlook it? I am referring to times when he may be thoughtless, unfair or insulting or is even harsh or critical. A man is entitled to many freedoms but he does not have the right to mistreat you. You are a human being worthy of the highest respect and consideration, and it is important to both of you, and to your relationship, that you maintain your self dignity. It is, in fact, difficult for a man to feel kindly towards a woman whom he can mistreat. Knowing how to handle these difficult situations is one of the charming arts of Fascinating Womanhood and will be taught in a later chapter.

3. *When a man does something wrong:* Another time to react to a man's faults is when he does something unkind, dishonest or sinful, showing a lack of character. You may be well aware of his better side, and feel that you do accept him at face value, but if you now completely overlook his misdeed, it displays a weakness in your own character. The way to respond to his improper conduct is this:

At first show reluctance to believe it. Say that you thought it was impossible for a man such as he to do such a thing. If you are compelled to believe it, indicate that you know it is contrary to his true nature, and was only the result of carelessness or thoughtlessness. *You must be immensely disappointed at his temporary lapse, but your faith in his better side must be unshaken.*

Don't Fall onto His Level

When a man shows his weaker side, as we have just mentioned, there may be a temptation for the woman to lower her standards to meet his. She may feel that she will cause the man to feel "more accepted" in this way. This is a serious mistake! He will not respect her for it. A man likes to consider a woman as "finer, better and holier" than himself and therefore it would be a disappointment to him to see her fall from her level onto his. He cannot consider her an angelic character unless she holds to her ideals and maintains her high standards.

LOOK TO HIS BETTER SIDE

As you come to accept a man you can stop worrying about his faults. This is made easy if you will look to his better side and concentrate on that. Try to imagine him painted partly bright and partly dull. Then turn the dull side out of view so that only the bright shows. You know the dull is there but you are not looking at it. You see only the bright. By recognizing and continually believing in his better side you can help a man, a child, or any individual to grow.

WHY DO WOMEN TRY TO CHANGE MEN?

In many instances women try to change men because they become irritated with their faults. They may have little habits or quirks in their personalities that are difficult to "put up with." At other times a fine woman of high caliber will try to get a man to change "for his own good." She may feel that he is missing his best opportunities, or failing to reach success due to a certain lack of ability or a fault that stands in his way. If the man is truly blind to his mistakes, or his lack, a woman may wake him up, as has already been explained, but if he is fully aware of his inadequacies, she should let matters alone, lest she drive him away.

Another reason a woman may try to change a man is due to a fault that lies *within her.* She may have an attitude of *self-righteousness,* may feel that she is essentially better than he is. She may love him a great deal, but in the overall, considers herself a little finer, smarter, more alert, more diligent, more careful than he. Although some of these traits she may excel him in, she should never make the mistake of feeling that she is a better or finer person than he is. To do so is to be self-righteous. The Sadducees and the Pharisees in Biblical times had this same self-righteous attitude. They were faithful to attend their church, pay tithes, pray, read the scriptures, fast, observe any number of rituals, but the Savior called them "hypocrites," not because of their faithfulness, but because of their self-righteousness.

If you have had this tendency to "overrate yourself" and "underrate men," whether it be the men you are interested in as companions, or your brothers and father, stop and ask yourself if you are in any position to judge a man's worth? Are you, indeed a finer person than he? The very heart of Christian doctrine is: *It is ourselves we must change.* The scriptures explain that each individual should cast out the beam from his own eye first, that he may more clearly see the mote in his brother's eye. When we become aware of our own faults, and take responsibility for them, we lose our self-righteous tendencies and find it easier to accept people as they are.

How a Woman Tries to Change a Man

Many disagreeable girls make the mistake of offering pushy suggestions or blunt remarks that drive men away. But more often than not, girls are more subtle in their approach to men. They are more apt to drop a gentle hint or give a carefully worded suggestion about how the man needs to improve. Even though these latter forms may sound more acceptable, they are nevertheless offensive to the man and will most likely interfere with his feelings for her. A man is sensitive to any attitude a girl may have towards him. Any thought that he is not acceptable just as he is may drive him away.

Another way a woman tries to change a man is by *using other men as shining examples.* She may use a brother, a father or an outstanding man of the community, or even a hero from history, as a shining example of manhood. By holding another man up as superior, she subtly hopes that the man will try to copy the other man's virtues. She may not be fully aware of her motives — they may be only in the back of her mind. Holding up another man as a hero is an indication that she does not accept him at face value, that in reality she wishes he were better — more like the other man.

You may not make these mistakes with your men friends, but since you probably live around your father, brothers, etc., it is wise to learn as much as possible about this subject and apply it to all men you associate with. There will be a number of rewards if you do. In the first place you will promote a much better relationship with men in this way. Your brothers will be apt to want to sit by you in church, and your father will be much more willing to do things for you and there will be a much better feeling between you. The second reward is that you will begin to form habits that will help you in your associations with men for the rest of your life, not only with the man you may wish to marry, but with your own sons. Then, third, you will help all men in your life to be better men. As you look to their better side you will help them to grow into finer manhood. Important also is that you *express* your acceptance of the men in your life, especially those you live with. Tell your father or brothers that you are happy they are the kind of men they are. Then look to their better side. The following are steps to remember in learning to accept men, just as they are:

STEPS TO ACCEPTANCE

1. Get rid of your self-righteous attitude.
2. Don't try to remake men, improve them, give pushy advice, drop hints or subtle suggestions about how they need to improve.
3. Don't use other men as shining examples.
4. Look to his better side.
5. Express your acceptance in words:
   a. Tell him that you are happy he is the kind of man he is.
   b. Express appreciation for his finer points.

CHAPTER IV

Admiration

CHARACTERISTIC No. 2

The center of a woman's happiness is to be loved — but the center of man's is to be admired.

Deep in his heart every man longs for admiration — of his abilities, his ideas and his dreams. This admiration is his greatest happiness, and the lack of it one of his most distressing miseries. Although it is all important to him, it isn't something which he can get for himself. It must be given him by those who respect and love him. He likes receiving it from any and every source, but it is most essential from the woman he loves.

A man will often do and say things deliberately in the presence of a woman, hoping to receive admiration. But these things often go unnoticed. Usually a woman is too busy or too mentally occupied with her own world and problems to notice anything to admire. We don't often bother to find out what is in a man's heart, what he thinks and dreams about. The woman who offers the perfect admiration is the woman who wins his heart and soul.

THE YOUNG BOY

This need is manifest in the young boy and is essential to his confidence and growth into manhood. It helps him to experience love for his parents. Unfortunately there are many young boys whose parents fail to admire them. A life of correction without praise some young men endure, but the longing is always there. When such a boy matures he needs admiration more than ever, for doing without it in his youth has caused a lack of confidence. If the woman he marries can offer the needed admiration, his troubles are over. If not, he often becomes a lonely creature.

THE YOUNG MARRIED MAN

Especially is the need for admiration apparent in the young married man just beginning his career. He expects to be an all-conquering success; no project is too wild, no dream too fantastic. He is full of plans and proposals, assurance and enthusiasm. What he doesn't expect to do, after a little preliminary preparation, of course, simply isn't worth doing. He can find a hundred flaws in the way older heads are managing things now — but you just wait until he gets his chance and revolutionizes matters. Meantime, life isn't worth living if he can't find someone to whom he can tell all this, how things ought to be, how they will be when he gets his chance.

Most of his youthful associates are too much occupied with their own aspirations to listen to his. Older people will only laugh at him. Where can he find an uncritical listener and confidante? *The cry of his soul is for admiration.* The woman who gives it to him is no less than an angel.

THE OLDER MAN

As a man grows older, if he has not been admired, he often learns to do without it. He becomes, it would seem, hardened, incredulous, and less sensitive to the lack of admiration. The older a man becomes, however, the more bitterly he resents this apparent indifference to the bigger and nobler elements of his character. He represses his craving for admiration because he does not believe it is to be had, but the craving for it is just as strong and persistent as it is in the younger man.

WHAT HE WANTS YOU TO ADMIRE

What a man wants you to admire more than anything else are *his manly qualities.* If you admire traits which are admirable in both men and women, he will be disappointed. For example, if you admire him because he is kind, thoughtful, pleasant or well groomed, he may appreciate your praise but it will do little to really stir him, or affect his feelings towards you. *It is his masculinity that he wants noticed and admired.*

Physically his manly qualities are his large build, his strong muscles, his endurance, his deep pitched voice, his heavy jaw, his manly beard, his mustache, his heavy walk, his large hands, etc. We see his manly strength and endurance at work in sports, weight lifting, swimming, lifting heavy objects, managing difficult equipment, sawing logs, taming horses and even some of the more common things such as mowing the lawn, painting, opening tight jar lids, turning screws or wielding a hammer. Men's clothes are also a part of the physical. They are heavier, rougher and more tailored than women's — and therefore masculine.

Mentally his manliness lies in his achievements, skills and abilities, his judgment, cleverness, determination and his leadership ability. His manliness is also demonstrated in his hopes and aspirations for his future and his striving to reach these goals. We see masculinity in the student who achieves in his school work, the mechanic, the salesman, the carpenter, the doctor, the lawyer and all of the other fields men engage in. We see manly skills at work in repairing motors, winning a debate or receiving some honor for outstanding service or some talent displayed. The man who faithfully goes to work from day to day to provide for his family, fulfilling his role as a man, is due admiration for his efforts.

Spiritually his manliness is demonstrated in his sense of honor and duty in men's affairs, his courage and devotion to a cause, his sense of fair play, his noble deeds, his standards and aspirations or any high ideals which have to do with a man's life. Few men possess all of the masculine traits mentioned, but all men possess some of them. These are the ones we should notice and admire.

Why is admiration of masculinity so important to a man? Because it makes him feel *manly,* and this realization of his masculinity is one of the most enjoyable feelings a man can experience. When a woman supplies him with the much needed admiration she becomes indispensable to his happiness, and he will seek her out again and again for the comfort her companionship gives to him — the feeling of manliness he experiences in her presence. In fact, one of the keys to a man's heart is admiration of his masculinity.

WAYS TO ADMIRATION

There may be a number of things which you can readily notice to admire about a man, especially those physical traits which are so apparent. But some of the finer traits may be obscure and difficult to know, especially if your acquaintance has been rather brief or superficial. You must know something about him before you can admire him, and you must know a *great deal* about him if you are to appreciate him for his true worth. The following are suggestions to help you discover his admirable traits:

1. *Observe him:* The first thing to do is to observe him. If you will keep your eyes and ears open you will notice many things about him which are manly, things you may have formerly overlooked.

2. *Listen to others:* Try to make a point to listen carefully to people who know him well. You can deliberately open a conversation with his close friends and family. Do not be inquisitive, but steer the conversation into subjects which will reveal his nature and accomplishments.

3. *Listen to him talk:* The greatest opportunity you will have to admire him is when he talks — about subjects he is interested in or about himself. These conversations will reveal many things worthy of admiration. If a man has a good listener he will enjoy talking. The following advice will help you become a good listener.

HOW TO LISTEN TO A MAN

Follow this rule and you can be a good listener: *Do not listen only to what he is saying, but to the man who is saying it.* If he is talking about politics, religion or world events, notice how absorbed he is in the subject. As his ideas unfold, look for idealism and devotion to the things he believes in. If his attitude shows impatience with how things are, this may be an indication that he has ideas of his own, ideas which need to be expressed and appreciated. He may display a special knowledge about a subject, knowledge which comes from intelligence, experience or dedicated study.

If you cannot comprehend all of what he is saying, look for the traits of his character which you can admire. His conversation will reveal them. In fact, if you only follow his subject and appreciate that, and not the man who is thus expressing himself, he will be apt to be disappointed. You may rest assured that he is not talking only to have his subject appreciated. He wants admiration to be bestowed upon himself as a man and not merely upon his subject.

A woman need not be well educated or possess high intelligence to follow a clever man's discourse. In his pleasure at having himself admired the man seldom notices that his conversation is not understood. Even when he does notice it he relishes it as in the following words by Maeterlinck:

What care I though she appear not to understand?

Do you think it is for a sublime word I thirst

When I feel that a soul is gazing into my soul?

If you learn to listen to a man correctly it doesn't matter if the subject is interesting or dull. You can converse on world affairs or the intricate details of his business career and you will be able to maintain an interest. In fact, you can safely guess that if he deliberately talks "over your head" he is doing so only to arouse your admiration.

If you once get the habit of looking for the masculinity in the men you meet, you will not find any of them uninteresting. You will welcome the most tedious monologue as giving you an opportunity to observe the man's character, and to seek out his admirable qualities. You will develop into a most appreciative listener and will invite, unconsciously almost, the confidences of nearly every man with whom you converse.

Remember too, that if you can't see anything manly in him, he won't see anything womanly in you. It is the manly things that you are to look for in him, the manly things that you are to appreciate. The greatest attraction of the exceptionally feminine woman is that she can observe and admire the masculinity of every man she meets. She is constantly on the lookout for it.

CHAPTER V

His Sensitive Pride

CHARACTERISTIC No. 3

We have just learned of the man's great need to be admired — to be admired for his *masculine* abilities, skills, ideas and achievements. Now we must learn that a man is very *proud* of his masculine abilities. He likes to show them off, to call your attention to them in both conversation and actions. Like every male creature from the peacock and the rooster to the bull and the lion, he likes to strut before the female of the species and show what manly powers are his.

Although a man is proud of his masculinity and longs to have it noticed and appreciated, it is here he is most vulnerable for his manly pride is extremely sensitive. He cannot bear to have it belittled, ridiculed or treated with indifference. When a man is belittled, he suffers the pains of humiliation. It can be a sharp cutting sensation or a crushing feeling. Whatever the forms of humiliation, it is a painful experience.

You will remember that admiration gives a man a wonderful feeling of manliness, and in turn he feels tenderly towards the woman who makes him feel this way. Well, when this same masculinity, instead of being appreciated, is belittled, or treated with indifference, the man experiences an opposite feeling — a feeling of lack of manliness — and in turn he will not feel kindly towards the woman who makes him feel this way. Take every precaution not to do or say anything which will injure his pride, for nothing will more quickly drive a man away.

MISTAKES GIRLS MAKE

Don't make the mistake of making fun of a man's mustache or beard, or anything to do with his masculine appearance. Be equally careful not to belittle any of his accomplishments such as grades, term papers, sports events, the way he repairs a motor, his knowledge of certain subjects or even certain high goals he may have. Often girls tend to belittle men in the form of *humor*. In this case it may be difficult to detect the boy's hurt pride, for he may pretend to laugh to cover up the pains of humiliation. This only obscures her mistake and as a result she is apt to repeat it again and again.

The most common cause of hurt pride, however, is an attitude of *indifference*. In other words, when a man reveals some masculine accomplishment or skill, the woman may show a lack of interest towards it. She may indicate by a yawn, an expression or a glance out the window that she is not impressed. If the man happens to be telling her of something of which he is particularly proud, her indifference to his masculinity can wound him as if he were struck by a lash. It is not difficult to imagine, then, how he feels towards a woman who has injured the most sensitive part of his nature and robbed him of his manliness.

Mistakes of Others

Women are not the only contributors to men's humiliation. In the working world his pride may be brutally cut down. His ability may be questioned. In some companies backbiting is common. Some sadistic employers may undermine an employee. Then there is a struggle for position in which men sometimes discredit one another. Often it is a creditor or customer who offers cutting remarks. Some workers are derided by their superiors.

On the campuses, in the classroom we sometimes observe further humiliation. Professors or fellow students are sometimes insensitive to manly pride, although they are vulnerable themselves. In sports, men freely belittle one another. This is because they tend to build themselves up by tearing others down. When we see what a man puts up with in the world with his fellow associates, it seems inexcusable for women to further add to the pains of humiliation. Women, in fact, can restore manly pride, and must, if they are to be indispensable to a man's happiness. In speaking of the mistakes women make and the seriousness of belittling remarks and injured pride, tragedies have occurred because of it. Let me tell you of one such instance:

BELITTLED

Many years ago I knew a girl who was engaged to marry a man of outstanding ability. He appeared to love her dearly but broke the engagement and married someone else. For years it seemed a mystery to those who knew the couple, but later I learned the truth. She lost him because she belittled him. She laughed at his big ideas, made fun of his actions on the basketball court and joked about his performance in plays. Such a constant eroding of his pride was more than he could stand. This man has become extremely successful, which indicates that in his young years he must have had a tremendous masculine pride.

We have learned thus far that a man needs desperately to be admired for his masculinity and that it is indeed the "cry of his soul." He is very proud of these manly qualities, but also very sensitive about them and cannot bear to have them belittled, ridiculed or treated with indifference. If you intend to become our ideal of Angela Human and offer to a man the perfect undertstanding and influence his feelings towards you, it is important that you realize fully his nature and never commit the unpardonable sin of ridicule or indifference. Such an act is apt to drive him away completely. If he does overlook a single act, he is not apt to show forth patience if it is repeated again and again. If you do have this habit of belittling men, or showing indifference, it is essential that you rid yourself of this tendency or you will make little progress in winning the attentions of men.

CHAPTER VI

His Reserve

A reserve is a barrier that a man builds around himself, making it difficult to "get next to him." By reserve we do not mean bashfulness or timidity. The latter peculiarities apply to comparatively few men. Reserve, on the other hand, is an attribute of all.

In order to understand reserve we must again refer to the subject of admiration. We have learned that to admire a man fully we must listen to him talk, so that we can observe the finer parts of his character and we will have an opportunity to admire these traits. But it is not easy to win a man's confidence so that he will talk about subjects that are near and dear to his heart. The reason for this is that his reserve stands in his way, a reserve that causes him to hesitate and withhold confidences.

His reserve is caused by fears, the fears of ridicule, contempt and indifference — those things that we learned about in connection with a man's pride. Because of fears, he forms a wall of reserve which makes it difficult to get him to talk. Although he may long to confide, so that he can be appreciated for his masculinity, he hesitates because of his reserve, or his fear of ridicule. Nothing is so frightening to a man as the horror of making a fool of himself.

A man of high caliber is most reluctant to expose his intimate secret hopes and ideas to indifference or antagonism. The fear of such humiliation is nothing less than appalling to him. He therefore sternly subdues every impulse to seek admiration by forming this wall of reserve. Nothing but the absolute certainty that his ideas will not be met with contempt or indifference will induce him to throw off his armor of reserve and reveal to others the things that mean the most to him. And even if he does dare, the slightest hint of misunderstanding or disrespect will shatter the illusion and drive him behind his wall of reserve again.

In order to understand the delicateness of the situation, take an example of a young girl who has successfully won a young man's confidence and he is unfolding his secret hopes and dreams. As he begins to reveal the finer traits of his character she has a most wonderful opportunity to acknowledge his manly qualities. But let her but indicate by a yawn or a glance out the window that she is not interested and the poor man will act as though he has been struck with a lash. It may be the first time in his life he has ventured to express his feelings. To him, therefore, the confession is a matter of prime importance over which he has probably pondered for days. The ideas themselves, and the motives underlying them, have long been the mainspring of his being. If the girl looks indifferently upon such a crisis and fails to recognize its significance to him she has indeed so far as he is concerned *a heart of stone*. Therefore, no matter where or when he meets her in the future, he will not again risk a similar rebuff.

Such is the case with every man. His longing for understanding, great as it is, is not sufficient to make him throw off his habitual cloak of reserve except in rare instances. And even then he will quickly resume it again unless he can bask in the full glow of an all comprehending understanding. The one characteristic, therefore, seems to be directly opposed to the other. Together they constitute a problem difficult enough to tax any girl's wits.

If you are to win the interest of men, you will have to first eliminate his armor of reserve so that he will confide his innermost feelings to you and you will be able to admire his masculinity, as has been explained. There are a number of things you can do to remove this reserve. They are the following:

How to Break Down the Wall of Reserve

1. *Accept him:* If you give any indication that you are not satisfied with him just as he is, he will not feel like exposing his innermost feelings to your unappreciative attitude.

2. *Admire his masculinity:* Your admiration will do more to break down his reserve than any effort you can make.

3. *Don't belittle him or show indifference:* Make sure you do not make mistakes which only strengthen the reserve he already has.

4. *Don't be critical of others:* If you are scornful, with an eye open for every fault you can find in those around you, he will be afraid to expose his own intimate feelings to your criticism and contempt. When you are with him you must not tell him about your quarrels with your acquaintances and about your poor opinion of this or that person. You must not betray envy or jealousy or contempt. You must not make light of anyone. Even when you cannot approve of what someone does or says, you must show your appreciation for his motives or basic character. The more ability you can manifest as a critic, the less inclined the man will be to expose himself to your criticism. He likes to believe that his confidences will meet with a generous and admiring interpretation, not with a faultfinding one.

5. *Appreciate the good in others:* If you appreciate the good in others, he will not fear ridicule or contempt when he confides his ideals and ambitions to you; he will begin to confide things about himself without any invitation on your part. Search for the good in everyone you meet and express your appreciation of them. This is the easiest way to develop a beautiful confidence-inspiring character. Unless you do this it will be impossible for you to play the part of Angela Human, the woman who is most attractive to men.

6. *Hold confidences sacred:* You must hold sacred the thoughts and feelings of others, and not confide in him matters that other people have confided in you. If you disclose the secrets of others, he will take it for granted that you will disclose his also and thus subject him to the same misunderstanding, ridicule or indifferences that he seeks to avoid. Unless he thinks that he is confiding his innermost hopes and ambitions to one who will not betray them to others, the man will not confide them to you no matter how sure he is of your personal admiration of him. Even though he knows you admire him, how does he know others will? They might ridicule the things you admire. He does not want to risk the contempt of anyone. In your associ-

ations with him, then, you must not uncover secrets which have been told to you in confidence.

When the man does disclose something about himself which you can admire, do not imagine that his reserve has disappeared altogether. You will need to further break down his reserve. You do this by making certain that everything he confides to you is met with admiration. Otherwise his first confidences will never be followed by another. If your response is always appreciative, he will add another confidence and another until at last, if your reaction is never disappointing, he will lay bare before you every motive, ideal and hope that stirs within him. Admiration is too rare for him to deny it to himself, once he has had the full enjoyment of it.

Remember, however, that underlying the desire for admiration is always lurking in the background that reserve, ready to spring out at the first sign of indifference or criticism, even when the criticism is only apparent in the girl's attitude towards other people. You can therefore understand how difficult it is for a girl with a weak, faultfinding or indifferent character to keep the reserve in the background and to maintain the man's interest.

CHAPTER VII

Sympathetic Understanding

A man needs sympathy in a number of ways, and they are the following:

1. *His responsibilities as a man:* A woman ought always to understand the responsibilities a man faces in his future. Since most men plan to marry, they have, at least in the back of their minds, a picture of what this responsibility entails. They know that they will be faced with the social and economic responsibility of a wife and children for a lifetime. They also know that their family will look to them to be their guide and protector, and that they must grow into manhood if they are to fulfill this position. They may not spend a great amount of time worrying about it, but they are nevertheless aware of it. They know that if they are to succeed in this role as man, they must make adequate preparation.

A woman's preparation for the future is different. She is planning for marriage also, but this does not require economic responsibility. If she is employed, she knows that it need not last a lifetime — that others will not depend upon her for their daily bread. If she is attending college or planning a career — a career out in the world, she knows that others will not depend upon her success, and that she will not be disgraced if she fails. She may change her mind, set down her burden at any time, without appearing a failure. She does these things — assumes these responsibilities by choice, without pressures for the future. Of course she may face unhappy or angry parents if she fails in school — but this problem she knows is only temporary. If she makes a success of her marriage, she will win their appreciation.

But with men — their college, career or their jobs are serious business. If they fail, they fail in their preparation for the future.

Success in life is at stake. They *must* succeed if they are to fulfill their roles as men and provide for loved ones adequately.

Now the main reason a woman needs to understand masculine responsibility is this: Men sometimes become depressed about their futures and at such times need the confidence and reassurance of a woman. They need to know that someone believes in them — believes in their ultimate success.

Another reason a woman needs to understand is that this responsibility a man faces about his future can sometimes be a difficult obstacle to marriage. He may give every evidence of desiring marriage and yet hesitate because of the responsibility he faces. A woman, if she knows what he is experiencing, can be a comfort to him and help remove this barrier to marriage, as will be explained in a later chapter.

2. *His desire for status:* A second way we need to understand a man's needs for sympathy is in his desire for status. By status we mean a position of honor or acclaim. Man has within his nature the drive to excel, or to shine out brightly, or to do something of note which will set him apart from other men. This is true, not only in the human male, but in male members of the animal kingdom. The pecking order in the barnyard, the hierarchy in a colony of baboons and the ranking within a herd of elephants is more of a driving force for the male than is the sex function. Men also have the longing to take their place in the world of men. This drive for superiority over other men is a masculine trait. Women desire appreciation but they seldom have tendencies to gain superiority over one another.

He Wants to Be a Hero in Your Eyes

Not only does a man want status in the eyes of the world, but more than anyone else, he wants to impress the woman he loves or is interested in. He wants to be a hero in her eyes. He may win the acclaim of the whole world, and all of the honors of earth, and yet would be disappointed if he could not impress the woman he loves. So, in your associations with men do not make the mistake of using another man as a shining example. Do not refer to your brother, or your father or some man in the community as the shining example of manhood. Do not even extol some admirable man in history. Do not give some other man the acclaim that he would like to receive, the acclaim of a hero. He may not have earned such honor yet, but he would like to feel that other men are not a competition to him in your eyes. He would like to feel that it would be possible for him to impress you as the shining example of manhood.

And even worse, do not allow *yourself* to be a competition to his acclaim. Do not excel him in any of the fields in which he is trying to win acclaim. If you are the one who stands out as notable among your fellow men — the one who has won the honor and acclaim, this is a serious threat to the position he hopes one day to win. We see this problem apparent with many famous women, especially movie and stage actresses. If they marry men who can outdo them, either in the field of acting or in any other occupation, then things are in their rightful place, but if men simply cannot meet the competition of their wife's acclaim, it is a serious threat to the male ego and can make him most uncomfortable and unhappy. How can he impress you with his meager efforts if you have already won the honors of earth, or if he is convinced that you can or will in the future? Be particularly careful, then, of the male ego, and the inborn desire for acclaim or status and never appear as a threat to this position or allow another to appear as a threat. This delicate nature of the male ego is something that must be understood and protected in our associations with men. Man's ego is vulnerable, and therefore it is here that we can either build or destroy.

In man's drive for status try to understand his desire to impress the world and also you. He wants money and security, yes, but he also wants honor and acclaim, especially for you. He does not expect it before he has earned it, but he expects you to recognize his promise for the future, that one day he will achieve the goals he has set. This struggle for status explains the added preparation a man feels he must make while he is young. It also explains why men later on in life become dissatisfied with a job that provides money and security, but little acclaim. It helps us to understand and sympathize with a man's striving for achievements as he goes along — the badge of merit, the champion cup and the honorary award.

3. *Sympathy for the discouraged man:* A man has a special need for sympathy when he is discouraged. This tendency to be depressed is common among men. Whether rich or poor, handsome or homely, learned or ignorant, few men escape this unpleasant experience. In fact, the more learned, talented and aggressive men tend to have the most intense suffering. Abraham Lincoln had periods of depression, in which he merely sat and brooded and read the newspapers. Most men of great responsibility have periods of real discouragement. But all men, both old and young, have times when they are depressed, times that need to be understood.

When we realize the complex world a man lives in, it is easy to understand why they become discouraged. If he is a young man, his future responsibilities may occasionally worry and discourage him. In his striving for acclaim, he may have lost, rather than won, some honor he has been striving for. Then his sensitive pride is always at stake. He is subject to insults, ridicule and the keen competition of his associates. He may be worried about money, or his family, or some special demands he cannot meet, or difficult problems he cannot seem to find solutions to. Or it may just be a bad day for him.

A woman has the power to break this spell of gloom, and the man senses this and turns to her for sympathetic understanding. A clever woman need not know the *cause* of his problems. She only needs to know the art of giving true sympathy. This art can be learned, by understanding a man's nature and just what it is he needs when he is discouraged.

How to Give True Sympathy

True sympathy means "sharing feelings." You are able to "feel with him," or "experience with him" even "suffer with him." This understanding of feelings is a great comfort to him and seems to ease the pain.

The way to do it is this: Come to him with warmth and friendliness and try to let him know that you understand just how he must feel. If he is very discouraged, tell him that "this is a dark hour that will pass." Try to maintain a pleasant attitude and whatever you do, *"Do not let his gloom rub off on you."* Remember, one of the chief functions of a woman is "to shed joy around, and cast light upon dark days." This does not mean that you appear exuberant while he is depressed. This would cause him to feel that you lack sympathy completely. He wants you to feel *with him,* but to lift his spirits with your spirit of hope and pleasantness.

If you find that you have not lifted the man's spirits, then do not be discouraged. This does not mean that you have not been appreciated or helpful. Sometimes it takes awhile for a man to "snap out of it," even though he has a sympathetic ear. He may need time and you will have to extend it to him. In the meantime, continue to show forth a sympathetic attitude.

SOME THINGS NOT TO DO

Many women do not know the art of giving sympathy. It is not that they do not try but rather that they do not know how. They make all kinds of mistakes, say just the wrong things and often none of the right things. Their greatest mistake is that they try to help him solve his problems, offer too many suggestions, offer to help lift his burdens or remove his obstacles. These things may be appreciated, but they are not sympathy and not what a man needs from a woman. Practical help is not what he needs. He needs sympathy and the reassurance of your understanding and faith in him.

Also, do not make the mistake of *minimizing his problems.* Do not say, for example, "You worry too much," or "Your problems are just in your imagination," or "Life is not as tough as you think." These attitudes not only show a lack of sympathy, but are belittling to his masculine pride. If you, a mere woman, can be so fearless in the face of difficulty, how can he feel like a man?

Also, it may not be wise to take the attitude of "count your blessings," for if you remind him that "he has two eyes, two hands and all the facilities to solve problems or make a success and he ought to be ashamed for letting life get him down," his worries will seem inexcusable. Not only will he feel a lack of sympathy from you, but he will be humiliated in your eyes. The fact that he has "blessings" can make his discouragement seem worse than ever, less justified. If he is reminded that in spite of his many blessings he has let life get him down, how can he possibly feel adequate as a man? Your lack of understanding sympathy, and your tendency to rob him of his masculinity will cause him to feel uncomfortable in your presence when he is discouraged. He will tend to avoid you in these moments of despair. You will have failed to give him one of the greatest gifts a woman can offer a man — an all comprehending sympathy. What the man wants is for you to understand his problem and sympathize with his feelings about it. Take the attitude, "Life is tough, how do you men put up with it?" and he will be encouraged to face life with a manly spirit.

It is interesting to note that when a woman is discouraged, she is different. She, of course, wants sympathy for her feelings, but she wants more than this from a man. She looks to him for help and guidance in times of trouble. She wants his suggestions and his help in solving problems. Men are her protectors and her guides, and she leans on them for helpful advice because she is a woman. But do not expect that men are like we are. They have a sensitive masculine pride. Having a woman solve their difficult masculine problems only makes them feel ineffectual and incomplete as a man. This does not mean that she cannot offer suggestions when he asks for them. But when she gives advice it must be given in a feminine manner, as will be explained in the next characteristics. The main thing he seeks, however, is not her advice — no matter how great it may be. He seeks her comfort, solace and understanding when life is discouraging. And she can best mend his feelings by "shedding joy around and casting light upon dark days."

CHAPTER VIII

The Role of Man

CHARACTERISTIC NO. 6

His desire to be superior in his role as man.

Man was created by his very nature and temperament to play a certain part in life — a masculine part. It was intended from the beginning of time that he be the *guide, protector and provider* for his wife and children. Women were created for a different role — that of *wife, mother and homemaker.* The masculine and the feminine roles are complementary to each other. Neither one is more important than the other, but both are essential. Yet they are different from one another. In marriage they have been compared to a lock and a key. They join together to form a perfectly functioning unit.

The important thing to remember about Characteristic No. 6 is this: Not only does a man have a desire to play his part as a man — as a guide, protector and provider, but *he desires to be superior to woman in his role as man.* In other words, he wants to be a more capable leader, a stronger protector and a more competent provider than she is. He does not desire to excel her in her domestic duties or her role as mother or any of the feminine arts. He only wants to excel her in anything which requires masculine strength, skill, competence or ability. I would like to point out most emphatically that a man does not desire to be superior to a woman as a person, or to be more respected and honored than she. He only wants to feel superior in his role as a man, and this is only because it gives him a sense of masculine fulfillment.

MAN THE LEADER

There is ample proof that man is the intended leader of his family. The first commandment which God gave unto woman was, *"thy desire shall be unto thy husband, and he shall rule over thee."* The Apostle Paul tells us that woman is to *"rever-*

ence" her husband and he says, *"Submit yourselves unto your own husbands."* The Apostle Peter tells us *"Ye wives, be in subjection to your own husbands."* The Apostle Paul compared man's leadership of his wife to Christ's leadership of the church. *"For the husband is the head of the wife, even as Christ is the head of the church. Therefore, as the church is subject unto Christ, so let the wives be to their own husbands in everything."* Because men were born to be leaders, they also inherited dominant masculine traits. Men are by nature aggressive, forceful and determined and more decisive in their judgment than women. Of course, there are exceptions to this rule, for the training and circumstances of childhood can interfere with a man's attaining these masculine characteristics. All the more reason for women to recognize the need for these hidden traits to come forth and help the man reach fulfillment as a man.

But the main thing to remember is that regardless of how much the leadership abilities may have been subdued — a man has an inborn desire to be superior to a woman in his leadership role. He wants to be more aggressive, more decisive and determined than she is, and only when he is playing this superior role will he feel manly in her presence.

In the days of courtship, men have always taken the dominant position in their relationship with women, for they seek women out socially, ask them for dates and propose marriage. The man is the pursuer — the woman the pursued. The woman does not ask the man — the man asks the woman. This has been the proper order of life since the beginning of time, for man was given "dominion over all the earth" and woman was created to be his "helpmeet."

Many girls, especially in our modern times, make mistakes in their relationships with men — mistakes that drive men away. Many of them are aggressive and thereby appear as a threat to the man's position. We have all heard of the term "forward" in describing aggressive girls, but few know what it really means,

THE FORWARD GIRL

A girl who is forward has the following tendencies: She appears overly eager to win the attentions of men. By flirting, hints, suggestions or even directly asking, she indicates that she is interested in the man and wishes that he would take her out. She demonstrates an interest in him long before he has had a chance to develop an interest in her. She leads rather than follows and in so doing steals his masculine position. There is a time that the man will want her to show an interest in him — to return the feeling that he has for her, but he does not want her to be more aggressive than he is.

Some other tendencies of the forward girl are to spend a lot of time talking about marriage, or how much she would like to have children, etc. These appear to a man as hints that the girl is serious about getting married and therefore "looking." It will probably cause him to feel "on guard" in her presence. Of course, if the man leads you into the subject of marriage or family life, it is all right to express your views, if you do not dwell on the subject too long or appear too eager. But otherwise, you are more interesting to men and more feminine if you avoid such subjects and appear interested in him.

Girls who call boys on the phone, or hint for dates, or even ask boys out, etc., appear "forward." There are a few who make the mistake of being forward in affection, like "kissing a boy goodnight," or taking his hand, or putting her arm around him, etc. Remember, the man is the pursuer, the woman the pursued.

If you have any tendencies to be aggressive, you will have to drop these habits lest you frighten men away. The rule is, never travel faster in love than he does. In romance the man leads and the girl follows. This means that you will have to subdue any inclination to "wear your heart on your sleeve." When he calls on you socially, do not rush to the door in uncontrolled exuberance! Hold your feelings in reserve until you are certain that he feels equally keen about you. And even then do not express feelings greater than his own.

This is not to suggest that you at any time appear unfriendly. But when you are friendly, do not single him out as one in whom you have special interest. Let him see that you are friendly with everyone you meet and that he is just one more man whom you happen to like very much and enjoy being with. This will set his mind at ease that you do not have designs on him. Allow him the privilege of being the aggressor. When you do you help him to feel superior in his masculine role and as a result he will be more apt to develop an interest in you.

EXCEPTIONS TO THE RULE

There is an exception to this rule and it is when the man is extremely shy or timid. He may be afraid of women or at least socially ill at ease around them and therefore does not play the part of the aggressive male. This does not mean that he does not have it in his nature, under some circumstances, to be the pursuer, but during the early stages of an acquaintance his shy nature subdues his natural masculine traits. Young boys especially are apt to be shy around girls, but there are some mature men that have never lost this disadvantage.

In the case of the shy man, whether young or old, a woman may, in the beginning of their romance, have to break all rules and show a marked interest in the man. He may have suffered severe lack of confidence around women and have the false notion that he is not attractive to them. The woman's interest, therefore, is an encouragement to him that he does have some traits that attract women and this will cause his outer veneer of bashfulness to disappear.

A good example of a situation like this is in the movie "Goodbye, Mr. Chips." The leading man, Mr. Chips, was a schoolmaster who had had little experience with women. Although he was attracted to the young lady in the story, he was extremely reserved and shy. He did not know what love was all about nor did he have the confidence to find out. The girl perceived that he did have a genuine interest in her and that his reserve was only due to his lack of confidence. She therefore took an aggressive position, invited him to a dinner party, managed to get him alone and under the spell of a moonlight night hinted a proposal of marriage. She realized that unless she did something to bring the man into romance he would shy away from it completely.

So, when a young woman is faced with the problem of bashfulness in men, it is permissible to be aggressive, at least to some degree. But, as soon as she has "unfolded" the man so that his timidity disappears, she should then retreat into her feminine position and allow him to take the lead.

It is best for a girl to always view the man as the leader, even in single days. He may not be using his position fully at present, but women should respect it, even in youth. One way to show respect for leadership is when the man turns to her for advice, as men often do. When men seek our opinions and wisdom, we should give it to them, but it is important that we offer them advice in the right way — a way that keeps men in their masculine position as a leader.

How to Give Feminine Advice

When you give advice or opinions, do so as a *fountain* that bubbles over in a park. Let him take as much or as little of your advice as he would like. Use no pressure or forcefulness. Have no unbendable opinions. Do not speak with strong conviction in a way that will cause him to feel obligated to take your advice. Give him "take it or leave it" advice. Use the words "I feel," or "I believe," for they are indicative of insight, which is a feminine gift. And remember the following don'ts:

1. *Don't appear to know more than he does:* This means that you should not map out a course for him to follow, analyze his problems or decisions or make a lot of suggestions.

2. *Don't be motherly:* Avoid giving him the feeling that you are sorry for him and therefore would like to rescue him from his problems — protect him from the hard world.

3. *Don't talk man to man:* When men give one another advice they "hash things over." Brutally honest, they are apt to tear into the heart of a problem. Being on an equal plane, they say such things as "Let's come to some conclusions," or "Why don't we go over it again," or "I think I know the big problem." When a woman takes this attitude she appears on an equal plane and threatens his position. Remember, in giving a man advice keep the man in his dominant position so that he will feel superior in his masculine role as the leader.

When you are in the presence of men who demonstrate the masculine traits of leadership, allow them the privilege of being the aggressive male, and also express admiration for this masculine quality — at least occasionally. For example, if he is firm, has strong convictions on an issue, or if he makes decisions with fast and decisive judgment, don't miss the opportunity to say,

"I notice that you make decisions with decisive judgment. I have always admired this trait in men and notice that it is somewhat lacking in feminine women."

In your relationships with men, eliminate all signs of aggressiveness, determination and unyielding opinions. This does not mean, however, that you should not be firm in your beliefs and in your moral convictions. It only means that when it comes to a man's position as a man, and as a leader, that you allow him to be the man and that you take the part of the feminine submissive woman. In this way you help him to feel superior in his masculine role.

Man the Protector

Another part of the man's masculine role is that of being the protector. When we consider the man's body build and his brave capable character, it is apparent that one of his purposes in life is to be the protector for women and children. He is larger, has stronger muscles and greater physical endurance than women. Women are delicate, fragile and weaker. They are like fine precision machines, created for the more delicate tasks and which run smoothly and efficiently when used for the purpose intended.

In all periods of time women have needed protection from the dangers, strenuous work and the difficulties of life. In the early history of our country the very conditions under which people were forced to live made manly protection necessary. There were dangers everywhere. Savage Indians, wild beasts and snakes created situations which called for masculine ability. Protecting their loved ones, however, made men feel heroic and brave and an enjoyable sense of manliness.

Protection Today

The important thing today is that we let the man play the part of the chivalrous male. We do not have the real dangers we had a generation ago, but we do still need men. Women are still afraid of spiders, mice, lightning, thunder and strange noises. Even though these dangers are only in our imaginations, if women think that they are real, they need the protection of men and men are only too willing to offer it.

Women also need to be protected from lifting heavy objects, moving furniture or anything which requires masculine strength and ability. On certain occasions women need to be protected from offensive people who may make unreasonable demands. She turns to men in times of danger, strenuous work or in difficulty.

MISTAKES WOMEN MAKE

Women of today do not always turn to men for protection. In our generation they have made the mistake of becoming independent, capable, efficient and able to "kill their own snakes." We see them lifting heavy objects, repairing automobiles, changing tires, driving heavy equipment, fixing the roof, doing carpentry and many other masculine tasks. We see women competing with men in the working world, or in masculine sports or games. Day in and day out they are proving that they do not need masculine care and protection, that they are well able to take care of themselves.

It is difficult to describe how seriously women rob men of their masculinity by becoming independent. A competent woman stands as a threat to the male ego — to his position as a man. When he comes in contact with a capable, efficient woman, well able to meet him or defeat him on his own grounds, he does not feel like a man any longer. It is an unpleasant feeling that he does not care to repeat.

The woman also loses ground by becoming capable and independent. As she begins to take on an air of self-sufficiency she tends to lose some of her essential feminine charm. A feminine woman is tender, delicate and gentle and needs the protection of men. When we see a generation of women who have become capable — able to kill their own snakes, it is not surprising to see that they have lost respect in the eyes of the men and that men do not offer them the chivalry that they did a generation ago.

The important thing to remember is this: Men *enjoy* protecting women. Do not think, therefore, that it is an imposition on a man to protect a dependent, feminine woman. *The most pleasant sensation a real man can experience is his consciousness of the power to give his manly care and protection. Rob him of this sensation of superior strength and ability and you rob him of his manliness.*

If you are going to observe Characteristic No. 6 — The Man's Desire to be Superior in His Role as Man — it will be essential to recognize his need to be your protector and to allow him this privilege. Do not make the mistake of trying to excel him in anything which requires masculine strength or ability and do not take on the capable and independent air of being able to kill your own snakes. To do so is a threat to his position and makes him feel like the "inferior" male rather than the "superior" one. If you want to help the man to feel superior as your protector you will take on the delicate nature of a feminine woman and *need* his protecting care. There are a number of things that you can do to make it easier for him to assume the masculine role, for example:

HOW TO LET HIM BE A MAN

Take every opportunity to allow him to play the part of the man. Let him open doors for you. If you are in a car, be sure to sit still until he comes around and helps you out — no matter how long it takes him to remember to do so. Be sure to always offer a gracious thank you. When he arrives to take you out socially, if you have a coat, hand it to him and turn your back so that he will be encouraged to help you with it. Boys can feel pretty awkward in offering their chivalry, but we can help to make it easier by "expecting it," and never shying away from their offers. Never lift a heavy object in a man's presence. If he does not offer, ask him to lift it for you. Men will not mind. They enjoy helping women. Lean on them for everything that requires masculine help, strength, skill, ability or protection. To prove the importance of helping a man feel masculine, let me tell you the following experience:

ROMANCE REVIVED

A girl of my acquaintance was going with a young man that she liked very much and they were getting quite serious about each other. Suddenly he stopped going with her for no understandable reason. She pondered the thought for quite some time, wondering what, if anything, she had done to drive him away.

About this time she attended one of our Fascinating Womanhood classes and learned about the importance of not competing
with men in the masculine fields and was able to pinpoint her
mistakes. She recalled that he had been bothered because she
had excelled him in math — a field that he had some pride in
himself. She also recalled trying to outdo him in sports, and
trying to impress him as an intellectual, hoping that he would
be impressed with her above-average knowledge. Instead, one
day he said, "Janie, you are so smart it makes me sick."

Shortly after completing the Fascinating Womanhood course
she chanced to meet him again, displaying a more feminine
attitude. He was friendly and asked her for a date. By this
time she knew just what to do and what not to say. They dated
again frequently and one evening he said to her, "Janie, you are
different than you used to be. I can't put my finger on just
what it is, but you are different!" Well, she knew. She had
dropped her display of intellectual powers and ability and allowed
him the privilege of showing his. She had stopped being competitive with him and it paid off, for they were soon married.

This does not mean that a woman need be under par mentally. Men are more attracted to highly intelligent women, but
they do not appreciate someone who appears to be a "brain"
or an "intellectual" and can out-do them in their own fields
of study or interest.

Never compete with men in sports, or in the working world,
or rival with them for some honor or contest or prize. In other
words, do not try to out-do men in any of their fields of endeavor,
fields in which men are supposed to excel. There are two main
rules if you are to help a man feel masculine in his role as man.
They are:

1. *Need* his masculine care and protection.
2. *Do not excel him* in anything which requires masculine
   strength, ability or skill.

When you do this, when you make a man feel like a man;
you give him the wonderful feeling of superiority in his masculine role.

MAN THE PROVIDER

We now come to the role of the man as the provider —
another part that he needs to play in his masculine role, and

another part in which he needs to feel superior to women. Earning the bread has been his responsibility since the beginning of time, for soon after man was created God gave him the command "Thou shall earn thy bread by the the sweat of thy face." This instruction was not given to the woman, but to the man. Since this time, the man has been recognized as the provider, not only by custom but by law, for in the event of divorce the man is required to pay alimony. This proves that today, even though women everywhere are working, we still recognize the man as the provider. Most men know that when they marry they will assume this full economic load for a wife and children. A man's wife may work at times and others may assist him, but it is not their direct worry. He alone is responsible.

In understanding the man's position as the provider, let us refer again to Characteristic No. 6, The Man's Desire to be Superior in his Role as Man. In applying it to this portion of the man's role, then, the Man desires to be superior to the woman, as the *provider*. There are two ways that you can help a man feel superior in his role as the provider and they are: 1. *Need* him as a provider, and 2. *Do not excel* him as a provider. Let us now discuss these two methods:

1. *Need him:* A man knows that part of his role is to provide the living. He knows what this responsibility entails and that it will be a day-in, day-out affair that will last his lifetime. But he also knows that he was blessed with the capacity to do the job and to do it reasonably well. He has the courage, the emotional stability and the stamina to face his man-sized job. He considers a woman the more gentle sex and knows that she was created for a feminine responsibility. She was born to be a loving mother, tender wife, to settle quarrels, inspire children, give birthday parties, and to manage the intricate details of a household filled with myriad responsibilities. Men would not like to fill this feminine place in life. They would feel entirely inadequate. They were made to be men, to press their way through life in the face of difficulty, to go out into the world "to get the little rabbit skin to wrap the baby bunting in." They would like to feel that gentle women *need* their manly care, that they are dependent upon them to provide the living. They would like to feel that they alone are competent to fill this

role and that they can do a superior job to women in doing it. They would like to feel that women *need* them, as men.

This generation of women have failed miserably in giving the man the feeling that he is *needed* as a provider. About one-third of our working staff are women. They are trained for work in almost every field that men engage in. They have become office managers, doctors, lawyers, congressmen, presidents, policewomen, carpenters, truck drivers and janitors, to name a few. They have invaded the entire working world of men. Women do not appear to need men. They can "get their own little rabbit skin, to wrap their baby bunting in."

When the wife becomes the capable, independent woman of the working force, who can adequately take care of herself, who does not need a man to provide for her, you can understand that the man cannot possibly feel superior to her as a provider. It is difficult enough, in fact, just to feel her equal.

There are, of course, pressing emergencies when women have to work and should be willing to help out. But few situations really demand the woman's supplementary income. Usually the reasons are that women are not satisfied with the income that their husbands provide. The assistance that they give their men in their manly role, however, does not counteract the harm it does to his ego. She says, in effect, "You do not provide for me adequately, so I must help out." If he cannot provide even the necessities, he does not feel *adequate* as a man, *let alone superior.*

The solution lies in retreating from the man's world. We should not be trained to be working wives. We should prepare ourselves to be wonderful mothers, and homemakers, and citizens and individuals that are an example and an inspiration to our associates. We should learn to understand men, to know how to make them happy, how to build up their self-confidence so that they can make a success in their own world of men. A woman can never really fit into the man's world. She may succeed in having an adequate job, and even receive a measure of recognition for outstanding service, but she will always be a "second-rate man."

2. *Do not excel him as a provider:* The second way that you can help a man feel superior as a provider is to not excel him

in his own field. Here again women have made serious mistakes. Not only have they invaded the man's world but they are competing with them for excellence! They are competing for advancement, for honors, awards and recognition. They are competing to "do a better job" than men do. They are trying to outdo them in almost every field and thereby stand as a threat to the man's position. In some instances the wife brings home a larger pay check than her husband's. You can imagine what this does to her husband and his struggle to feel like a superior male. She is defeating him on his own ground.

When we steal from men their rightful places as our providers, we tend to "demasculate" them. A man can suffer a most unhappy feeling when he thinks he is lacking in masculinity. The fact that he may not be responsible for the situation does not lessen his feeling of inadequacy. When the woman proves that he is not needed, he feels inferior, less of a man. The feeling of adequacy in his masculine role is essential, not only to his basic happiness, but to his ability to succeed in life. It is also important to his feelings for his wife — to the success of their relationship.

Equally serious when the woman works, is the harm which comes to her. When she attempts to play a part not intended for her she sacrifices her own special beauty and grace. The moon, when it moves from its sphere of night into day, loses its luster, its charm, its very poetry. And so it is with woman, when she attempts to play a part not intended for her. Gone is the luster, the charm, the poetry that says, "she is a phantom of delight."

Children too suffer when the mother is gone out into the working world. Nothing can replace the mother's love in the life of the child. When we see the harm to the man, to the wife and also the children it should be a deterrent to us in encouraging our young women to plan for careers. Problems would be solved if they would plan to be mothers, homemakers and useful citizens and be an essential part of the feminine world.

Just Reasons for Working

There are a number of just reasons for women working. Certain family emergencies require a temporary assistance from the wife. These, no one would argue, are times a woman "must work." Also, the young wife who is helping her husband obtain an education is justified in working. Her work will help him become an adequate provider. She does not propose a threat to his ability, but displays, instead, trust in his ultimate success.

Single women are also justified in their intermediate days between their father's household and their own. They are not proving their independence, for they are only providing for themselves. They are saying, in effect, "I can support myself, but I could not manage a household and help support a family also. Therefore, I will need a man to provide for me when I am married."

If you want success in your associations with men, therefore, dispense with any thought of a career. Your future happiness will not depend upon receiving money or acclaim, but upon your successful relationships with men and eventually marriage. These are the only things that count in the life of a woman. Do not, however, give him the indication that you are planning "marriage" as a career, for this could cause him to feel that you are taking him too seriously and it might frighten him away.

If you talk about the future, do have plans, but not the all encompassing plans of a career. Talk about plans to get an education, to develop your talents or even to work. These are safe subjects as long as they do not propose a threat to his career. Lead him into conversations about his own career and help him to see that when he does take his place in the working world, he will undoubtedly be a success. In this way, by projecting his thoughts into the future, you will help him to picture himself as a successful provider.

In reviewing Characteristic No. 6, then, we have learned of the man's craving to act the part of the man, the ideal man who is the guide, protector and provider. At no time can he act this part as well as when he is guiding, protecting and providing for someone who seems *dependent* upon his manly care. There will be much more said about this in the chapter on femininity, but in summary we can give the following suggestions:

If you want to help a man take his position as the superior male, dispense with any air of competence or fearlessness, or the ability to kill your own snakes. Instead, develop a quality of *dependency* for his masculine care and protection. Let him lead in your romance and subdue any tendencies to be aggressive or forceful or "forward." If you do engage in any activities which might be competitive with men, such as schoolwork or sports, *do not excel him.* Remember the rule: need him, and do not excel him in anything which requires masculine strength, skill or ability. In this way you help him to feel superior in his role as a man. The following is an outline of these rules:

How to Help Him Feel Superior in his Role as a Man

1. Admire his masculine strength and ability.
2. Do not show indifference or ridicule for his manly skills, strength or abilities.
3. With yourself: Don't be aggressive, independent, competent or efficient in masculine things, or show any ability to kill your own snakes.
4. Be *dependent* and *need* his manly care and protection.
5. *Do not excel him* in anything which requires masculine strength.
6. Recognize him as the leader: In romance let him lead and you follow.

Summary of Understanding Men

We have learned that in order to become the kind of woman a man wants, the kind he can love and cherish, we must have the ability to "understand men." We must know their characteristics, peculiarities and vulnerabilities and their basic needs and feelings, so that we will know just what to do and say in our associations with them. We will be able to avoid mistakes which drive men away, and instead learn the secrets which will bring them to our side. The following are the basic characteristics we must understand:

Six Characteristics of Men

1. His need to be accepted at face value
2. His need for admiration
3. His sensitive pride
4. His secret reserve

5. His need for sympathetic understanding

6. His desire to be superior in his role as man

The woman's gift of understanding is one of the most moving forces which brings a man to her side and causes him to seek her constant company. She also fills a great need in his life as she becomes indispensable to his happiness and helps him grow into manhood. The following experiences which were sent to me by letter, will illustrate:

How Understanding Helped a Young Man Grow

"I've been going out with this fellow for seven months and the change that's come over him is remarkable! When I first started going with him he was extremely reserved and self-conscious around everyone, especially me. He even blushed when he was spoken to. He also appeared as if he were half asleep or dull, with listless eyes. Our dates were spent in almost complete silence all the way there and back. I couldn't put up with this and I am sure he was also uncomfortable, so I started to exercise Fascinating Womanhood principles, especially admiring his manliness.

"Now he is alert and alive, has self pride and a healthy male ego (not too much or not too little) and a good sense of humor. I didn't even know he was there before. He's really beginning to act like a man! He has a certain sparkle in his eye that appears as complete adoration every time he looks at me. Sometimes it is so strong that I can't meet his gaze. He is so considerate and always protecting me and watching out for me. He's always writing little poems and dedicating songs to me. He's so sweet and loving now. I love him!

"One night his final wall of reserve came tumbling down. Mabye you would call it a Pandora's Box reaction, except the thoughts reserved were ones of gratitude and not past resentments. Here is what he said: 'You helped me stay happy through the hard times this year of hurting my leg and failing in my grades. . . . You're always so happy. It radiates . . . I feel I've grown up so much since I've met you. . . . You've inspired me to break the school record in track and will inspire me to do it again in the fall. . . . I get along with people so much better now. . . . I don't know what I would have done this year without you. . . . You're so cute when you get mad and bite your lip and open your eyes wide.'

"Then when he was kissing me goodnight, with his voice full of emotion and tears, he passionately whispered, 'I love you,' and I believe him. I am so happy now, too, and I wouldn't be able to have all of this and more without the help of these principles of understanding men."

An Old Friend Returns

"After studying Fascinating Womanhood I realized how many things were wrong in the way I related to men, so I began to practice the principles, which for a long time seemed so foreign to me, as I had lived such a self-centered life.

"Two weeks ago I heard that an old boyfriend had been through a divorce and was coming to see me. I began to saturate myself with the teachings, made some feminine clothes and grew excited with the anticipation of seeing him again. Via letter I apologized for some of my mistakes when dating him 10 years ago and began to admire him. I told him I believed he had qualities of leadership which I had not recognized previously.

"When he arrived 5 days ago a miracle took place in me. The principles of Fascinating Womanhood became a natural part of me — not foreign anymore and I was able to be the kind of woman I wanted to be and the kind he wanted. As I accepted him, admired him and gave him his freedom to be himself I saw the most beautiful change begin to take place in him. I saw him become and reveal himself to be the kind of man I knew he wanted to be. He shed fears he had developed from his previous unsuccessful marriage. A new manly, domineering strength entered his life.

"By the end of 5 days we had expressed love for each other and asked God to help us to know His will about our lives. I feel like such a feminine woman and admire him as such a masculine man. This is the most wonderful experience I have ever been through."

CHAPTER IX

Inner Happiness

In our study of the ideal woman, the kind a man wants and the kind he will love and treasure, we come to the second quality, that of inner happiness. Men just naturally seek the company of girls who are happy, as we all do. This inner beauty not only captivates the man's interest, but gives his spirits a lift, too, since happiness tends to be "catching." As you will remember in the story of David Copperfield, Agnes shed such a peaceful influence upon David that it "soothed him into tears."

Inner happiness is a quality of serenity, peace of mind and tranquility. Agnes possessed inner happiness for she had "a placid and sweet expression" and "a tranquility about her, a quiet, good, calm spirit." A girl who has inner happiness is not necessarily free from problems, but she does have the power to face these problems, or disappointments or sorrows with a spiritual calm.

A girl who does not have inner happiness is easily upset, troubled, or even disturbed. She may be gloomy over small matters or discouraged with herself, or in a turmoil about things. She cannot stand the stresses or strains of life, the disappointments or problems. When a man is in the presence of such a girl he may, if he has good character, be sympathetic towards her and even try to cheer her up, but he is not apt to be attracted to her. Remember, one of the functions of a woman, as far as men are concerned, is to "shed joy around," and this is difficult if not impossible to do when one is not genuinely and inwardly happy.

Inner happiness is a quality which must be earned. It cannot be "put on," as a smile. It is involuntary and comes as a result of a noble character. The blueprint for attaining this noble character will be explained in the next chapter. Do not be discouraged, therefore, if you are an unhappy person who is troubled or gloomy by nature. You are this way because you are doing something wrong — breaking the rules. It is due to some weakness in your character. But regardless of what kind of person you are now, you can build a wonderful character in the future. If you have not been angelic, you can become angelic and in so doing will automatically earn inner happiness.

The road to happiness, then, lies in the development of our spiritual side. It does not lie in any other direction, regardless of how many people may think otherwise. It is quite important to understand these "mistaken roads" to happiness, so that you will not be fooled or sidetracked into them.

MISTAKEN ROADS TO HAPPINESS

Most everyone of us is trying to be happy. It is one of the most central desires that each one of us has, and yet few people attain true happiness, which only proves that most people are pursuing it in the wrong direction. The trouble lies in the fact that we seek happiness on the road to pleasure. We think that if we just had a charming wardrobe, or more beautiful hair, or a prettier face, then we would be happy. Or we may feel that if we could live in a particular community or had money for the comforts and pleasures of life, then we could be happy. These things do, of course, have a certain value, but they are not the requirements for inner happiness. There are women who have none of these material things and they enjoy inner peace. On the other hand, some who have them all are miserable.

The word pleasure comes from the word *please*. Pleasure is derived from those things which please the *senses*, such as the eyes, nose, ears, mouth and sensual feelings. We must recognize that there are both good and bad pleasures. The good pleasures are such things as sunshine, rain, flowers, nourishing food, the laughter of little children, music, wholesome recreation, the arts and many more of the finer things of life. There is good pleasure in attractive clothes, beautiful homes, gardens, furniture and the conveniences of modern equipment such as vacuum cleaners, washing machines, etc. These things are enriching to life, but we should realize that they bring *pleasure* rather than true *happiness*. This can be proven by the fact that people who have all of the pleasures of earth, may yet fail to find happiness.

Bad pleasures are those things which are derived from sin, or those things which do us harm, rather than good. They are such things as indulgences in immoral sex, bad literature, improper food, drink, smoking, riotous living, improper entertainment, etc. These things do nothing good for either the body or the spirit and should be avoided completely.

The Road to Happiness

Happiness is quite different from pleasure. It arises from a different source. While pleasure arises from those things which please the senses, happiness may even come from unpleasant experiences, such as pain in childbirth, or the weariness, pain or toil by a father to secure comforts for his loved ones. Pleasure may be derived from sin, while happiness is a direct result of the struggle to overcome sin.

Happiness comes from dedicated effort to fulfill our responsibilities in day to day living — no matter how great or small these duties may be. It comes from overcoming our weaknesses and from reaching worthwhile goals and achievements. It is a result of losing our selfcenteredness and becoming interested in the lives of others and developing a genuine love for them. Inner happiness is a direct result of the development of character. To review these sources of happiness:

1. Overcoming our weaknesses, or sins
2. Fulfilling our life's responsibilities
3. Losing our selfcenteredness in our love for others
4. Reaching worthwhile goals or achievements
5. Developing a worthwhile character

Inner happiness is independent of others and outside circumstances. It is within the reach of each one of us through a dedicated effort in the right direction.

Happiness for Women

The way to happiness for a woman is the perfection of her angelic side. As she develops a kind, gentle, sympathetic character, yet one with strength of will, womanly courage and a sense of responsibility, she will grow towards this inner happiness essential to the ideal woman. Then, as she learns to understand men, filling a need in their lives and bringing them greater happiness, she in turn attains the virtues of acceptance, understanding and appreciation, which further add to her happiness.

The greatest source of her happiness will come with the successful fulfillment of her total feminine role. As she becomes an understanding wife, a wonderful mother and a devoted and successful homemaker, she will attain this inner happiness in full measure. Success in the feminine role is her real glory and brings her an inner peace and satisfaction that cannot be met otherwise. Her happiness is not reached without it, for the woman who neglects these sacred duties for other interests, fails as a person and thereby does not earn genuine happiness. She may gain satisfaction from other activities and success outside her home, but they cannot compensate for her failure as a woman. In the words of David O. McKay, "There is no success in life to compensate for a failure in the home."

If, however, the woman becomes narrow in her feminine world, occupied entirely with her own family and their comforts and pleasures, with no thought for anyone else, she will limit her happiness. She must branch out — extend her arms to others, especially those in need of her help. As she gives to those in need, not neglecting her own family, she becomes a person of great worth and earns the highest happiness. The source of happiness for a woman, then, lies in the following:

Source of Happiness for Women

1. Fulfilling her God given responsibility as a wife, mother and homemaker
2. Understanding men
3. Developing a worthy character — overcoming weaknesses and sins
4. Losing her self-centeredness in service and love for others outside the home

(You can see that all of these sources are on the Angelic side.)

You may have heard the statement, "We are just about as happy as we make up our minds to be." Although there is some merit to this positive outlook, the statement is not entirely correct. A wicked person cannot acquire happiness through this positive attitude, nor can one who is neglecting his duties or living a selfish life. You cannot obtain inner happiness by determination alone. You must lay the proper groundwork by living righteous principles.

Happiness is based upon eternal laws. If we are not at peace within, it is because we are not obeying principles upon which this inner peace is based. Inner happiness is available to everyone and is acquired by understanding and applying its principles.

The Unhappy Woman

If you will notice women who are unhappy you will agree that they are not attractive to anyone, so it is easy to see that they would not be charming to men. Especially is it noticeable in the eyes, for a dullness and unhappy expression is apparent, even though they may try to cover it up with a smile. A tendency to poor posture, lackadaisical manner and shuffling of the walk are other signs. Girls who are unhappy are apt to be critical, harsh and quick to judge. They are negative thinkers, and sometimes whiners, and complainers. They appear older, for they have lost their sparkle. If they are extremely unhappy there will be an inner turmoil that is noticeable and also depressing. All of these traits destroy the charm of a girl and make her unattractive to men. A man may be aroused to sympathy for an unhappy woman, but he will not be fascinated or enchanted by her or have a tender feeling which inspires love.

The Happy Woman

A girl who has inner happiness is quite the opposite. There is an inner radiance to the eyes, a serene expression in the face. She has a lightness to her walk, a winsome manner that is inspired by the attitudes of optimism, faith and love. She smiles easily, is content, is slow to criticize. She is trustful and patient and her spirit radiates tranquility, serenity and peace. Her appearance is uplifting to all who view her and fascinating to men.

In reaching the quality of inner happiness, I have said that it must be earned, and that it is earned by the perfection of a wonderful character. All of the virtues of character add to inner happiness, but there are two which I would like to mention as especially essential to women. They are the following:

TWO ESSENTIAL VIRTUES TO A WOMAN'S HAPPINESS

1. *Accepting ourselves:* In the process of becoming Angels we are still human beings and therefore we are apt to make mistakes and failures. We do such things as burn food, spend money foolishly, break an expensive object, lose something, or we are late for an appointment. These errors can cause us to become quite upset with ourselves. Even little things disturb us and rob us of happiness. It is not fair for us to be "hard on ourselves." If we can learn to be forgiving of others, we must do the same for ourselves. Just as we learn to accept men that we associate with, we must learn to accept ourselves as human beings and allow for our mistakes and weaknesses.

I read about a man who loved to travel the world over but was quite upset at times about a problem he faced in foreign lands. In some countries he was deliberately overcharged for purchases. These deceitful people took the joy out of his travels to a degree. By thinking about the problem, the man determined to set aside a certain amount of money for each trip "to be robbed of." From then on he was able to enjoy his trip.

The businessman allows in advance for business failures. We should allow for some mistakes as well. Tell yourself that each year, each week, and even each day you will make your share of mistakes or unwise decisions. When you plan a wardrobe, remember that you may not choose wisely with every item. We learn by experience and this means we make our share of mistakes.

Accepting ourselves, however, *does not mean contentment.* It does not mean that we accept ourselves as foolish, unwise, weak or inferior human beings, making no effort to improve. This attitude would block our progress. It *does* mean that we accept ourselves as human, likely to make mistakes and use poor judgment at times, although we do make an effort to improve. In our efforts to improve we should not become discouraged if old habits are difficult to break. In the swim upstream we are occasionally pushed back by a wave or an opposing current. But this is our road to perfection.

2. *Appreciation of the simple pleasures of life:* Another virtue essential to happiness is an appreciation of the simple joys of

life, such as rain, sunlight, or fresh crisp curtains. It is not so much these simple pleasures themselves that contribute so much to a woman's happiness as it is her ability to *appreciate* them.

The appreciative woman will enjoy drinking water from a tin cup while another feels she must have china dishes. One woman will enjoy sitting on an apple box in her back yard, letting the warm sun shine down upon her shoulders, while another may feel she must have patio furniture to be happy. An appreciative woman will enjoy the sounds of the forest or the birds and the leaves rustling, while another must have grand opera. One will enjoy a simple wardrobe of cottons while another, less appreciative, lives for the day she can buy her clothes on Fifth Avenue. One feels joy in pushing her baby carriage in the park, while another must have the bright lights and gay places. One will enjoy the simple cottage, while another must have a modern home with a view. Little children have this ability to enjoy simple pleasures. A ray of sunshine, a tub of water to splash in are common things they enjoy. The appreciative woman who learns to enjoy these common pleasures is never left wanting.

In summarizing the subject of inner happiness, be reminded of its essential value in feminine charm and that men especially are attracted to it. It is earned by the development of our angelic side, or our spiritual qualities. If you do not have happiness now, it is largely due to some weakness in your character and not to outside circumstances. You may earn it by putting forth the necessary effort.

Happiness is promised to each one of us for God has said: "Eye hath not seen, nor ear heard, nor entered into the heart of man the things that God hath prepared for those that diligently serve him." Serving God, as far as a woman is concerned, means fulfilling her role as wife, mother and homemaker and loving her fellow men.

INNER HAPPINESS IS AN UPWARD CLIMB. IT IS LIKE SWIMMING UPSTREAM AND IS FOUND IN THE GREAT EFFORTS AND ACHIEVEMENTS IN LIFE. IT IS EARNED BY A PERSONAL VICTORY OVER OUR WEAKNESSES AND AN UPWARD REACH FOR THE PERFECTION OF THE SPIRIT.

CHAPTER X

A Worthy Character

In winning the interest of men we cannot overlook the importance of good character. It is, in fact, *essential* in becoming "the kind of woman a man wants." Men always either consciously or unconsciously look for traits of virtue in women and quickly detect any signs of weakness.

Good character is the foundation of a charming *personality* in both men and women. If you will notice people who have "winning ways," you will observe that their charm is based upon traits of character. They are inclined to be kind, generous and considerate, with a genuine love and concern for others. When a person loses the tendency to be self-centered, and develops a real interest in his associates, he can't help but win their friendship and respect. His good character has created for him a winning personality.

In a young woman, good character provides three things in winning the attention and interest of men. First, her worthy character provides the very basics for what a man is looking for in a woman. Then second, it is the framework of a winning personality. Her goodness, her kind consideration of others, her honesty and her strength of will are essential elements of her feminine charm. Then third, her good character earns for her a serenity in the face, a womanly beauty in her manner and her bearing that is especially appealing to men.

Contrast this with a girl who is selfish, deceitful and critical. Not only will she not be good "wife material" in the eyes of a practical man, but she will have a personality that repels men rather than attracts them. As a result of her poor character she will not have the beauty of serenity but instead will have a hardness about the face that spoils her appearance. All of the expensive clothes and good grooming imaginable cannot counteract or hide the unwholesome expression in her face.

Our Models for Study

Agnes, you will remember, had an angelic character. David Copperfield always associated her with a "stained-glass window in a church" and worshipped her from the time he first beheld her. Deruchette was known as the "living form of a benediction," and "sweetness and goodness reigned throughout her person." Amelia was "a tender little domestic goddess" whom men were inclined to worship. These girls must have had inspiring characters to have inspired such reverent feelings from the men in the stories.

And if you will refer to CHAPTER ONE in which I have described "true love," you will remember the worshipful love that John Alden had for Priscilla. "There is no land so sacred, no air so pure as the air she breathes, and the soil that is pressed by her footsteps." Also, the young woman that Victor Hugo loved inspired holy feelings in his heart for he writes: "If she only allow me to give my life to anticipating her every desire . . . if she but permit me to kiss with respect her adored footprints." These feelings of reverence could only be inspired by a woman of true worth and great character.

The Pedestal

A man wants a woman of such high character that he can "place her on a pedestal" and worship her from below. Not only does he expect her to be good, but he wants her to be better than he is. He would like her to be kinder, more patient and forgiving than he is. He rather considers himself to be the more unrefined creature of the human race. If he becomes thoughtless, harsh or critical he may be willing to overlook it in himself, but is disappointed to see a woman, the angelic creature of the earth, fall onto his level. But before a man can place a woman on a pedestal *she must develop a character worthy of that position.*

As you are reading this chapter you might be inclined to think, "This quality of womanly charm is not too essential for me to know. I have been trained all during my youth in the development of the virtues. *I have a worthy character!* The other things in this book are of far more value to me. I am honest, kind and benevolent. You see, I have a fine character."

Such a thought indicates one's failure to understand what good character includes. The virtues mentioned above are essential, of course, but the attainment of a worthy character includes much more. Dora was kind, honest and benevolent, but she did not earn the worshipful love of David Copperfield. Few women earn the eminence of the pedestal! There are many virtues of character, all worth every effort to acquire. The following, however, are ten of the most essential. Several are particularly important for young women.

Qualities of Character Essential to the Pedestal

1. *Self-mastery:*
   "He who rules within himself and rules his passions, desires and fears, is more than a king."   —Milton
   Self-mastery is the foundation of a worthy character. We cannot even apply the knowledge which is in this book if we do not have the will to apply. Self-mastery in the highest sense means control over one's thoughts, feelings, desires, passions, fears and actions. It means deciding what is right or wise to do and then having the will to do it. It means sticking on diets, controlling our words, schooling our feelings, keeping confidences or secrets that have been entrusted to us. It means being on time, fulfilling responsibilities assigned to us, holding to the standards that we set for ourselves and reaching our goals.

   So important is self-mastery to the spiritual achievement that the greatest person of all time felt a need for it. Jesus Christ did not even begin his ministry until he first went into the wilderness and fasted for forty days and forty nights. During this time He gained spiritual strength and was able to endure severe temptations. He gained mastery over himself which was necessary for the completion of his mission in life.

   There are numerous ways of gaining self-mastery. One of the most useful is the example set by the Savior, that of fasting. By depriving ourselves of food for a period of time we gain a self-control that strengthens one for the challenges of life. Usually a 24-hour fast is sufficient and all that many people can endure to begin with.

   There are other methods of strengthening self-control. Many philosophers have advised that we "do something difficult each day" to strengthen the will. Taking cold showers, doing irksome tasks, demanding definite quotas of ourselves are some of the things that we can do to gain self-control, so that when severe temptations come we will have fortified ourselves to resist them. Most of us have had experience setting goals for ourselves, only to find that we let one thing and then another interfere with their accomplishment. This is due to a lack of self-mastery, in most cases. As we practice measures of self-control, such as fasting or doing difficult things, we will gain a self-mastery which will greatly aid us in "sticking to" our goals and eventually attaining them.

2. *Unselfishness:* Another mark of fine character is that of unselfishness. The dictionary describes *selfishness* as "caring unduly or supremely for oneself; regarding one's own comforts, advantages, etc., in disregard, or at the expense of that of others."

Tiny children are by nature selfish. If you will notice, they can gather up every toy in sight and claim them for their own, without the slightest conscience for another child who may be crying at the top of his voice. But, as they are taught they learn unselfishness, learn the joy of sharing and giving. And as they grow towards maturity they tend to lose this childish fault. Our growth towards becoming a finer person, in fact, is directly parallel with our ability to overcome selfishness. Unfortunately there are some who find it difficult to drop this trait and carry selfish tendencies throughout a lifetime. Whereas it is tolerable in little children, it becomes almost unbearable in a mature adult.

Young girls should take care lest they retain this childish fault of selfishness. Being young, they may still be inclined to think too much about their own clothes, comforts and social success with little regard for the feelings and needs of those about them. To be selfish is to live a narrow life. It is wrong and a real weak point of character.

To be unselfish requires self-sacrifice. In fact, to give when there is no sacrifice would hardly be called unselfish. For example, if you give away clothes that you dislike or do not need, it is not unselfish since there is no sacrifice. But if you give something of your own, which you like and want, but which you recognize that someone else needs even more than you do, this is an act of unselfishness.

There is perhaps nothing which builds the angelic character of a woman more than unselfishness. It enlarges her spirit, enriches her life. Women such as this are blessings to this earth and in return they attain a beauty of spirit which is charming in their personality and which men admire greatly.

3. *Love and concern for others:* (Benevolence) Going a step beyond unselfishness is to have a genuine love and concern for others, especially those whom you associate with from day to day. We live in a world of people who need our help in various ways. Some need actual assistance, but many more need only a word of encouragement or just the strength of a warm friendship.

One of the marks of a girl of fine character is her love and concern for her parents. If you have not been thoughtful of them, spend time thinking about your father and the responsibilities he faces in providing for the family, etc. Then remember your mother. She is not just a piece of furniture. She is a human being with needs and feelings which should be understood by her children. Your kind assistance and concern for her welfare will be uplifting and will have more far reaching effects than you may realize.

Another mark of character is a concern for older people, for they are often desperately lonely and need the brightness of youth to cheer them. I remember years ago knowing a young girl who was a friend to all of the older people. She was charming and had many friends her own age, but she would always stop in church to converse to this or that older person, to laugh with them, pay attention to them and cheer them with her spirit. Everyone soon learned to love her for her generosity and considered her a girl of great worth.

In giving love and concern for those outside of your family circle and of your own age, you will need to take reasonable care. It would not be wise for you to become friends with "just anyone." Certainly some people would be of improper influence and a few might even be dangerous. It will require some discrimination, therefore, to determine just whom you will be safe in befriending. Remember, however, that it is "only a few words of encouragement" that you need give in most cases, and not a close friendship. It is not necessary to accept social invitations from those you befriend.

Brotherly love has always been rather difficult to define. It is not something superficial, given out of a sense of duty. Real love is a *feeling*, one of the strongest feelings in the world. A man and a woman may have it for one another (aside from romantic love) or a parent may have love for his children but it is also experienced outside the family circle. Those who never love go empty-handed through life, strangers to the most moving feeling in existence.

The greatest enemy to love is a faultfinding attitude. It is impossible to love someone at the same time you feel resentful or critical towards him. The way to love is to accept a person as he is, both virtue and fault and then look to his finer side and concentrate on that.

Those you bestow love upon will be quick to perceive it. They will be able to detect by the tone of your voice or the soft look in your eyes, your feeling of genuine love. But even without these outward expressions love is easily felt. It is the most wonderful feeling that human beings can experience and one that people everywhere hunger for more than they do for food. Giving true brotherly love is the greatest service that you can render.

4. *Chastity:* The word chastity specifically means "to not engage in sexual relations with anyone outside of marriage, or with anyone to whom you are not legally and lawfully wed." This is not man's law, but God's law, and was intended to last for all generations of time. This law of chastity was created for our well being and happiness and is especially essential to the happiness of a woman, for a number of reasons.

Contrary to this law of God, there has come into existence a "new morality" which teaches an opposite doctrine. This new code teaches our youth that chastity is no longer important, that they can engage in "free love" with anyone, and that marriage is no longer required. It is strange that they think they can take a god-given law, that has been tried and proven for thousands of years and toss it out, without ill effects. One need only to look around to see the results of the "new morality." Are those who engage in it people of worth? Are they the builders of the nation and the strength of society? Do they create homes that will inspire children to be better citizens and to have higher goals? No, they are the "free loaders" who are drifting downstream. They are not the lifters of society, but the leaners. When they speak they have nothing to offer the youth that makes life richer and fuller. They only offer a life of indulgences and frustrations. It is best, young girls, to listen to those who know the answers — those who know the way to true happiness and peace.

There are several strikes against this new morality that each young woman should understand. In the first place, it does not lead to happiness. Whether we realize it or not, there are certain definite laws in operation in this life which cannot be changed or altered. One of these laws is that you cannot be happy unless you are morally clean. *It is impossible,* no matter how you may think otherwise. In fact a rejection of moral codes can even lead to mental and emotional disturbances. This information does not come alone from the clergy or from religious experience, but from the professions of human relations and psychology. For example, Dr. Max Levine, M.D. and Psychiatrist of New York Medical College has said:

"I speak not as a clergyman but as a psychiatrist. There cannot be emotional health in the absence of high moral standards and a sense of human and social responsibility."

Another strike against the new moral code is that it can alter a woman's looks. It is impossible to have the tranquil angelic beauty that men find so attractive without being sexually pure. Of course, men can be attracted to other things about a woman. He can, for example, lust after her body or he can admire the physical structure of her face but this has nothing to do with his admiration for true womanly beauty of appearance. He finds such beauty only in the angelic woman who is pure and chaste.

Another strike against the new morality is that sexual indulgence is destructive to the character. Not only does it in itself corrupt the character of the individual, but it becomes a weak link in a chain that can lead to other weaknesses. When a person relaxes his sexual morals he opens the door for other deviations. It becomes easier to be dishonest, irresponsible and disobedient.

Still another strike against it, as far as women are concerned, is that it is foolish. Marriage was designed for a purpose — as a protection to a woman. It is highly foolish to give yourself to a man outside of marriage. Too many hearts have been broken, too many lives ruined when a girl yields without the protection of marriage. In other words, when a man is free to "help himself" to "love her and then leave her" without the obligation of marriage, he may find it easy and desirable to do so.

Some girls foolishly think that they must yield to a man sexually because they may lose him if they don't. Actually just the opposite is more likely to be true. When a man can indulge himself in sex without the obligation of marriage, he is apt to "take his full measure" of her and then walk away, free of the responsibility of marriage. She is more apt to lose than win.

There are, then, several convincing reasons for remaining chaste. First, we cannot have inner happiness without it. Second, we cannot attain true womanly beauty of appearance without it. Third, our strength of character depends upon being sexually pure. And fourth, considering the wise and foolish aspects, marriage is a protection to a woman, a protection she would be foolish to forfeit for the temporary pleasures of premarital sex.

5. *Honesty:* It is difficult to say which of the virtues are the most important but honesty is certainly one of them. One cannot lead a moral and wholesome life if one is not honest. Most of us have been trained in the basics of honesty, in that we would not think of stealing or telling lies. These standards, however, do not necessarily make us an honest person, for we may be dishonest in the more subtle forms.

Some of the more obscure forms of dishonesty are such things as cheating on tests, making excuses which are not entirely true, lying about our age, failing to return money or goods which do not belong to us, or which have been given to us by mistake, taking pay for jobs we did not complete, failure to leave identification for damaged property (cars, etc.), giving false reasons for improper conduct, failure to take the blame for bad behavior, etc.

If you will think about these things carefully yŏu will soon see that our failures are caused by *fear* — the fear of humiliation, embarrassment or loss of money, comforts or goods. In order to overcome these dishonest tendencies, it is important first to gain some moral courage, so that these fears can be overcome. Then, one has to develop a sense of values, and be convinced that honesty is worth far more than material goods, comforts or our personal pride. To be honest in spite of any inconvenience or embarrassment to us is the attitude of a wholesome person who lives a worthy life. There is an old statement, "Do what is right and let the consequences follow." This is the frame of mind necessary for a person who is determined to live an honest life at all costs. And whatever the temporary "consequences" may be, the overall results of an honest life will be rewarding a thousandfold, not only for the strength of character gained, but for the well formed life that comes as a reward.

Another form of honesty is *sincerity*. Men in particular appreciate this quality in women. A man admires a woman who is at all times herself, who does not put on the false front of trying to be someone else. There are some girls who make the mistake of being one thing at home and trying to be quite another when they are out socially with men. A girl may be afraid that if the man were to see her as the plain little Jane that she really is he would be disappointed. So she takes on another character — another image. She may be "groovy" or "mod" or "sophisticated" or anything but the type of personality that she really is. At home she may be a relaxed, demure and charming girl, one that a man could truly love, but this image may not seem exciting enough to her. She must be "in," so that others will see that she is really not just a plain little girl after all. This effort is not only a waste of time but it can do harm to her image. Her false front seldom deceives anyone. The fraud is usually quickly detected and interpreted as insincere. The man, you can be sure, will be immensely disappointed to discover that she is a *phoney*.

Now there are some girls who actually have the characteristics mentioned. They may be genuinely "groovy" or "mod" or "sophisticated." If the quality is real it can be charming and will impress men so. But remember, these girls are the same all of the time — at home or out socially. They are not frauds or phonies. They are just themselves. Whatever your true personality, try to discover it, polish it up so that it will be at *its best* and then give it to the world without apology.

6. *Humility:* Humility is *a correct estimation of ourselves as we really are, and as God sees us.* It means viewing ourselves not less than we are, or more than we are, but just as we are. It means an evaluation of our good points and recognizing our weaknesses, then measuring our total worth as a result. It does not mean "groveling" or denouncing ourselves as inferior human beings. It is an honest evaluation.

True humility is one of the most essential elements of a noble character. All of the really great people in this life have had humility, regardless of their position or outstanding qualities. They have been able to see themselves in a true light, have been able to recognize their greatness and yet have acknowledged their weaknesses. No one is so great or good that he has no need of humility.

There are a great number of people, however, who lack this virtue, who are very proud of their position, wealth, accomplishments, talent or other advantages and who take pleasure in feeling superior to others and delight in causing others to feel less than themselves. This tendency to be proud and haughty is a great evil and one which God has denounced. In the book of Proverbs the Lord is quoted as having said, "Six things doth the Lord hate, yea, seven are an abomination to Him." The first one on the list is "A proud look."

If you intend to develop a character worthy of a pedestal it will be important to take stock of yourself to see if you have a tendency to be lifted up in pride. There are a number of ways that we tend to be proud. Three of these to carefully consider are:

a. *With worldly goods:* It is difficult for those with money and lavish possessions to keep from being lifted up in pride. There is a natural tendency for women who are dressed in expensive and stylish clothes and who drive the latest model automobiles and who live in luxurious surroundings, to feel superior to women who have less. In some cases they take pleasure in parading their fine possessions before those who have little material wealth, making them feel inferior. Such a lack of humility is an indication of moral and spiritual weaknesses.

b. *With knowledge:* Another source of unwholesome pride is knowledge which can come from higher education, native ability, gifts, talents and what some consider higher intelligence. A recognition of these special gifts or accomplishments is not wrong, but a feeling of superiority can be, and demonstrates a lack of humility. People who are highly intelligent and have great stores of knowledge are seldom proud and haughty about their abilities, but usually have a noticeable amount of humility. They realize that in spite of their talents, there is yet a vast sea of knowledge which is undiscovered, and which they may feel limited to explore. They recognize the greatness of those who have come before them and those in the future who may yet discover knowledge that would dwarf the present day accomplishments. They live in between a realization of their own contributions and an awareness of their limitations. They also realize that others in their own day know far more about certain subjects than they. Their knowledge, great as it is, is limited to specific fields.

c. *Humility in righteousness:* There is a tendency to be lifted up in pride because of the goodness of our lives. We may be making an honest effort to live a pure and wholesome life, to hold to high standards and overcome weaknesses. When we compare ourselves to others who do not appear to be making an effort according to our terms, we are naturally tempted to feel superior to them. To feel humble in this situation is extremely difficult but is a real mark of character. The thing to do is to tell ourselves that "we are no judge of a person's true worth." This person may now appear to be weak and irresponsible, but he may yet live a life more worthwhile than our own. He may have hidden qualities that have not yet come to life or been brought to the test. Also, we must consider the person's background. He, or she, may not have had the advantages of proper training. They may not have been inspired by good parents and other family members, to a better way of life. If given a proper chance or equal opportunities to your own, they may show their better side.

When we are tempted to be critical of someone, we can keep ourselves humble by remembering our own faults and imperfections. We may be superior to the person in some ways, but not all. As a total person we are unlikely to be better than they. At least we are in no position to judge another person's worth. True humility brings with it the qualities of patience, forgiveness, acceptance and love. It is almost impossible to love someone without humility.

In our striving for a worthy character and climbing to the position of the pedestal, we should not lose our spirit of humility or we will lose one of the foundation stones of character. No matter how righteous we become there is always someone to whom we can compare ourselves who is more worthy. There is always some greater nobility which we can be striving to attain. These attitudes promote a feeling of humility.

7. *Moral courage:* Moral courage is the ability to live according to our own convictions. It means a firmness or determination to live that which we believe with a disregard for the pressures of others to persuade us to live otherwise. It is one thing to set standards for ourselves and quite another to have the moral courage to be true to these standards. For example, you may determine that you will not drink alcoholic beverages, or eat desserts, or snack late at night. Then you find yourself in a situation where people are persuading you to break your rules. Due to fear, or the risk of being different from the group, you are tempted to break your standards, or to yield to their influences. This is due to a lack of moral courage.

Another example is when you set goals for yourself, with the best of intentions of reaching these goals. You may determine to do well in your studies this semester but find that others rob you of the time to study. First one person will drop by and fail to take the hint that you are busy. Then you receive numerous phone calls or demands which occupy your time and attention. It may be difficult to resist these distractions, but a failure to do so is a lack of moral courage — the courage to tell your friends that you have important things to do.

Quite often our failures to hold to the things we believe in or want to do are not so much a matter of will power, as they are a lack of moral courage. We yield to the pressures of other people. Because we hesitate to offend them or because we want to be accepted by them and to be like them, we succumb easily to their influences. A person of strong moral courage, however, will not yield to the influences of his associates, but live his life according to the dictates of his own conscience. He does not "go with the group."

8. *Forgiveness:* To forgive is to be willing to pardon a wrong that someone has committed against us. Unfortunately, it is not within our human nature to be forgiving. For example, when someone has been critical, has said some unkind things about you behind your back, the tendency is to "punish" him the next time you see him by being cool and unfriendly. In this way you "get even" or level the score. There is a certain feeling of *justice* in giving "pain for pain," which we cannot deny. But, although it may seem fair, is it right? The Master taught us many hundreds of years ago that we should "resist not evil" and instructed us to "do good to those that hate us and pray for those who despitefully use us."

Forgiveness is a higher law — one that goes beyond justice. Since this higher law runs counter to human nature it requires effort and self-discipline to live it and to overcome the tendency to "fight back." The best way to learn forgiveness is to remind yourself of your own faults and weaknesses. This will make you much more patient and forgiving of others.

People of fine character and personality invariably have the virtue of forgiveness; they are able to rise above the trivial things in life and concentrate upon the good and the beautiful. Those with especially noble characters are able to "forgive much" in others, are able to take into their circle of love those who may not deserve it. Admirable and angelic women have always had this quality.

The unforgiving do harm to others but they do an even greater disservice to themselves. As they hold resentments and ill will within themselves they bring destructive effects to their own bodies and spirits. There have been many instances in which unforgiving persons have become enraged with anger towards their offenders, and have grown ill and died. Many also, have held resentments which have made them emotionally or mentally ill. This only proves that the unforgiving are the real losers.

The important thing to keep in mind is that forgiveness is essential to a noble character — one worthy of the pedestal and attractive womanhood. If you want to be the kind of a woman that men worship, you will have to lose all tendencies to hold grudges and resentments towards your associates and be willing to overlook their faults and offenses. Their actions and weaknesses are not your responsibility. Your responsibility is only to forgive them.

There are times, however, when we as human beings do need to rise up and defend ourselves against offenses or improper treatment. I am speaking of times when we have been criticized, insulted or misjudged too far, to the point of it being damaging to the spirits. There is, or should be, a human dignity in every human being that commands proper treatment and respect. When mistreated too far it is admirable to rise and make a proper defense. At first this may seem inconsistent with forgiveness, but it is not if properly understood. When we rise to defend ourselves, we can still do so without rancor or bitterness. We can be forgiving even at the time we are speaking, but we can, in all fairness to ourselves, command fair treatment. In doing this we earn respect for ourselves and also from our associates. This spirit of self-dignity will be explained in the next point of character.

9. *Self-dignity:* Those who have self-dignity have a proper respect for themselves, never place themselves in an inferior position, nor will they allow others to reduce them to an inferior position. They have a stability of spirit, a feeling of self-worth which keeps them from being treated as an inferior.

Those who lack self-dignity tend to be *too willing to please.* In an effort to win friendship of another person, they do many special favors. We see an example of this in young children. A neglected child may try to win favor of a well thought of child by giving him gifts and doing special favors. He lets him in front of the lunch line, shares the prize Easter egg, lets him grab the last swing on the playground and a thousand and one other things he is not deserving of, in an effort to win his friendship. Unfortunately this does not win the favor of the well thought of child, but usually only awakens a feeling of lack of respect because of the child's inability to appear as an equal.

People of all ages make this mistake. College students, for example, sometimes loan cars and clothes to those they consider their superiors, in an effort to win their favor. An unpopular boy may loan his car to a boy he considers socially respected; a plain shy girl may loan her clothes to a girl she considers better looking and more popular; or she may offer to do her dishes, sew her clothes or cater to other requests in an unconscious effort to win her friendship. Sadly enough, instead of winning favor they are more apt to be further spurned for their lack of self-respect.

Once in a while we may meet a person who strives valiantly to please us in other ways. They meet us with ingratiating smiles, listen eagerly every time we open our mouths, anticipate our every wish, laugh mirthfully at every jest and magnify our every accomplishment. They humble themselves to the point that we are afraid they are going to "lick our hands," and in spite of a hundred and one things they do for us deserving of gratitude we can't help but dislike them for their lack of self-dignity because they appear as our inferiors rather than our equals.

Their fault lies in thinking too much of us and too little of themselves. We are glad to accept the approval of our equals but are little flattered by those who consider themselves our inferiors. If the person is a woman we can't help expecting her to respect herself as a human being, queen of all earth's creatures and the equal of every other human being. When, instead, we see her cringe in self-effacement before us, we are naturally disappointed.

Those who lack self-dignity also tend to be *too servile*. Take for example the woman who makes a slave of herself for her family and for her friends. The poor thing is always called upon to do this or that or the other thing and is never heard to hesitate or complain. Instead of being thanked for it, she is rewarded only with grudging toleration. When we see this divine creature, a woman, transformed into a mechanical drudge, we can't help feeling a certain contempt for her for falling so far below our standards. In her slavery to others she seems to be only paying a natural tribute of an inferior to her superiors and accordingly undeserving of neither thanks nor respect. This does not mean that we should be unwilling to do our share of the hard work or menial tasks. It only means that we maintain a spirit of self-dignity in our labors and that we not allow others to impose on us unduly or push work onto us that rightfully belongs to someone else.

Another way a girl may lack self-dignity is in the tendency she may have to *belittle herself to friends.* Such remarks as "I'm so dumb," or "my nose is too big," or "my hair is so stringy," or "my mouth is so large," or "my complexion is broken out again" are expressions which discredit herself to others. These negative statements only reaffirm her weak points, both in her mind and those of her friends and indicate a lack of self-respect. She may, of course, be just "fishing for compliments," but this motive does little for her picture of self-dignity.

Another sign of lack of self-dignity is the tendency to be *easily pushed around, walked on or abused.* It is not in our human nature to respect those who can be trampled on and men especially do not respect women who will allow this mistreatment. They admire women who have some spunk and enough self-dignity to defend themselves. A later chapter will deal with this special problem and will outline just the right way to handle these situations in a way that will preserve self-dignity and charm and at the same time add to her relationship with the man.

Still another evidence of lack of self-dignity is in placing oneself in the position of *pleading or begging,* since it reduces one to an inferior position. Self-dignity implies a "queenly attitude and bearing" and is a matter of character as well as charm. It in no way indicates a lack of humility but rather shows a proper respect for self, as we would for any other of God's creatures.

I have explained the different situations in which women lower *themselves* to an inferior position. Sometimes, however, *others* are to blame for placing you in the position of disadvantage. There is a tendency for those who have more money, clothes or talents, to take on an air of superiority which is quite discomforting. Knowing how to deal with these persons in a way which will preserve our self-dignity is all important.

The Snob

A person who has money or material advantage and who deliberately uses them to make another person feel inferior is known as a snob. These people seem to derive a fiendish joy from parading their possessions or accomplishments before others that would shame a savage gloating over his beads. Sensitive and gentle women are apt to be discomposed somewhat in the face of such rude vanity. With a little thought, however, you can succeed in giving the snob the contempt and indifference she deserves. The secret is this. As long as you respond to her tactics with obvious pain she will be rewarded and will continue her coarse pastime of gloating over her supposed superiority. The minute, however, that you stop showing pain at her jibes, she will lose all pleasure in making them and transfer her attentions, unfortunately, to another. Moreover, she will respect you for your self-dignity, your refusal to be made to feel inferior. She cannot help feeling a wholesome admiration for those who are superior to her attack. Your attitude of mind is really the most important factor in determining how either the snob or anyone else is going to treat you.

Whether in the forms just mentioned or in the many modifications of them, lack of self-dignity is always distasteful. Unless you respect yourself as the divine creature nature intended you to be, others cannot respect you. Unless you have respect for yourself you cannot maintain the proper bearing in your associations with others, either in family or in social life. No matter how admirable your other attributes, society will regard you as alien. Finally, without self-dignity, an otherwise admirable character is discredited.

In building self-dignity it is important to first take a good look at yourself. If you are a weak, lazy irresponsible girl who never does anything upon which to build a respect, you are defeated before you begin. You will first have to work to *be* at your best if you expect to build a self-respect which will make you feel equal to others. First straighten up your character and make something of your life and strive to be a person of real worth. Also, always appear at your best. If your hair, your clothes and your posture are respectable, you will naturally feel more respect for yourself. If you can live in such a way as to build a genuine self-respect, regardless of any material disadvantage you may have such as lack of money, physical appearance or lack of social prestige, you will build a self-dignity which will make it easy for you to feel equal to every other human being.

10. *Gentle, tender quality:* A quality of character especially important for women is *gentleness*. It is the framework upon which we build true femininity. Men of fine character also have the quality of gentleness, but in them it is mixed with strength. A charming woman of fine character is expected to have gentleness in abundance, without reservation. This does not indicate weakness or a lack of moral fiber or firmness. Gentleness is a part of the feminine nature — and essential to fine womanly character.

The quality of gentleness is a combination of several other virtues such as sympathy, benevolence, understanding, compassion, long suffering and kindness. These qualities combine to form the gentle, tender quality we speak of here. The opposite of this virtue would be the traits of harshness, criticalness or bitterness which are so undesirable in human relations and also so unattractive in women.

If there is anything which will destroy feminine charm and along with it the illusion of an angelic character, it is a fierce frown, a hard expression about the mouth or a bitter tone in the voice. These outer expressions indicate a hard unyielding character and one which is not represented in our ideal of the angelic women.

The women that we all admire, both men and women alike and especially little children, are those wonderful angelic creatures who are soft spoken, who have firm but gentle attitudes, quick to forgive our offenses, slow to criticize us for our mistakes, who lend to the household an atmosphere of peace and harmony due to their gentle natures. These are the angels men speak of in their memoirs. Usually these same men admit that they did little to deserve the kind, gentle understanding of such a mother or a wife, but they appreciate her all the more because she gave them more than they deserved.

This gentle, tender nature should be showered upon all of our associates, not merely those who deserve our kindnesses.

Christianity teaches that "God maketh the rain to fall upon the just and the unjust" and oriental teachings compare the perfect life with the lotus blossom — which sheds its fragrance upon all within its reach. If gentleness is to be a genuine part of our character, then, it is for all human beings, not merely for our own families and circles of friends and those whom we may happen to want to shed it upon. Gentleness is, in fact, a part of real character only when it is habitual, every moment of the day with every person we meet.

How to Acquire a Beautiful Character

There are many other virtues of character. These are only 10 of the most essential. You can acquire a beautiful character in the same way that you would acquire any other accomplishment, by diligent effort. However, with worthy character, it would be difficult to make any measure of progress without the assistance of earnest and daily *prayer.* The goal is too high and the forces of opposition too strong to gain any real success without the guidance of God from day to day. You may be able to become a good pianist, a good tennis player or public speaker by persistence and exercise alone, but the perfection of a wonderful character is not entirely within our reach without faith in God, and His divine assistance. He will be your strength in times of trouble and temptation and will lend to you His spirit to mellow your character as well as to give you strength and honor.

Since there are many virtues worth attaining, it will be best to take them one at a time. Decide which is your weakest point and then work on that for a month or two, or as long as is necessary to make some real progress. Then go on to another and another, and back again to your weaker ones. You will be aware of improvement as you begin to draw others to you by the force of your angelic personality.

Is Good Character Beyond Your Reach?

Do not fear that the attainment of a fine character is beyond the realms of possibility for you. Your character is not fixed or unchangeable. It was made to grow, to unfold until you become an angelic woman. *You can become a worthy person.* It is up to each person to believe in this goal and in his god-given potential to reach it. We never know what is in our character — it is always more or less an unexplored mine in which there are depths we never dreamed of. To be sure, we are familiar with only a few surface details which trick us into imagining we know ourselves; but let a great crisis come, let us be thrown upon our own resources; let a dear one meet with disaster or let a great responsibility be suddenly thrust upon us and there arises from the unexplored depths below the surface, qualities of character which neither ourselves nor others ever suspected. On such occasions we seem to acquire a different personality.

If you will deliberately explore the depths of your own character you will be surprised to learn of the latent qualities which you can bring to the surface and of the injustice you have committed by underrating yourself. You will perceive that you have been smothering your real character under a woodenlike exterior that was caused by a lack of belief in yourself. You will realize that with dedicated effort you can have an angelic character and make yourself desirable to men.

But, you may insist, "I am just an ordinary human being, with serious faults of character. I am not an angel. I can't aspire to the 'living form of a benediction.' I can never hope, with my ordinary character, to arouse such reverence and adoration as the authors of Deruchette and Amelia."

But, are you so far from being an angel as you think you are? You may not have done anything in the past which deserves particular reverence, but how do you know what you will do in the future? How do you know that your character, if it were put to a serious test, wouldn't prove as worthy of worship and reverence as that of any woman living? Look at the millions of ordinary girls who have become our world's extraordinary mothers. Most of them had to grow, had to be put to the test before they became great mothers. But their potential was there, during their youth. They only *became* great mothers. There have also been wives who have proven themselves to be the inspiration for their husband's success and greatness. They are angels — their husband's refuge and his strength in times of trouble — his joy in times of triumph. These angels were once ordinary girls whom no one particularly recognized as noble in character. They only *became* angels. Each one of us has within us the seeds of a fine angelic character if we but believe in ourselves and work to bring it into being.

How Do Women of Poor Character Win Men?

Do not become confused with the thought that there are many girls who do not appear to have angelic characters, yet who somehow contrive to win men. The answer to the question is this: The girl may appear to be ordinary to you and to others, and even to herself, but her lover has found some evidence of true character that he admires. Either he has discovered a beautiful trait, or she has revealed her true character to him, whereas she withholds it from others. She may appear an ordinary girl to the world but when she is with him, the man she loves, she reveals her finer side, a side that he appreciates.

Amelia and Deruchette, in the eyes of themselves and others, were perhaps just ordinary girls. They seemed angels not to all men, but only to one or two. Similarly, the girls who seem to you so faulty, but who nevertheless have won a man, may not be angels in your estimation or their own, but they are in the estimation of their adorers. Men seem to seek out in the object of their affections the spark of divinity inherent in every human being; once having found that spark they seem blind to a thousand faults. The fact that lovers can see in each other qualities that are invisible to others has given rise to the notion that love is blind.

Every man ascribes fine character to the object of his affections. No man who really adores a woman can conceive of her as anything but an angel, a goddess, the very essence of purity and goodness. That this quality is necessary to true womanly attractiveness has been insisted upon by every poet and lover that ever lived.

There are a few women with base or evil characters who still manage to win a man. If this is the case, they have either deceived the man into thinking they have a worthy character, or they have attracted a man of equally low standards. In either case a state of real love cannot exist, for true love is based upon a feeling of worship. They have forfeited the real rewards for only a physical gratification.

Be Sincere and Consistent

Do not think that you can be successful if you merely pretend to have a fine character. Insincerity is a form of dishonesty and a serious weakness of character. If you are to win the interest of men your character will have to be genuine. If you only *pretend* to have a fine character your fraud will most likely be detected. If you insist upon keeping a skeleton in your closet it is bound to rattle around occasionally and betray your insincerity. However well satisfied you are with your deception, a shade of darkness will flit across your eyes, a grating tone creep now and then into your voice or a cruel line appear at the corner of your mouth. The betrayal may be only momentary but it will be unmistakable. You will therefore have to *acquire* a true character if you are to be successful with men.

If you are to be successful, you will also have to be consistent. You cannot be angelic on some occasions and unwholesome on others. You cannot have a Sunday character and an everyday one. Once you begin to strive for a lovely character you will have to try to stick to it every minute of the day and every day of the week. There will be times, being human, when you will slip back into old undesirable habits, but this is normal. If you continually strive for a fine character, progress will be certain.

Let Your Light Shine

Not only is it important to *have* a fine character, you must convince *the man* that you have one. To do this *let your light shine,* as mentioned in the Bible, or in other words, *display your angelic side.*

Now there are many girls who have fine characters and although they display them to their families and close friends may never reveal them to the men in their lives. It has apparently never occurred to them that men can only appreciate what they can *see,* or *detect.* If women are to arouse the admiration of men to the point that they will place them on a pedestal, they must *display* their angelic side. It is important, therefore, that you *"let your light shine"* or put your character *on a candlestick,* rather than *under a bushel* where no one can see it. Do those things which you do naturally for your family and friends, so that men can appreciate you as they do.

Try not to confuse *letting your light shine* with the serious fault of *blowing your trumpet before you,* as also mentioned in the Bible. This fault was offensive to God. It was a method used by the hypocrites to impress others by calling attention to their good works. They misrepresented themselves and deceived others into thinking that they were better than they were. The image that they presented to others was not the image that they really were.

On the other hand, *letting your light shine* is a virtue. It indicates that you really do have a fine character, or *light,* and that you are showing to others the person that you really are. This method has been advocated as a means of "inspiring others," or encouraging them to good works by example. A young lady, when she has a fine character and displays it to her associates, will inspire them to be better.

There are different ways of "letting your light shine." If you acquire the ten traits of character mentioned here men will perceive your character by the angelic "light" which radiates from your face. However, they will not be altogether convinced of your true worth until they see your true character in action. The following are some methods of "letting your light shine":

How to Let Your Light Shine

1. *Hold to your ideals:* If you will hold to your high standards and ideals, in your normal experiences with men you will have many occasions which will reveal your angelic side. These will come without any conscious effort on your part. You will be brought to many tests and will meet these tests. Men will gradually come to know your true worth.

2. *In conversation, reveal your true self:* In your conversations with men, you will be able to reveal your standards, high ideals and goals. As you talk about this and that, you can get on to subjects which reveal your true character and how you feel about life. Deliberately steer the conversation into the subject of standards, family life, morals, social responsibility, etc., so that he will be able to get acquainted with your angelic side. He will begin to detect the framework of a beautiful character by just what you say.

3. *Appreciate his character:* Another method of proving your own worth is to appreciate *his*. If you appreciate him *only* because he looks polished and well groomed, or because he is a lot of fun, you do little to indicate that you have fine character; but if you appreciate him because he is *honest, dependable* and *fair,* you prove that you claim these attributes as your own.

4. *Appreciate the character in others:* Your estimation of others is a real indication of your own character. For example, if you are faultfinding and harsh in your judgment of your friends, you give yourself away as a person of weak character, lacking the qualities of forgiveness, patience and humility. Also, if you appreciate only the superficial traits in others, such as a nice hairdo, good taste, or some talent that could belong to the weak as well as the strong of character, you will not appear as a person who appreciates the real values of life. But if you recognize and treasure *unselfishness* in others, or *benevolence* and *patience,* etc., then you prove that you have a fine character or you would not be so quick to perceive it in others.

Shaking the Pedestal

As I have stated in the beginning of this chapter, when a man considers the ideals of womanly character he expects her to be *better than himself* and therefore deserving of a place on a pedestal. Now in man's relationship with women he tends to *shake the pedestal,* or to *test her character.* He wants to see for himself if she is as angelic as she appears to be, to see if she will hold fast to the position of the pedestal. He may not be fully aware of his motive for shaking the pedestal, but consciously or unconsciously he must find out for himself her true worth.

In testing her he may, for example, suggest that she lower her standards or deviate in some way from her true character. He may try to persuade her to keep unwholesome company or attend a low standard movie or if she does not drink he may offer her an alcoholic beverage. If she remains true to her ideals, his admiration for her is reaffirmed. Remaining on the pedestal is only further proof that she belongs there. If, however, she lowers her standards and falls from the pedestal to a lower level, he is naturally disappointed in her.

We women must realize the seriousness of the man's attempt to shake the pedestal or to test our character. If we fall, not only do we injure ourselves but we lose favor in the eyes of the man. An impressive example of pedestal shaking is found in the novel *The Portrait of Dorian Grey*.

The girl in the story was, for the most part, angelic in character. She and Dorian Grey loved each other and were engaged to be married. Just prior to their proposed marriage he tempted her by asking her to engage in pre-marital relations with him. At first she was shocked; then disappointed, she turned to walk away. As she reached the door she hesitated, thought about it, and an immense fear seized her, a fear that she may lose him if she refused. She turned around and came back to him and yielded to his request. The next day Dorian Grey expressed his great disappointment in her and his reluctance to marry her. He shook the pedestal but she fell off. The poor girl, broken-hearted and rejected, committed suicide.

CONCLUSIONS

As I have stated, a man can truly love only a woman of angelic character, one he can place on a pedestal and one who can inspire a feeling of worship in his heart. I have pointed out ten essential virtues of character and suggested that you work diligently to acquire them in your preparation of becoming the kind of girl a man wants. I have also suggested that you display this true character by "letting your light shine" so that he will be convinced that you belong on a pedestal. And finally, I have warned you that a man may shake the pedestal at times to test you, to see if you are the worthy person you appear to be. If you acquire a fine character and meet the test, you will have one of the essential elements of Angela Human, the kind of girl a man adores.

CHAPTER XI

The Domestic Goddess

The fourth quality of Angela Human is her domestic or homemaking ability. This means that she must be able to cook, sew, manage a household, care for children, handle money wisely and a myriad of other things that go to make up the homemaker. These qualities are only a small part of the ideal woman, but they are essential. There are, of course, some women lacking in these qualities who still manage to win men but they do not represent our ideal, the kind of woman a man will love and cherish. There will definitely be something missing as far as men are concerned.

Domestic qualities are found in our studies of Agnes, Amelia and Deruchette. Agnes was "as staid and discreet a housekeeper as the old house could have." Amelia was a "kind, smiling, tender little domestic goddess whom men are inclined to worship." Deruchette's "presence lights the home" and "her occupation is only to live her daily life." Then the author says, "When womanhood dawns, this angel flies away; but sometimes returns, bringing back a little one to mother." These three girls, who represent at least in part our ideal of Angela Human, had qualities of the domestic goddess — qualities that men notice and admire in women.

WHAT MEN WANT

It is important that you understand just what it is men want in women, in different stages of their relationship. When a man first becomes acquainted with a girl, for example, he is not particularly interested in her ability to cook and sew. Her ability to be good company is far more important at this stage. But later on, if he becomes interested in her, or considers that there is a good possibility that he might become interested, he will begin to take a closer look. At this stage he is looking for "good wife material" and the domestic qualities will weigh heavily in the girl's favor. He will begin to notice her ability to cook well, her neatness and orderliness, her ability to handle money wisely, etc. It is an advantage if a girl can have a good knowledge of these subjects, but if not, she should at least have an *interest* and a *willingness to learn*.

A man does not want, however, a girl who is *overly domestic*. If she appears to be the "wholesome farm girl" whose whole life revolves around cooking, sewing, etc., she will appear somewhat lacking in class and sophistication. A man wants her to have a good knowledge of the domestic arts, but he would like them to be *second nature* to her. She accepts them as a necessary responsibility to the success of her life and, although she enjoys her domestic role and finds fulfillment therein, she enlarges her circle of interests to include music, the arts, an appreciation and love for people, an interest in world conditions and she also accepts a certain social responsibility for the problems of the world. To be anything less than this is to be narrow and selfish and therefore unattractive to men.

A man also does not want a girl who thinks *only* of the material parts of homemaking such as cooking, sewing, decorating, etc. He wants a girl who has a true sense of values, who counts love and daily fun as important as a clean house and good meals. He wants a girl who can make a house a home. There are too many women who think only of the *mechanistic* part of homemaking, are too concerned about the "letter of the law" things and not enough about the spiritual values of a home. Their home becomes an empty shell and, although they may have polished floors, clean sheets and cupboards, they are not successful homemakers for they have ignored the very heart of the home — love, understanding and kindness. After all, the only thing that counts in life is people and the home should serve only the purpose of making a family comfortable and happy and serving both their material and spiritual needs. The men you know may have observed this emptiness in some homes and may have definite ideas about its tremendous lack. They may not want to take a chance of repeating it in their home of the future and therefore are very aware of any tendency a girl may have to be material minded in her attitudes about home-making.

A man also does not want a girl who looks at homemaking as an *escape* or a *retreat* from the realities of life. If she is "tired of studies, social responsibility and demands made on her time" and will be happy when she can relax with her simple home duties, he may not have a good impression of her domestic attitudes. He may picture her in her future home, walking about the house in a lackadaisical manner, watching T.V., taking coffee breaks, or leaning over the back fence discussing recipes with neighbors, and totally lacking in the picture he has of the ideal homemaker. He imagines his future wife to be enthusiastic and devoted, putting forth great effort to make his house a home. He wants her to give life the best she has, not the least.

A man does not want a girl who advertises her domestic interests. For example, she may say, "See my new dress, I made it myself," or "I fixed the most delicious dish for my room-mates," or "I can't wait until I have children," or "marriage is the main thing I want in life." Although these are indications of your domestic interests, your efforts to "sell yourself" cause you to appear to be *manhunting,* and is apt to frighten him away. Especially is this a mistake early in your acquaintance before he has had a chance to get to know you and to appreciate your charming qualities.

If you are attending college and are majoring in the fields of home economics, family life, child development, etc., don't make the mistake of deliberately telling him about it lest you appear to *advertise* your domestic side. If he does ask you, tell him the truth but say something like this, "Yes, I am majoring in home and family life, because I feel that every girl should be prepared for responsibilities that lie ahead."

A man likes a girl to be rather modest about her domestic interests rather than to advertise them. For example, a girl who tends to apologize for her cooking is more attractive than one who brags about it. The modest girl implies, "Oh, I am not very good at this yet, but I intend to be some day." She promises better performance in the future and gives the impression that other things have taken her interest right now.

Now I would like to try to give you the full picture of just what a man wants and doesn't want in a woman, as far as her domestic side goes. First, he wants to know that she has a basic knowledge of homemaking skills, or at least has a desire to learn. And he would like her knowledge to include a broad picture of homemaking, with spiritual values emphasized as well as the material. He would like the assurance that some day she will give this part of her life the best that she has and that she will enjoy doing it. But, he does not want her to be *overly* domestic. He wants her skill and knowledge to be second nature with her, but not her entire life. He wants her circle of interests to include other things outside the home. He also wants her to have charm, sophistication to a degree and to be an intriguing companion as well as a homemaker.

A man wants a girl who knows more about the feminine arts than he does. He does not appreciate it if she asks him questions such as "what would you like to eat?" or "what kind of tomatoes should I buy?" or "which fabric is better?" He may want to give suggestions generally about your appearance or cooking, but does not want to provide the answers to women's problems. To do so makes you appear unqualified in your own field and gives him the impression that he knows more about it than you do. Just as we expect men to be more capable in the masculine things, more qualified as leaders, protectors and providers, men expect women to excel them in the feminine arts.

A man also likes a woman who does not reveal all she knows about a subject. She should not play her full hand, and this includes her domestic knowledge. A woman is more interesting if she is somewhat of a mystery and keeps some of her qualifications to herself. She should reveal only a small part of that which she knows and subtly indicate that she has a whole store of knowledge yet to come which he knows nothing about. In this way he will detect that there is more than appears on the surface, that there are hidden qualities that will be intriguing for him to discover. A woman of mystery is much more interesting than the woman who tells all and then that appears to be the end of it.

Now, a word about careers. A girl who is planning a career for herself outside the home is in danger as far as men are concerned. If she focuses all of her interests and attention on her career and indicates that this is where she intends to find happiness and fulfillment — implies that "staying at home tending children, etc., is boring," then she is not the tender little domestic goddess that men dream about. It may be difficult to detect the man's disappointment in finding out this fact about the girl, for he may even express an interest in her career and future plans. And although he does admire women with wide interests, he does not appreciate a woman· who rejects her feminine role in preference to the man's world.

If you want to be a domestic goddess, prepare early in life and learn at least the basic homemaking skills. Do not wait until you are married to learn to cook and sew and keep the house clean. Learn to do these things well and to enjoy doing them so that when the right man comes along they will be second nature to you. And since in reaching the goal of Angela Human it is expected that you be more than a mere homemaker, that you go beyond the call of duty and become a "domestic goddess," it is important that you know just what this term implies. The following are suggestions to get you started in the right direction. Much more study than what is outlined in these few pages will be required to be skilled in homemaking and be our image of the domestic goddess.

How to be a Domestic Goddess

To be a Domestic Goddess you have to go beyond the mere call of duty and do your jobs *well*. If you give the bare stint of requirement, merely feed and clothe the family and sweep and dust, or do a half-hearted job of cooking and homemaking, you will not be our idea of a Domestic Goddess. The woman who succeeds is the one who really makes something of her responsibilities. She adds a kind of glory to her work that sets her apart as a goddess, and this glory comes primarily from doing her jobs *well*.

Besides this, a Domestic Goddess adds some *feminine touches* to her duties. Typical of her are doilies, soft curtains and pillows, and in cooking she includes foods which have delicious aromas. In motherhood she is gentle and tender — qualities that are so typical of the truly feminine woman.

A Domestic Goddess is also *happy* in her role as wife, mother and homemaker. Deruchette, Amelia and Agnes were happy in their homemaking roles. Deruchette flitted about as a little bird, from room to room, Amelia was a *smiling* little domestic goddess and Agnes had a peaceful calm spirit about her. They did not dislike their daily duties. They enjoyed their domestic life, just as they enjoyed being women. We also should enjoy these domestic tasks, doing dishes, scrubbing floors, etc., and should never make negative remarks about them, especially in the presence of men, lest we lower their estimation of us as women. I remember hearing a man say that the main reason he did not pursue a certain girl any further was that she had made some comment about dreading to do the dishes. Also, while in her home her brother had asked her to bring him a glass of milk and she had refused. She told him to do it himself. Women should delight in waiting on men — it is part of their calling as women.

In summary we can say that a Domestic Goddess has principally three main qualifications. She:
1. She does her essential homemaking tasks *well*.
2. She adds some feminine touches.
3. She enjoys her domestic responsibility.

The following are some general suggestions to help you get started in doing your home duties *well* and also in adding some *feminine touches:*

HOMEMAKING

The following will result in greater efficiency in homemaking:
1. *Concentration:* The management of a household requires concentration. One cannot daydream and ponder problems and at the same time expect duties will be performed with efficiency. There are specific tasks, like ironing, cleaning windows and doing dishes in which daydreaming is possible, but most of our tasks, especially any amount of tidying or organizing, requires *thought* as well as hands. So put other things out of your mind and concentrate on getting the job at hand done and out of the way. What is often interpreted as lack of homemaking ability is usually mental laziness.
2. *Organization:* Basic good homemaking depends upon being organized. This means having a place for everything, a time

for everything and some type of plan or schedule to follow. I know that women dislike rigid schedules, but lack of planning can lead to disorder, hurry and a waste of time. It is doubtful that there is anything about housekeeping so appreciated by men as a well organized household, where homelife runs smoothly and without confusion. Some women feel that working diligently and quickly will accomplish the goals of homemaking. These virtues are important, but being organized is the secret of a successful homemaker. Time spent in organizing and planning saves hours of time in actual work.

3. *First things first:* Also important is the habit of putting first things first. This means to concentrate on the more essential tasks while placing as secondary those things of lesser importance. If you will list your six most important homemaking responsibilities and then arrange them in order of their importance, then use it as a guide each day, it will increase your efficiency, for example:

A. Appearance	D. Washing and ironing
B. Meals	E. Imperative shopping
C. House neat	F. Auxiliary things

Although young girls will not have the full responsibility of a household yet, they at different times share this responsibility of homemaking. Learning how to manage their portion of homemaking will help them to assume this responsibility later.

In learning to put first things first, it pays to be aware of *time wasters*. Such things as talking on the telephone for long periods, sewing to excess, spending hours of time browsing through shops, are often the cause of essential home duties being neglected. Some may justify these duties on the grounds that they *enjoy it*. Personal sacrifices, however, are often required when one determines to become a Domestic Goddess but such is the necessary step one takes in becoming Angela Human.

4. *Simplicity:* You will have to simplify life and get rid of a lot of clutter if you are to excel as a homemaker. Clean out your closets and drawers and live simply. This makes domestic chores easier and more enjoyable.

5. *Work: Nothing* worthwhile in life is easy and it certainly is not easy to be a good homemaker. You can expect

it to be work, but you can also expect that it will pay rich dividends. Work is good for a woman physically, mentally and spiritually, to say nothing of the comfort and pleasure it brings to the family who lives in a clean well ordered home. These are the five essentials of good homemaking.

Be Genuine: As a girl goes out into the world she is usually wise enough to represent herself as a clean and tidy girl. She is careful to have nicely washed hair, clean ribbons and clothes, etc. Some girls, however, are quite another thing at home. They may have dirty bedrooms, messy closets and drawers and unclean habits. When they take off their clean clothes — their immaculate exterior — they reveal unclean underwear. It is easy to see that they misrepresent themselves in public.

If you want to represent yourself in the proper image, be genuine and consistent. You will be the same thing at all times in your life. You will not only present a clean image to your public but you will actually *be* that image in your own home. To do less than this is a form of dishonesty, and not only is it weak in principle but your insincerity will likely be detected by your associates. In being consistent you certainly do not want to represent to the public the messy image that you may be portraying at home, so the only thing to do is to change your home habits to meet your clean immaculate appearance and truly be the girl that you represent to others.

The Feminine Touch: In addition to a clean, well organized home, the Domestic Goddess provides some feminine touches to housekeeping. Things like soft pillows, frilly curtains, bowls of fruit, doilies, gingham curtains, soft rugs, artistic pictures and ornaments reveal the feminine touch.

SEWING

Girls of today are fortunate in that there are so many fine classes in sewing. They learn the most effective techniques and shortcuts to making a garment look really professional. These techniques, however, wonderful as they are, will not provide the secrets of being fascinating in appearance. A girl may sew the finest seam, produce the most finished garment imaginable and still fail to be attractively dressed. The real secret is in learning what you look well in, your best color, style and materials and the overall effect.

If you will examine the dresses of some girls who do all their own sewing and who are beautifully dressed, you will not necessarily find perfection in sewing as you would imagine. There is great merit in learning to be a fine seamstress, and I do not wish to discredit this feminine skill, but techniques alone are not enough.

I remember noticing while in a public gathering an extremely attractive girl with a striking dress on. I felt at first glance that her dress had certainly been purchased at an exclusive dress shop and that she paid a high price for it. But on closer scrutiny, I noticed that her zipper was not exactly straight, and that there were other signs that it was hand made. This did not detract from the effect, however. She was stunning, dress and all. It was quite convincing to me that if you design a dress that is as special as this one was, the construction will somehow pass.

In learning to design dresses that will please men, not only should you take into consideration yourself, just which colors you look well in, which styles and materials, but beyond this the dress should have a certain quality. It has got to be a dress that men like and this means that it has got to say "I am a woman" or "I am cute," or "I am umphy," or even "I am sexy." This does not mean that it be in any way immodest or improper. It simply means that it will be special to men so that men will notice you in a positive way.

In contrast to this, dresses that do nothing to men are those that are too practical or bland. They do not say anything at all. They are just something to fill a need, to cover the figure or to solve a problem. Clothes need not be gaudy or loud in any way. But they should be special in some way and have some quality that fascinates men. We will learn more about clothes that men like in a later chapter.

If you want to put more thought to this subject you can learn it by observation. You can notice girls who have dresses that "say something." Notice girls you meet, and clothes that are displayed in shop windows. Also browse through magazines and make a collection of dresses that have that special quality. You will gradually learn the type of clothes that fascinate men. Remember, that what looks well on another woman, may not be for you at all. Your observation will lead you to an understanding of clothes that attract men and you will be able to apply this understanding to your own type and figure.

There are many things written on the subject of planning wardrobes, but remember, if you pursue these subjects, that most of them are written with the idea of pleasing women rather than men. The clothes men admire are based on freshness, femininity and girlishness.

I wish to stress that it is important for girls to learn to sew. There are occasions all during her lifetime when sewing will be of real value, even though she may be able to afford to buy her clothes most of the time. Emergencies can arise when sewing is a real answer to problems.

COOKING

Men are inclined to put cooking at the top of the list of domestic arts. They want good food, well prepared, and they want it "on time." It is important to learn a number of dishes and menues that men like. They tend to like beef stew, roast beef and potatoes, fried chicken and biscuits, crisp green salads and apple pie with ice cream. They do not tend to like casseroles, weenies, cold cuts and prepared foods. If you would like to get more ideas of foods that men like, talk with a woman who has reared a large family of boys. She is likely to have some good recipes.

If you want to add feminine touches to your cooking, include foods which smell delicious. Things like onions frying, homemade bread, cinnamon rolls, etc., arouse sentiment and appreciation. These things set a woman apart as a domestic goddess.

HANDLING MONEY

Another gift of the domestic goddess is "knowing how to handle money." After marriage she will be expected to do much of the buying, especially for the household. She will have to learn to "make a dollar stretch." Men tend to notice a girl's tendencies to be extravagant or wise with money. Actually one of the man's greatest fears in taking the step of marriage is the fear of financial responsibility. A woman who is extravagant will propose a real problem to his future. Thrift is a virtue in women, and one that we should cultivate in our youth. Here are a few ideas and rules to follow:

If you are making money or have an income, after you deduct your basic monthly expenses, try to save at least half of what you make. This seems simple and easy, but actually it requires considerable self-discipline to follow this rule. There will be many temptations to buy things which we do not need and go beyond our intended savings plan.

Another rule is to buy or make *good* clothes and then *take care of them* so that they will wear as long as possible. Don't wear your nicest clothes "just anywhere." If you do you will soon find that you need more, that you are without something suitable to wear. Have enough casual clothes so that you can save your really nice things for special occasions. Have some things for "roughing it," also clothes to be worn outside for things like mountain climbing, bicycling, horseback riding. These should be sturdy clothes that wear well. Do not wear your "special" slacks for these occasions. To do so is poor economy, and not even appropriate for the occasion. Keep clothes clean and mended. They wear better this way.

The economy wardrobe includes some clothes that are plain and basic, that can be dressed up by a change of accessory. These are the clothes that you will rely upon when you are tired of everything else. You can change their appearance by a change of scarf, necklace, a different collar, etc. Some basic plain skirts are also economy and can be coordinated with many different tops.

Don't be hasty in your buying. If you definitely know what you want, buy it. But if you are at all uncertain, and if the item costs at least $20.00 or more, it is safer to go home and think about it. The next day if you still want it buy it. Here again, this is not as easy as it sounds. There will always be the temptation to "buy it now" and save time. You will save more money, however, if you make this a rule in your buying.

Don't buy anything which is not what you really want. Also beware of sale items. They are usually "left overs" that no one else wants. They are seldom real economy. Some stores even purchase inferior merchandise, just for sales. It is best to buy good clothes and then take care of them.

Beware of letting money slip through your fingers on small items which you think you need. Especially avoid shopping at the 5-and-10¢ stores and drugstores. These things add up quickly.

If you buy your own food, note that wholesome food is usually low in price. Whole grains like brown rice, oatmeal, cracked wheat, are highly nutritious, easy to fix and inexpensive. Legumes like dried peas, lentils and beans are also inexpensive. Fruits and vegetables, of course, are essential, but meats, packaged mixes, certain prepared frozen foods and all kinds of prepared foods are higher in price.

MOTHERHOOD

Part of the domestic role is motherhood. To be a wonderful mother is one of the most important contributions that a woman can make to our society. Do not think that leaving the home and centering your life around a career, making some notable contribution to the world there, can compare to the success of rearing a family of fine sons and daughters, inspiring them to high standards and goals, helping them to grow both physically and spiritually, giving them love and sympathy in times of trouble and finally helping them to take their place in the world. On the other hand, deserting your post as a mother, and as a result causing a whole family to fail to reach their potential, or even fail as individuals, *is the mistake of a woman's life* and no success she may achieve out in the world can compensate for it. This is not to say that a woman cannot be successful as a mother and still have a career, but it will be extremely difficult to do as fine a job as if she had centered all of her interests in her family. Also, the mother who stays at home may still fail as a mother, if she neglects her children. We must realize that our most sacred responsibility is to be a successful mother and to rear to maturity the precious souls that God has given us and to do the finest job of mothering that we possibly can. If we do, we will have, in their maturity, *peace of mind.*

Not only is it our sacred responsibility to rear children, and to do it wholeheartedly, but we must realize that men admire this dedication in women. A man will notice and admire a woman who loves little children, and who wants children of her own. He himself may even resist the idea of a family, but he does not find this attitude attractive in women. The idea of the Domestic Goddess is not only to *be* a mother, but to have an overabundant willingness to do so and to be the most wonderful mother possible.

How to Find Happiness in Domestic Role

I have said that one of the qualities of the *Domestic Goddess* is her ability to find happiness in her work. With the right attitude, and control of life's activities, this can be achieved. The following suggestions are good rules to follow:

1. *Have a proper attitude:* It is best to face your work with a *realistic* attitude. Just as we learn to accept people as part good and part bad, our work consists of some jobs that can be enjoyable and some that may be just plain drudgery. We can't expect a job as varied as homemaking to be all pleasant. But if you will look around you, you will find that every occupation has its boring, monotonous tasks and it is best to face them for what they are, a necessary responsibility. It may insult an intelligent woman to tell her she must find her joy in washing diapers and scrubbing floors. She must remember that her happiness does not come from a mere segment of homemaking — it comes from the *overall accomplishment.*

Many of our duties, however, are a source of real enjoyment. Caring for children, cooking delicious meals and cleaning the house can be a happy experience. There are women who delight in scrubbing floors and walls, washing and ironing and cleaning closets. Little of our work is unpleasant, but if it seems so to you, it is best to face it with an honest attitude, realizing that the world's work consists of a certain amount of drudgery.

2. *Don't become crowded for time:* If you want to enjoy homemaking allow yourself enough *time* to enjoy it, rather than to hurry through a job just to get it over with and out of the way. It is almost impossible to enjoy a job if you are rushed. And even though you are a single girl, you are always faced

with a certain amount of housework. You probably have your laundry to do, your room to clean, your closet and drawers to keep straight, mending, sewing, ironing and probably at least some cooking. It is best to control your time and learn how to enjoy these tasks while you are young.

While you are single there are many things which require your time other than homemaking. You are probably either working or attending college. Your work or your studies will have to have top priority until you are married. Your social life is also important at this stage. But there are many other things of questionable value and some are a complete waste of time. Belonging to organizations and outside activities may not be worth the time involved. This will be up to you to decide. Time spent talking on the telephone, browsing through magazines, watching T.V., or even extensive sewing can be a waste of time, if done to excess. If these things rob a young girl of time to keep her things clean and organized, they should be questioned for their value in her life.

It will be a challenge, however, to have enough self-discipline to keep outside activities and demands at a minimum. You will have to develop a keen sense of putting first things first and giving cleanliness and orderliness some priority.

3. *Go the second mile:* The third part of learning to enjoy domestic duties is to *do them well. If you will find joy in your tasks do them well.* This means to go beyond the call of duty and do more than is required. Do not do just the bare stint of requirement — just enough to get by, for there is no special merit in this, nor is there any real enjoyment. The real joy comes in going the second mile and in doing a "grade A" job. This doctrine was taught hundreds of years ago by Jesus when he said, "If any man compel thee to go one mile, go with him twain." Going the second mile lifts the burden out of work and makes it seem easy and enjoyable. Jesus also said, "My work is easy and my burden light," which only further emphasizes that if we go the second mile our work will seem easier and more enjoyable.

In reviewing the method of becoming a Domestic Goddess, remember there are three requirements:

Method of Becoming a Domestic Goddess

1. Do your tasks *well.*
2. Add some feminine touches.
3. Be *happy* in your domestic duties.

We have also learned just *how* to enjoy homemaking, so that we *will be happy.* We have learned that we should have a *proper attitude* about our work, to face it realistically for just what it is — part enjoyable and part drudgery. Our happiness comes in the *overall accomplishment.* We have also learned that if we are to enjoy working, we will have to allow enough *time* to enjoy it, and this means not allowing ourselves to be crowded for time — or eliminating non-essentials that waste our time. And last, we have learned that if we are to enjoy our homemaking we will have to do a *second mile job* — or go beyond the call of duty.

How to Find Joy in our Tasks

1. Proper attitude towards drudgery.
2. Allow time to enjoy homemaking.
3. Do your jobs *well.*

If you will give thought to this subject and apply reasonable effort even though your social life and education are more important at this stage, you will form habits that will be valuable to you later on, when you are married. You will be on your way to being a Domestic Goddess.

A Matter of Character

You may never have thought of this before, but good homemaking is *a matter of character* since it requires thoughtfulness, unselfishness, consideration of the feelings of others, organization, diligence, understanding, patience, kindness, forgiveness and almost every virtue in existence. A woman has a most wonderful opportunity right in her own home to develop her character by being a wonderful homemaker.

On the other hand, poor homemaking displays a serious weakness in character. The woman who neglects the care of her family and housekeeping is usually *self-centered* and *inconsiderate* of the needs and feelings of others. She may selfishly spend her time in her own pursuits, pleasures and comforts, talking on the phone, browsing through shops, or just being lazy, rather than things that would make her family more comfortable and happy. The poor homemaker also lacks organization which is a serious fault. God, who is our pattern of perfection, sets before us the work of his creations — a work that is a masterpiece of organization and system. Our lack of order, then, is un-godly and lacking in character.

Also the poor homemaker lacks knowledge. If she continues to fail, without a diligent effort to gain knowledge of this important responsibility, she demonstrates a weakness of character, for we have been taught "If [we] lack wisdom, ask of God, who giveth to all men liberally." This instruction is from the Bible. There is no excuse for a woman's lack of knowledge in her domestic world. If she doesn't know she can learn, and has a right to ask her Heavenly Father for help. The role of the Domestic Goddess is a spiritual qualification; this is why it is on the Angelic side of the ideal woman, the kind a man wants.

Beyond the Domestic Goddess

Remember that although the idea of the Domestic Goddess is essential to our picture of the ideal woman, a man wants more than just a homemaker. He wants a playmate and an intellectual companion. He also wants her to have a broad interest in life and all that is in it — its many problems, its many faces and its wondrous beauty. Only in this way will she be interesting and challenging to him.

The ideal woman needs to be a part of the world outside the home, needs to feel a certain debt to society — a sense of social responsibility. If she stays too close in her own little world she tends to become selfish and narrow. If her time and energies are consumed with her children, her house and her husband, without a thought for the world beyond, she will not only be uninteresting but unhappy. Her real happiness lies in her fulfillment as a wife, mother and homemaker, but giving beyond this — stretching forth her hand to those in need — *enriches her life.*

If you will remember in the beginning of this chapter I explained that men are not attracted to women who are overly domestic, who limit their interests to cooking, sewing and homemaking, etc. They are attracted to women with *broad interests,* who do their homemaking duties as *second nature.* This is our picture of the Domestic Goddess.

We now come to the end of our study of the Angelic qualities, the side of our ideal woman that awakens in a man a feeling of worship and the side that brings him true happiness. But we have to realize that although these qualities are essential to him and to his true love for a woman, a man wants *more than an angel.* He also wants a woman who is *human.*

THE HUMAN SIDE

The human side of our ideal woman is composed of a myriad of charming and fascinating qualities. It is her girlishness, her dependency upon man, her delicacy and her femininity. It is also her joyfulness, vivacity and her teasing playfulness. Add to all this a rosy glow of vibrant health and a dash of spunk and sauciness and an underlying attitude of trust and tenderness and you begin to build a delightfully human creature, one that will win a man's heart.

The human qualities fascinate men. They enchant him, captivate him, amuse him and also arouse in him a tender feeling — a desire to protect and shelter. They set off a spark, or a driving force in a man that can cause him to do what appears to be foolish things. It is now that love is blind. This is the mad infatuation and indulgence that can lead him to a pinnacle of joy or destruction.

The Human qualities, in some instances, will cause a man of intelligence and character to marry a girl of inferior qualities — perhaps some brainless doll whom he finds irresistible. One would expect such a man to choose a more sensible companion, but her Human appeal has made love blind. The fascination David Copperfield had for Dora was due to her Human characteristics and caused him to turn from the angelic Agnes to marry Dora. The Human qualities have tremendous appeal. If anything can be said for them, it is that they have more power over the average man than the Angelic.

They are not difficult to acquire; they are not foreign to your nature, for they are woman's natural instincts. If you do not have them, it is because they have been suppressed. They are not "unholy" for they enrich a man's life and when combined with the Angelic cause a man to experience *celestial love*.

CHAPTER XII

Femininity

Femininity is a gentle, tender quality found in a woman's appearance, manner and actions and her general attitude. No other quality has so much appeal to men, for it is such a direct contrast to his own strong and firm masculinity. This contrast, when brought to his attention, causes him to feel manly and this realization of his masculinity is one of the most enjoyable sensations he can experience. The extremely feminine woman is charming to men and the woman who is completely lacking in it may even be repulsive to men.

Femininity is acquired by *accentuating the differences between yourself and men, not the similarities.* You apply this principle in your apearance, your manner and your actions and even your attitude. The more different you appear from men the more feminine you become.

1. The Feminine Appearance

To be most fascinating to men, women should wear only those materials and styles which are the least suggestive of those used by the men and which therefore make the greatest contrast to men's apparel. Men never wear anything fluffy, lacy, or gauzy or elaborate. Use such materials, therefore, whenever you can. Men never pay much attention to the extremes of style in men's clothes, but they expect women to be the opposite — to be among the first to adopt the new fashions, providing these new styles are modest and becoming.

Materials: Avoid such materials as tweeds, herringbones, hard finish woolens, denims, glen plaids, faint dark plaids, pin stripes, shepherd checks and geometrics, since these are materials that men wear. These materials can be used, however, if distinguished by an extremely feminine style or color. Otherwise they can give no help in making men realize how un-manlike —

how womanly — you are! They cannot strive to bring out any contrast between your nature and his.

Do wear soft woolens, soft or crisp cottons, soft and drapery synthetics, floral prints, polka-dots, animated designs, etc. The extremes of femininity are such things as chiffon, silk, lace, velvet, satin, fur, angora and organdie. Every woman should include as many of these in her wardrobe as she can afford and find appropriate to wear. These should be worn when trying to make the most feminine appeal to men.

Colors which are extremely feminine are pastels and vivid colors since men generally do not wear them. Those colors to avoid are the drab and dull colors used by men, such as browns, greys, deep blue and charcoal. These colors may be used effectively, however, if they are cut in an extremely feminine style, or trimmed with soft or bright accessories.

In selecting floral or designed prints try to avoid anything which is overly loud and gaudy and therefore lacking in good taste. Men do tend to like vivid colors on women, but those that are both vivid and beautiful are hard to find. Therefore, use extreme care in selecting a print, to make sure that it is in good design and does not dominate you.

Style: Avoid tailored styles or any suggestion of masculinity such as buttoned cuffs, lapels, and top stitching. These styles can be used, however, if combined with a feminine color or material, such as velvet or lace. Extreme feminine styles are such things as full skirts, ruffles, scallops, puffs, gathers, drapes, flowing trains and many others. These styles are not always in fashion, nor are they appropriate for every use. Do use them whenever you can, and if they are becoming to you. There are feminine styles that are always available which can be used for any occasion. The Victorian dress is feminine, for example, and conservative enough for most occasions. The dress itself, for that matter, is feminine, for men do not wear them.

It is difficult to advise a feminine style which would be suitable for all women since we vary in figure. A safe rule is to remember to accentuate the difference between you and the men and to avoid any style which has a suggestion of masculinity unless softened in some way by a feminine effect.

Should women wear pants? Young girls are in so many sports and activities that the custom for them to wear pants for these events seems to be universal and men have accepted the idea. When you do wear pants, soften the effect by color, material or accessory. You may have to wear a ribbon in your hair, for example, or a scarf at your neck. The most feminine pants, for special occasions, are made of such things as white lace, black satin, brocade, etc. They can be beautiful and extremely feminine.

Back to dresses, *trim* can give a feminine effect to an otherwise plain dress. Lace, ribbons, colorful tie, fringe, embroidery, beads and braids can accentuate femininity.

Accessories: Avoid purses which resemble men's brief cases and shoes of masculine style. Wear soft scarfs, flowers, jewelry and hair ribbons. In achieving a feminine appearance the important thing to remember is the "over-all impression" which you make. Work for softness, airiness, delicacy and striking contrast to masculinity. The effect can be fascinating to men. The following two examples will illustrate:

How to Turn Men's Heads

I remember hearing of a girl who bought a complete outfit in brown for street wear — brown shoes, tailored brown coat with a brown fur collar and a brown hat. It was perfect in style, in taste and in fit and her women friends admired it immensely. But as she went along the crowded street she attracted no attention from men. A little later she purchased a light blue coat of unusual material, smart in style and vivid in color. To complete the outfit she added light grey shoes and hat, with touches of pink and blue. Neither in her own opinion nor in the opinion of her friends was the outfit as tasteful or as harmonious as was the brown outfit. She was considerably surprised, therefore, when she wore the second and supposedly inferior outfit, to discover when she passed along the same crowded street that not a man would pass without an interested glance at her new attire. With the brown outfit, she could get on the city bus without a man offering her a seat, but with the vivid blue and grey outfit, one man after another, somehow, always felt impelled to sacrifice his comfort for her sake. She was considerably entertained and surprised to watch the great difference the change of outfits made with the men. The explanation however, is very simple. The first outfit was too much like what the men themselves wear, in color, in style and in this case even material. It could not be expected to make her appear as a feminine woman. The second outfit, on the contrary, consisted of combining colors and style that no man would ever dream of wearing. Naturally this outfit helped to emphasize the fact that here was a woman, as different from men as could be, a girlish girl, the essence of femininity the kind of woman a man likes to protect and cherish. Every man is interested in women who give such an impression in her outward appearance.

Another incident I heard about was of a young girl who went weekly to a local market, dressed in ordinary clothes. She was not poorly dressed, but neither was she dressed in any way that would attract the attention of men. One day, however, she bought a beautiful long dress of rich and beautiful colors in a gorgeous design. The dress was straight and to the ankles, of rich purple and deep pink, combined in a lovely artistic and large pattern. She wore her long black hair loosely down her back and a pink ribbon in her hair. When she went to the local market, on this single trip three different men employees stopped her and asked her if she would like to work at the market, said that they would recommend her as a cashier. She couldn't help but be amused that she had been in the market dozens of times before and not a single man had noticed her or stopped to talk to her — to say nothing of offering her a job.

Good grooming: Another part of the feminine appearance is to be well groomed. We need not dwell on this since there is much emphasis on grooming in our modern times. We need only mention that clean, well groomed hair, clean body and clothes are essential to the feminine appearance. This is not to say that men should not be well groomed also, but they expect women to be even more immaculate than they are themselves, and somehow it seems more of a disgrace for a woman to be slovenly and careless than for a man to be. If you see a young man who has just been playing basketball, sit down and relax before he combs his hair and straightens his clothes, it seems excusable. When it comes right down to it, men are inclined to be less concerned about their appearance and clothes than women. But they expect women to be the opposite — tidy and immaculate. In bringing out the charming contrast between yourself and men, you must have an all-absorbing pride in your appearance; you must endeavor to appear at your best every minute of the day and under all circumstances.

MODESTY

Still another part of the feminine appearance is modesty. In spite of the emphasis in our times on the "sex symbol," men do not respect woman who expose their bodies to the public. Not only should the body be reasonably covered but also the underwear. Men dislike hanging slips, bra straps that show and exposed underwear when a girl sits on a chair. Higher types of civilizations have always been modest — it seems to go with intelligence and refinement. Only savages and primitive tribes lack this refinement, except for certain unwholesome deviations in our modern society.

GIRLWATCHERS

I would like to include in this section an article which was printed in a San Diego newspaper about a group of young boys in a San Diego Junior High School, who formed a club called "Girlwatchers." Here is what the newspaper had to say about them and their views on femininity:

"There is a 'Girlwatchers' club at the Lakeside Junior High School in San Diego. It has a membership of 39 boys. Near the close of the last semester of school the club published and distributed to all girls on the campus the following proclamation:

"We, the boys of Girlwatchers Club, have been watching girls for the past four weeks. Some of what we have observed has pleased us. BUT, much of what we have seen displeased, disgusted and repulsed us. Therefore, we have agreed and resolved that some changes must be made. We feel the changes suggested are reasonable and fair. In general all we are asking is that girls again become feminine in their thoughts, words and deeds because they should be different from boys.

"We are tired of constantly being forced to look at girls' underwear. For example: pettipants hanging out; skirts not long enough to cover underwear during such normal activities as sitting, stooping, reaching up or running. Boys do not like the carelessness girls display when sitting with legs apart or lying on floors, grass, benches and retaining walls, constantly making others look at their underwear. This is no thrill for boys or anyone else — just obnoxious!

"We are disturbed by girls who wear improper hose. Too many are wearing hose not long enough. The viewer is greeted by the unlovely sight of hose tops, garters and bulging thighs all hanging below skirts. Ugh!

"We find girls draped in boys' or men's clothing unattractive and unfeminine. Many are wearing sailors' pea-jackets, boys' shirts with tails hanging out . . . and sundry other items of male clothing. Wear your own clothes and let us wear ours.

"We have been badly frightened too many times by girls who use makeup with little or no skill or even good sense. It is hideous! Use a little makeup, learn how to apply it. . . .

"We are concerned about girls choice of vocabulary in both spoken and written communication. We take a dim view of girls using both profane and obscene language in their conversation with each other and with us. Clean up your mouths or keep quiet. We think girls passing notes around is silly but girls passing obscene or vulgar notes is revolting and intolerable. Stop writing dirty notes — period!

"We are concerned about the large number of girls whose general behavior is becoming increasingly unfeminine and boy-like. Girls who greet us by pushing us, hitting us, pounding us on the back, chasing us or mussing up our hair or clothing leave us absolutely cold. Try just saying hello.

"Girls who ask us if we love them, if we'll go steady with them, or if we'll date them are nowhere. If we want to be with you we'll let you know. Don't call us, we'll call you.

"Girls who run everywhere all day and who come out in skirts at noon and try to play basketball or football with boys turn us off. Girls' atheltics are great but pay attention to time, place and costume.

"Girls who smoke, ditch classes, shoplift, and hitch-hike are well known to all of us and respected by NONE of us. Suggestion: Don't smoke, attend school, pay for things you need and walk where you are going."

The proclamation concluded with an announcement that girls failing to comply with it would be subjected to a "total boycott of all friendly relations" with the 39 boys. The boycott started with the posting of the proclamation on the school bulletin board Friday morning with the hearty approval of the school principal and boys' counselor. All girls got a copy in the home rooms and they all froze. They were still sore all day Monday but by Tuesday they showed so much improvement, particularly in connection with underwear that the boycott was lifted pending a Girlwatcher's meeting Friday.

Well, here is the young man's viewpoint, but men of all ages feel the same way.

2. THE FEMININE MANNER

The feminine manner is the *motions* of a woman's body, the way she uses her hands, her walk, her talk, the sound of her voice, her facial expressions, her laugh. It seems to be more important than that of appearance, for it is an even greater contrast to masculine strength and firmness.

David Copperfield was fascinated by Dora's enchanting manner; the way she patted the horses, spanked her little dog, or held her flowers against her chin were attractive to him. "She had the most delightful little voice, the gayest little laugh, the pleasantest and most fascinating little ways."

I have pointed out the importance of a feminine *appearance* in winning the notice of men, but if you do not add to this a *feminine manner*, the total effect can be disappointing or even humorous. For example, if you put a frilly feminine dress on a woman who has a stiff, brusque manner, she just doesn't fit the dress. We have all seen women who wear the most feminine dresses but who wear them as if they were on the wrong person. They do not carry themselves generally in a way to harmonize with their clothes. They are *professors in chiffon, bears in lace, or wooden posts in organdie.* You will, therefore, have to add to a feminine appearance a beautiful enchanting manner, if you are to be attractive to men.

A GLIMPSE INTO FEMININITY

In the novel *The Cloister and the Hearth* by Charles Reade, is an illustration of the thrilling sensation the feminine manner can awaken in a man.

"Then came a little difficulty: Gerard could not tie his ribbon again as Catherine (his mother) had tied it. Margaret, after slyly eyeing his efforts for some time, offered to help him; for at her age girls love to be coy and tender, saucy and gentle by turns . . . then a fair head, with its stately crown of auburn curls, glossy and glowing through silver, bowed sweetly towards him; and while it ravished his eye, two white supple hands played delicately upon the stubborn ribbon and moulded it with soft and airy touches. *Then a heavenly thrill ran through the innocent young man, and vague glimpses of a new world of feeling and sentiment opened to him.* — And these new exquisite sensations Margaret unwittingly prolonged; it is not natural to her sex to hurry ought that pertains to the sacred toilet. Nay, when the taper fingers had at last subjugated the ends of the knot, her mind was not quite easy till, by a maneuver peculiar to the female hand, she had made her palm convex and so applied it with a gentle pressure to the center of the knot — a sweet little coaxing hand kiss, as much as to say, 'now be a good knot and stay so!' 'There, that was how it was!' said Margaret, and drew back to take one last survey of her work; then looking up for simple approval of her skill, received full in her eyes a *longing gaze of such adoration* as made her lower them quickly and color all over."

This experience between Gerard and Margaret conveys the tremendous feeling that a woman can awaken in a man, and in this case it was accomplished by the feminine manner alone, principally the hands. You can imagine how fascinating a girl becomes when she adds to this a gentle voice, sweet expressions and soft looks. The feminine manner is one of the most important tools a woman can use in being attractive to men.

How to Acquire a Feminine Manner

You acquire a feminine manner by *accentuating the differences* between yourself and men, not the similarities. Since men are strong, tough, firm and heavy in manner, women should be delicate, tender, gentle and light. We show this by our walk, voice, hands and the way we carry ourselves generally.

1. *The hands:* Dora and Margaret charmed men with the use of their hands. Gentle motions, pats and maneuvers are peculiar to the female hand. Learn how to shake hands with men. Do so with gentleness and just enough firmness to convey friendship, then quickly draw it away. Never shake a man's hand with strength and vigor, regardless of how happy you may be to see him. Take a man's arm lightly and never use him as a support. To do so makes you appear as a block of wood. Avoid stiff, brusque movements, waving the hands in the air or using them firmly in expressing yourself. Never pound on the table to put over a point, and never grasp the sides of a lecturer's stand. Also avoid slapping anyone on the back.

2. *The walk:* Your manner of walking should be *light*. Imagine that you weigh only 95 pounds. Walk with knees slightly straight. This also encourages lightness and will make your walk cute and feminine. Keep head back over the spine, chest and chin high. Avoid slanting forward, rounding the shoulders or walking with knees bent, since this makes you appear heavy and matronly. Also avoid a heavy gait or long steps like men take.

3. *The voice:* With your appearance and your manner contributing to your femininity, you must be careful that the good effect is not spoiled by your voice. Usually a girl who is learning to walk and use her hands correctly will automatically modulate her voice to harmonize with her manner. If you have already modulated it, or if you already have a feminine voice, then you can forget about it. If, however, you discover that your voice is spoiling the impression you are endeavoring to create, take a little time and effort to change it.

The ideal feminine voice is gentle and variable, with a clear ringing tone and an air of self assurance. It is not a voice which is overly soft and timid, for these qualities suggest a lack of self assurance, something unattractive in women. The main thing to avoid is loudness, firmness or any of the qualities that men have. You must not let your voice suggest mannish efficiency, coarse boldness or the ability to "kill your own snakes." The voice should be just as appealing to the man's chivalrous desire to protect and shelter as the girl herself. No man likes a course, loud or vulgar tone in a woman any more than a woman likes an effeminate tone in a man. And no man likes a mumbling, dull, monotonous or singsong voice, because such a voice indicates to him that the character behind the voice is equally dull and uninteresting.

To speak correctly, speak with teeth apart. Pronounce consonants clearly and be expressive. Do not pronounce "a" and "e" with mouth stretched wide but let your mouth form a slight "o."

A beautiful voice also has a *ringing* quality rather than a flat, dull sound. To speak correctly and to achieve this ringing quality we should speak by using our *resonators* and not our vocal cords. Each person has two resonators, the upper and the lower. The upper resonators are found in the sinuses in the forehead and in the cheek bones. The lower resonators are found in the upper part of the chest. Many people use their resonators automatically. But if you do not, if your voice sounds dull or flat, you can learn to use your resonators by conscious effort. You will have a much more beautiful tone and your voice will not become tired when you speak for long periods of time.

If you have any difficulty with your voice, a few weeks' practice ought to help you greatly. Speaking aloud to yourself or reading aloud in the privacy of your room, endeavoring all the time to eliminate the objectionable features in your voice, should be effective. A half hour devoted to this once every day ought to be sufficient if it is kept up for three or four weeks. When reading, read with expression. Put laughter into your voice in the humorous parts, sorrow in the sad parts, enthusiasm, delight, eagerness, wonder, love, pity and every sentiment or emotion. And when you think of it, practice consciously the same expressions of voice in your conversation.

4. *The laugh:* It is more difficult for a person to change his laugh, although the tone will improve with the improvement of the ringing qualities of the voice. Avoid things, however,

which resemble men's laughs, such as loudness or a deep tone. Also avoid facial contortions, opening the mouth wide, throwing the head back, slapping your hands on your thighs, roaring or anything coarse or vulgar. If these extremes are avoided the laugh will probably be at least acceptable.

5. *The cooing or purring quality:* This is an extremely feminine quality that is reserved for only your man. Deruchette "made all kinds of gentle noises, murmurings of unspeakable delight to certain ears." It is an intimate type of conversation that is soothing and feminine.

6. *Facial expressions:* You have no better means of conveying femininity than through tender smiles, gentle eyes and sweet expressions. The opposite — harshness, bitterness, fierce frowns and tightness across the lip — all destroy feminine charm. Girls who are dainty and feminine, who suddenly take on a hard expression, always disappoint us, like an unhappy ending to a beautiful story.

Femininity has its real roots in character, in a virtue called "a gentle tender quality." If you have a gentle character, it will be easy to convey sweet expressions. If you do not, if you tend to be harsh and critical, to lose patience with people, it will be difficult to keep these unwholesome traits hidden from view, to keep them from spoiling your femininity. It will be wise, therefore to work on character, to acquire a better philosophy of life, a better understanding of people, to learn to accept them, to forgive them and be patient with them. The real key to this change of heart and attitude lies in *humility,* for through this virtue we learn to accept, to forgive and not to judge.

In the meantime, while you are working on character, try to control your facial expressions. This will help to train your character within to be more gentle. The face then acts as a sort of teacher to the character, reminding it to be patient and forgiving. It will be difficult, however, to keep this practice up for long if you continue to hold grudges and have ill will towards people. Be gentle and tender with everyone — your roommates, family and close friends — not just the men in your life. If you are one thing to a man and another to your friends there will be times you will betray your double personality.

It is not likely that the men you associate with will do anything themselves to irritate you and cause you to display an ugly expression. Young people tend to put forth their best company manners and conceal their weaker side. But if a man does do something which aggravates you, just let one fleeting bitter expression cross your face, or a hardness appear about your mouth, and he is apt to be extremely let down. Your hard expression, in his estimation, has been a small peek into your inner character and may give him the impression that you are not the tender creature that you appear to be on the surface. You will have to work to subdue these ugly expressions and at the same time remake your character so that femininity of expression will be yours. One last thought is this: When men offend you, I am not implying that you be bland or unresponsive, only that you not be bitter or harsh. A later chapter will explain how you can react to a man's offenses with a charm called childlike sauciness.

7. *Conversation:* You can do a great deal to strengthen your feminine image through conversation. If someone unfortunate is the topic for discussion, you can show forth sympathy and love. Do not make the mistake of giving an unsympathetic remark like "Well, he deserves it," or "He had it coming to him." Take every opportunity to defend people, to be long suffering and understanding, and in this way show forth your gentle feminine nature.

Avoid talking about people you dislike lest you be tempted to make some unkind remark. It will be difficult enough to remake your attitude towards this person without inviting temptation by bringing him into the conversation. Also avoid subjects which may lead to heated arguments. By avoiding negative statements and concentrating on kindly expressions, you can do a great deal to enhance your femininity and therefore your attractiveness.

REFINEMENT

One of the marks of a feminine woman is refinement. This means that she has "good social breeding" and a sensitivity to the feelings of others, that she never offends anyone by being rude, impolite, inconsiderate, crude or socially negligent. She is tactful, diplomatic and considerate.

To be refined, you must never use coarse or vulgar language, profane, swear, tell vulgar jokes, etc. What these habits do to your character is one thing but what they do to your feminine image is more serious in the eyes of men. Although these coarse habits are not becoming in men either, they are somehow more easily overlooked — less offensive than in women. Here again, men expect women to be the more refined creatures of the human race. Indulging in loud, coarse or vulgar talk not only causes a woman to fall from her pedestal but to fall from being the idol of femininity in men's eyes. Men have always expected women to be cultured and refined and have considered it beneath feminine dignity to utter coarse language. They are naturally disappointed, if not repulsed, by a display of crudeness.

Still another mark of refinement is to show a courteous appreciation for everyone you meet, regardless of age, situation, financial or social standing. Every person who is a human being is entitled to respect and reverence. The higher your conception of human beings generally, the higher will be your tendency to refinement. To show a lack of courteous appreciation of anyone is only to show a decline in the quick intelligence and perception expected of a cultured person. Nothing is more quickly calculated to give you a coarse, unrefined character than to ignore or shun another individual.

In order to demonstrate a real consideration for people, it will be essential that you never do anything to hurt their feelings. Never, for example, show indifference for the opinions of another, or downgrade things he says or does, especially things he considers important. Be considerate of all the feelings, opinions, accomplishments, ideas, traditions, religious customs, or "ways of life" of others. If, for example, you happen to meet a little old lady who has spent a lifetime devoted to a worship of traditions, don't show disrespect for her feelings by trampling on those traditions. Or if you have dinner with some honest soul who takes pride in her cooking, don't refuse a second helping or give any indication that you are any less than delighted with her meal.

If you are in the home of an exceptionally cultured or refined person, do not show a disregard for her way of life by boisterous conduct or heated arguments. On the other hand, if the hostess is fun loving and set on everyone relaxing and having a good time, show consideration for her thinking by being light-hearted yourself. The greatest mark of refinement you can show is a genuine delight in the company you keep with a respect and consideration for their way of living.

Also, learn to respect another person's *enthusiasm*. For example, if a gentleman happens to be telling you of an adventurous journey he is about to take and gets into a state of excitement as he unfolds the plans, do not "throw cold water" on his enthusiasm by acting coldly indifferent. Even worse, do not make a negative remark which would destroy his enthusiasm altogether, such as reminding him how expensive or foolhardy it might be. Instead share his enthusiasm. Or if he is merely eating a piece of pie which he enjoys heartily, do not make a cold remark like "Oh, I can't stand that kind!"

Still another lack of refinement is "cheekiness," an old fashioned word which means to be nervy or to impose on people. Cheekiness is an attitude of "expecting" favors, with a lack of consideration for the imposition it might be on the other person. Young people especially are apt to be guilty of this practice by asking for things to eat while in the homes of their friends, or by asking to borrow clothing, perfume, cars or even money. This is not to say that there are not emergencies when we are justified in asking these favors, or that others are not willing to grant them, but borrowing is ordinarily considered nervy and unrefined.

Also, be tactful and diplomatic in your remarks to people. Blunt honesty is never appropriate. Anything which must be said can be said with a kindly consideration for the other person. Refined women never ignore social invitations without a thoughtful acceptance or apology. They are courteous, with a respect for the feelings of everyone.

Timorousness

Timorousness is little understood by women of today, and yet it is a most bewitching charm of womanhood. It can be described as an air of timid fearlessness, of self-conscious modesty and of pretty confusion. In order to understand this feminine trait, let us refer again to the incident of Rebecca Sharp, when she had just rebuked Joseph for tricking her into eating hot peppers. When Joseph apologized with "No, I wouldn't hurt you for the world," she said, "No, I know you wouldn't," "and then she gave him ever so gentle a pressure with her little hand, and drew it back quite frightened, and looked first for one instant in his face and then down at the carpet rods, and I am not prepared to say that Joe's heart did not thump at this involuntary, timid, gentle motion of regard on the part of the simple girl." "And Oh," exclaims Thackeray, "what a mercy it is that women do not exercise their powers oftener! We can't resist them if they do." Men are never quite prepared for such an unexpected, mysterious feminine maneuver, which is so very different from their own nature. This is perhaps why they are so fascinated by it.

Another illustration of timorousness is found in the incident I referred to in *The Cloister and the Hearth*. In reviewing this incident, notice the trustfulness with which Margaret undertakes the intimate task of tying the strange young man's tie, the confiding, innocent attention to her work until the task is completed, then the sudden self-consciousness and appearance of timidity, modesty and pretty confusion when Gerard gazes at her in adoration.

You can practice timorousness around men by first unconsciously performing some task, then when you realize that the man is noticing you, suddenly becoming self-conscious and confused. Look first directly up in his face for a moment, and then hastily down or to the side. Devise different ways to practice this dainty little stratagem under many circumstances. There is nothing like it to contrast your girlish modesty with the man's insensibility, not only to make the man conscious of your femininity, but even more pleasant to him, conscious of his own contrasting manhood, before which young girls tend to become self-conscious.

BEWITCHING LANGUOR

Languor is a feminine characteristic and is a relaxed, calm, quiet air, similar to that of a cat relaxing before a fireplace. It is like a touch of velvet and is calming and appealing to men.

"Deruchette had at times an air of bewitching languor." Languor is a means of varying other feminine mannerisms. The opposite of languor is the nervous, high-strung woman who is always biting fingernails, jingling her keys, twisting her handkerchief or twisting her hair.

Outdoor Parties: One place that girls tend to let down their femininity is at outdoor parties and games. This may be due to the way they are dressed, usually in pants and casual clothes, which puts them in the spirit to be lax in their actions also. It is here that we are apt to see women slap men on the back, whistle, yell or speak loudly, laugh noisily, gulp their food down, sit with their legs apart or one leg resting on another as men do, roar at jokes, throw their head back when they drink, etc. Here is the time to really watch your femininity. Now, as we come to the end of this section on the feminine manner, I would like to give you some do's and don'ts to follow:

Do's and Don'ts for the Feminine Manner

DON'T

1. Don't use your hands in a stiff, brusque, efficient, f i r m or strong manner.
2. Don't walk with a heavy gait, long steps, round shoulders or slanting forward.
3. Avoid the following qualities in the voice: loudness, firmness, efficiency, boldness, over softness or timidity, dullness, flat tone, mumbling, monotonous singsong.
4. Don't laugh loudly or in a vulgar manner.
5. Don't use facial expressions that are hard, harsh, bitter or unyielding, etc.
6. Don't indulge in words or conversation that are harsh, bitter,

DO:

1. Use hands lightly.
2. Take a man's arm lightly.
3. Shake hands with men lightly.
4. Walk lightly, w i t h knees slightly straight.
5. Acquire a ringing tone to the voice, also gentleness, tenderness, self assurance.
6. Acquire facial expressions that are gentle and tender.
7. In both words and conversation, s p e a k with tenderness, gentleness, and show forth

DON'T	DO:
critical, impatient, crude, vulgar or unrefined.	kindness, patience, sympathy and love.
7. Don't slap anyone on the back.	8. Eat quietly.
8. Don't whistle.	9. Sit modestly.
9. Don't yell.	10. Be refined.
10. Don't talk loudly.	11. React with timorousness when men notice you.
11. Don't roar at jokes.	
12. Don't gulp food or eat noisily.	
13. Don't drink by throwing your head back.	
14. Don't sit with legs apart or with one leg horizontal across the other.	

CHAPTER XIII

Feminine Dependency

Feminine dependency is a definite quality found in a truly feminine woman, a sort of helplessness, weakness, submissiveness and dependency upon men for their masculine care and protection. More than anything else it is a *lack of masculine ability,* a lack of aggressiveness, competency, efficiency, fearlessness, strength and the ability to "kill your own snakes."

You will remember in our studies of understanding men that we recognize men as our guides, protectors and providers. This they were designed to be. We were designed to be women, to be wives, mothers and homemakers and therefore in need of masculine help to make our way through life. This need of masculine help and protection is called feminine dependency. The quality is very attractive to men. Dora was rather helpless and dependent upon men and for this reason made a strong appeal to David's gentlemanly heart. Agnes was too lacking in this quality. She was too self-sufficient, independent and too able to kill her own snakes to win David at this stage in his life.

Do not think that protecting a dependent woman is an imposition on a man. *The most pleasant sensation a real man can experience is his consciousness of the power to give his manly care and protecton. Rob him of this sensation of superior strength and ability and you rob him of his manliness.* It is a delight to him to protect and shelter a dependent woman. The bigger, manlier and more sensible a man is, the more he seems to be attracted by this quality.

HOW MEN FEEL IN THE PRESENCE
OF CAPABLE WOMEN

What happens when the average red-blooded man comes in contact with an obviously able, intellectual and competent woman manifestly independent of any help a mere man can give and capable of meeting him or defeating him upon his own ground? He simply doesn't feel like a man any longer. In the presence of such strength and ability in a mere woman, he feels like a futile, ineffectual imitation of a man. It is the most uncomfortable and humiliating sensation a man can experience; so that the woman who arouses it becomes repugnant to him.

A man cannot derive any joy or satisfaction from protecting a woman who can obviously do very well without him. He only delights in protecting or sheltering a woman who needs his manly care, or at least appears to need it.

How Men Feel in the Presence of Dependent Women

When a man is in the presence of a tender, gentle, trustful, dependent woman, he immediately feels a sublime expansion of his power to protect and shelter this frail and delicate creature. In the presence of such weakness he feels stronger, more competent, bigger, manlier than ever. This feeling of strength and power is the most enjoyable he can experience. The apparent need of the woman for protection, instead of arousing contempt for her lack of ability, appeals to the very noblest feelings within him.

Amelia

A perfect illustration of feminine dependency in woman is in the character of Amelia in *Vanity Fair*. The following is a description of her and the charm she possessed in men's eyes.

"Those who formed the small circle of Amelia's acquaintances were quite angry with the enthusiasm with which the other sex regarded her. For almost all men who came near her loved her; though no doubt they would be at a loss to tell you why. She was not brilliant, nor witty, nor wise overmuch, nor extraordinarily handsome. But wherever she went she touched and charmed everyone of the male sex, as invariably as she awakened the scorn and incredulity of her own sisterhood. I think it was her *weakness* which was her principle charm; a kind of *sweet submission* and *softness* which seemed to appeal to each man she met for his sympathy and protection."

Mrs. Woodrow Wilson

Mrs. Wilson was a tender, dependent woman, for her husband wrote to her: "What a source of steadying and of strength it is to me in such seasons of too intimate self-questioning to have one fixed point of confidence and certainty — that even, unbroken, excellent perfection of my little wife, with her poise, her easy capacity in action, her unfailing courage, her quick efficient thought — and the charm that goes with it all, the sweetness, the feminine grace, — none of the usual penalties of efficiency — no hardness, no incisive sharpness, no air of command or of unyielding opinion. Most women who are efficient are such terrors."

The Efficient Woman that Men Admire

Occasionally, we may notice men who seem to admire women who are efficient and capable. Don't let this confuse you. Although the man may have a genuine admiration for such a woman, it does not mean he finds her attractive. He undoubtedly admires her as he would another man — with appreciation of her fine ability.

The Capable Woman

There are many women, in all walks of life, who possess great personal magnetism, whom all, including the men, admire as great and powerful characters, but who can never change a man's admiration into love. One such woman, a famous Sunday School teacher of young men and women, illustrates this situation. Her magnetic personality and noble character were so much admired that hundreds of young people sought to join her class and thousands of men and women of all ages attended whenever she gave a public lecture. In spite of this almost universal respect and admiration, the average man would never think of seeking her private company, indulging in an intimate conversation or of making her his "little girl" to cherish and protect throughout a lifetime. Everyone knows of such women, healthy, charming, enjoyable, whom men admire greatly but whom they do not seem to be fascinated by. The reason for this is that they lack an air of frail dependency upon men. They are too capable and independent to stir a man's sentiments. This air of being able to kill your own snakes is just what destroys the charm of so many business and professional women, and it is the absence of this air that permits many unsophisticated, artless and less educated women to capture an intelligent and capable man.

The kind of woman a man wants is first an angelic being whom a man can adore as infinitely better than himself, but also an adorably helpless little creature whom he would want to gather up in his arms and cherish and protect forever. The admirable women that we just mentioned fulfill the first requirement, but fail to fulfill the second. Though it is absolutely necessary to fulfill the first, you cannot afford to do as these women do and neglect the second.

If You are a Big, Strong and Capable Woman

What if you happen to be a big, strong and capable woman, or have a powerful personality or in some other way overpower men? How, then, can you possibly appear to be tender, trustful, delicate and dependent? In the first place, size has nothing to do with the quality of feminine dependency. No matter what your size, your height or your capabilities, you can appear fragile to a man if you follow certain rules and if you will take on an attitude of frailty. It is not important that you actually be little and delicate, but that *you seem so to men.*

When the Large Woman Attracts the Little Man

Occasionally we will see a rather small short man, married to a large woman. It is interesting to observe that she does not seem large to him because she has given him the impression of smallness. Such a man is even apt to call her "his little girl." She has managed, in spite of her size, to give him the impression of delicacy. By letting him know that she can't get along without him, that she is utterly dependent upon him, he has been able to disguise her rather large, overpowering figure.

If you are a large, tall or strong woman you will have to work to disguise these features so that men will have the impression that you are little and delicate. And if you are an efficient and capable woman, you will have to "unlearn" these traits. As you begin to develop your feminine nature, the one you were born with, you will tend to lose some of your qualities of fearlessness and efficiency and supplant them with the virtues of true femininity.

SUBMISSIVENESS

The meaning of the word *submissive* is to be yielding, compliant, obedient, to yield to power or authority, or to leave matters to the opinions, discretion or judgment of another or others. The opposite of submissiveness is to be defiant, rebellious, intractable, unruly, ungovernable, obstinate or stubborn.

Since we expect men to be our leaders and therefore dominant and aggressive, we should be the opposite in order to be the most feminine. We should be yielding and submissive to their rule, their opinions and their judgment. After marriage a woman can apply this more fully, but while she is single a certain amount of this is important and will do a great deal to enhance her femininity in contrast to the man's masculinity. She should avoid any tendency to stubbornness.

Men find it extremely disagreeable to be in the presence of women who have unyielding opinions. They want women to express their viewpoints, and to defend them to a degree, but are offended when a woman takes such a firm stand on an issue that the man cannot convince her of anything regardless of his sound logic. It is better to be submissive to a man than to try to win an argument.

I do not wish to imply here that you be in any way yielding in your moral convictions and ideals. I stress firmly that under no circumstances do you submit to a man in anything which would mean a lowering of standards. To do so would be to fall from your pedestal. However, there are many things and situations in our relationships with men which are of no real consequence. A woman would do well to submit to a man in unimportant matters and thereby give him the satisfaction of being the dominant male. So, as often as you can, whenever it does not interfere with your moral convictions, show forth this feminine trait by giving in to his opinion and his rule.

FEARFULNESS

Another trait of femininity is being subject to little fears and uneasiness in the presence of small dangers. Feminine women, for example, are known to be afraid of bugs, mice, the dark, strange noises, etc., much to the amusement of men. In the presence of her weakness he naturally feels stronger. If she shrinks from a spider or hops on a chair at the sight of a mouse, how manly he feels that he can laugh at such tremblings and calm her fears. It does a man more good to save a woman from a mouse than a tiger, since he feels so much more superiority over the mouse.

Feminine women are also known to be afraid of the dangers of nature. An illustration of this is in the following incident a woman confided to me. Her husband owned a sailboat and was a competent seaman. He loved to take her into dangerous waters and heel the boat over on its side. She was terrified at such times and asked me, "Why does he do this when he knows I am afraid?" I explained that the very reason he does is because she *is* so afraid and he is so *unafraid*. Her fearfulness was attractive to him. I encouraged her to not try to control her fearfulness, to reveal it in more calm waters, and perhaps he would be satisfied and not take her out further. It would be a mistake for a woman to subdue the tendency to fearfulness in the presence of men. To do so would be to rob herself of one of her elements of real charm.

Feminine women are also uneasy in the presence of heavy traffic. If you take a tiny child down to a busy highway and hold it tightly in your arms while the heavy trucks and fast moving traffic rush by, you would be able to feel the tremorous fearfulness of the child. Similarly a woman, when she approaches an intersection, does not charge forth with all confidence, but hestitates on the curb for a moment, clings to the man's arm a little tighter, waiting for him to lead the way. Here again, the man appreciates her apparent fear or uneasiness and his ability to give protection.

You Need Not be Beautiful to be Feminine

You need not be beautiful to have all of the charms of femininity. There are thousands of rather plain girls with irregular features and faulty builds who succeed in being attractive to men because they are models of femininity. On the other hand, there are thousands of other women who are beautiful in their faces and features but who, because of woodenness or masculinity of their manner, never impress men as being especially attractive. When a girl is tender, soft, fun-loving, lovable and also innocent and pure, who stops to inquire if she has beauty in the classical sense? Regardless of her feature or form, to most men she will seem a paragon of delicious femininity. To them she *is* beautiful!

Even when the woman is so homely that the fact cannot be overlooked, the men are often attracted nevertheless. While they may not consider her beautiful, they may consider her pert, cute, charming, dainty, lovable and saucy and everything else that is highly fascinating. Very often such a woman has the most enchanting personality of all and succeeds in captivating the most sensible men, the more vivid and virile characters for whom beauty without personality has no attraction; and frequently such a woman can make a merely beautiful woman seem insignificant beside her. You must not, therefore, let the absence of beauty discourage you; nor must you let the possession of beauty, if you have it, lull you into a false security. The presence or the absence of beauty is of minor consequence in the attainment of true femininity.

How to Develop Feminine Dependency

In acquiring feminine dependency, you must first *dispense with any air of strength and ability,* of competence and fearlessness or efficiency and acquire instead an air of frail dependency upon men to take care of you.

Then you must *stop doing things that are masculine.* Stop lifting heavy objects, moving furniture, mowing the lawn, painting, fixing motors, cleaning cars, changing tires, balancing on ladders, or anything else along this line that you may be doing. Stop doing these things whether you are in the presence of men or not, and form the habit early in life to let men take care of the things that belong in their world. Then also stop being aggressive, dominating men or bossing them around or telling them what to do, etc. Also, don't make plans for the future that are definitely in the masculine categories, such as planning to be a director of a business organization, a leader in industry, a president, superintendent, policewoman, attaining some acclaim or honor in the fields of men or anything that is masculine. These invasions into the man's world turn men off towards women.

Also, *don't be competitive with men or try to excel them* in their own field. For example, don't try to outdo them in sports, in lifting weights, in running, in repairing equipment, etc. Also, don't compete with men for advancement on a job, for higher pay, or greater honors. Don't compete with them for scholastic honors in men's subjects. It may be all right for you to win over a man in English or Social Studies, but you are in trouble if you compete with him in math, chemistry, public speaking, etc. Men may admire women who excel them but they are not apt to ask them for a date. Why? Because they have defeated them in their own field.

The next rule is: *Need his manly care and protection.* Remember, a man does not enjoy protecting a woman who can obviously get along without him. He only delights in protecting or helping a woman who *needs* his manly care, or at least appears to need it. So in every way you can, indicate to him that you *do* need his masculine assistance. First, "always accept his chivalry when offered." Let him open doors for you, help you with your coat, pull up your chair, lift your boxes or books, help you over the creek bed, offer you his coat in the cold or a rainstorm, give you his seat on the bus, run errands for you, help you solve a problem or wait upon you for this or that. As often as you can, accept a man's offer to help you. Be sure to thank him and let him know how much it was appreciated and *needed.* If a man does not offer his help in a rainstorm or at the creek bed you will have to devise some way to let him know that you need his help. Either shiver in the cold or hesitate fearfully at the creek bed.

On many occasions you can ask for his help when needed. Ask him to open jar lids for you, or to lift a heavy object, or to advise you on a difficult problem or to help you with an assignment. Remember that it is not an imposition on a man to ask him for his masculine assistance. Men enjoy helping women because it makes them feel masculine. Take care, however, to confine your requests to things that women need men for and not for petty trivial things that women can just as well do for themselves. In every way you can, demonstrate your helpless dependency upon men, and let them know either by asking or by some outward appearance of weakness, delicacy or incompetence that you are in need of masculine assistance.

The next rule is this: If at some time or another you are stuck with a masculine job in the presence of men, *do it in a feminine manner* and thus show your helpless dependency. For example, if you must lift a heavy sack of groceries, or must change a tire, or hammer some nails, do so with all womanliness. This means to struggle with it or show some amount of incompetence. It is not up to you to perform masculine tasks with the skill that men do. They will never come to your rescue if you can do these things as well as they can. Be yourself, your true feminine self, and men will come quickly to the rescue because you appear dependent and in need of their help. Now here are the rules to follow in becoming a feminine dependent woman.

Developing Dependency

1. Dispense with any air of strength and ability and acquire a feminine, dependent air or attitude.
2. Stop doing masculine things.
3. Don't be competitive with men in their own masculine fields or try to excel them.
4. Need men and call on them when needed.
5. If stuck with a masculine job, do it in a feminine manner.

Practice your femininity on every man you meet until it becomes second nature to you. Do not be dependent upon only those whom you consider especially masculine men. The kind of women who are most universally attractive look upon any and all men as big, strong and masterful. Truly feminine women do actually feel the contrast between themselves and *every man* for his strength and superior capabilities.

What Feminine Dependency Awakens in a Man

The air of delicacy and dependency awakens in a man — tenderness. As he begins to do things for you, to shelter you, wait upon you, take care of you, the tenderness grows (providing you have not made mistakes that drive men away). Your very need of care has contributed to this feeling of tenderness. You can easily see the truth of this principle if you will think of other situations in which the strong take care of the weak. If you give your constant care and protection to a little bird or a dog or a kitten, you can't help but feel tender towards it. This is because he is so dependent upon you. A mother feels this way about her little children as she gives them her watchful care.

A woman needs also to care for a *man*, to wait upon him, to comfort him, to watch over him and keep others from taking unfair advantage of his generous nature, to keep his foolhardy courage from endangering his safety, to see that he does not neglect his health, and to make certain that his manly indifference to detail does not lead him into trouble. Thus she too feels that he is dependent upon *her* in a different sort of way, and she too delights in his need of her and of her ability to fill the need of such a big, strong yet helpless man. She too feels tenderness towards the one she is caring for.

It is only natural to assume, then, that as we grow in feeling by caring for our pets, our children and our men, that the man would also feel tender towards a woman to whom he gives his masculine care and protection.

The Sweet Promise

Although men are fascinated by frailty in women, there is a balancing quality that they also want to see. They would like the assurance that, with all the woman's helplessness in the presence of men, with all of her dependency upon him to take care of her, to protect her and to wait upon her, that she has somewhere hidden within her the ability to meet an emergency. He would like to know that in such circumstances she would have womanly courage, strength and endurance and the ability to solve difficult problems, that she would not, in this case, be helpless. This is known as the "sweet promise." The man needs to be able to detect it somewhere in her character.

There are many women who show forth this promise when put to the test. Take for example a young widow who is left with several small children to support. What does she do? She sets out single-handed to battle against all odds. She slaves and struggles, she dares and she suffers in her effort to provide for her children. When defeat stares her in the face she doesn't even whimper, but taking her lot as a matter of course, she grimly grits her teeth and braves the struggle again. No matter what pain she suffers from overwork, she has always a smile of comfort for the childish fears of her little ones; no matter how weary she is, she is always ready to forget her own weariness at the slightest hint of danger to one of her children. Look to the widows of this earth and you will find that many of them compare to the angels of heaven. This sweet promise is a quality which comes from the development of a noble character, for in it are courage, love, determination, endurance, faith, etc.

Planning an Education and Career

The best way for young girls to plan for their future is to plan a *broad education*. The background of a liberal education will assist a woman greatly in being a wonderful mother to her children, in helping to educate them and inspire them with an appreciation for life and in helping them to make the proper adjustments and preparations for their lives ahead. It will help her equally as a wife, since women who are educated are more interesting, more open-minded to new ideas and challenging thoughts. She will also be a better citizen, have a greater appreciation for life and a greater capacity for happiness. This is providing she has a *good* education and puts something into getting the most out of it.

As for being trained in homemaking and family living, these classes can be of value also. Somewhere along the line she will have to learn to cook and sew with skill and to manage a household if she is to be our ideal of a domestic goddess. Many young girls learn this art from their mothers, but if not she will need to have training somewhere, or have a determination to learn on her own.

And what about careers? It is plain to see that if a girl is to be the dependent creature that men adore she should not center her education and her life around a career. Not only will she be in danger of taking on the efficient masculine traits that so many professional women acquire, but by making herself independent she will lose one of the elements that attracts men to women — her need of his manly care.

There are, of course, some professional women who manage to stay feminine, either through a nature so strongly feminine that it cannot be subdued or by conscious effort. But an all-consuming career that is apt to place a woman in a position of leadership or great responsibility will be competitive with her femininity, since she will have to take on masculine traits in order to succeed at her demanding job. It is therefore a real threat to femininity for you to plan for a career.

There are some who justify a career on the grounds that they may be faced with an emergency someday when it would be necessary for them to work. Although this may be true, it seems rather foolish for a woman to bypass a broad education, one that would assist her in being a better wife and mother, and plan her life around some rare emergency. It is wiser to prepare to fulfill her feminine destiny — to create a happy home. Most women who have a broad college education are intelligent enough to solve the problems of an emergency.

SUMMARY

As we come to the end of the chapter on femininity, you should have gained a new insight into the subject. Femininity, as you can see, is much more than just ruffles and lace. Although a feminine appearance is important, it is of little use without the feminine manner; and neither of them will be of any merit without the beautiful quality of feminine dependency.

Of all the qualities a woman may possess, this one attribute outweighs them all. It will make a woman enchanting, cuddlesome, lovable and fascinating in men's eyes and altogether too bewitching to be allowed to go through life without the guidance, care and protection of a man. Without femininity you may have a magnetic personality and you may have a powerful character, but in men's eyes you will not be a woman. A man isn't interested in a great and powerful character. *He wants a woman.*

REMEMBER:

THE MAIN WAY YOU ACHIEVE FEMININITY IS BY ACCENTUATING THE DIFFERENCES BETWEEN YOU AND MEN AND BY NEEDING THEIR MANLY CARE AND ASSISTANCE.

CHAPTER XIV

Radiant Happiness

I have already told you of inner happiness which is a spiritual quality and must be earned. What then is radiant happiness? Radiant happiness is a human quality and is therefore voluntary. That is, it can be "put on" like a smile. It is such things as cheerfulness, laughter, singing, joyfulness, smiles, bright eyes, pleasant outlooks, hope, optimism and the ability to radiate happiness to others.

There are many women who are happy at heart, but it may never have occurred to them that it is important to show it. Do not make the mistake of putting your happiness "under a bushel" where no one can see it. Instead, put it "on a candlestick" where everyone in the room may be warmed by its influence and beauty.

Radiant happiness is one of the real charms that men find fascinating in women, counting far more than physical beauty of face and form. Beautiful girls should not make the mistake of resting on their laurels, hoping that their pretty faces alone will win the attention of men. Without a smile and sparkling eyes men will not likely be interested. Men admire pretty girls as they do beautiful pictures and scenes from nature, but they search for radiant smiling women to be their companions. Women who lack beauty of face and form due to irregular features, often turn out to be real charmers because they have worked diligently to make up for these defects by acquiring the qualities that really count with men. Amelia, you will remember, was chubby and stout, with a short nose and round cheeks, yet she succeeded in winning the love of all men who came near her. This was due to her smiling lips, eyes and heart.

There is great emphasis in our modern times upon the appearance, especially of clothes, hair styles, etc. This emphasis upon the "outer shell" is all very good, but if radiance is not also added it will be like serving a beautiful banquet, arranging the table with the finest china, silver and crystal, and then serving an inferior quality of food. For example, a girl can be dressed in the latest styles from the most expensive salons, with her hair arranged in the most feminine and alluring fashion, but if she also appears with a disagreeable or sour expression on her face she will be a "flop" as far as men are concerned. If, on the other hand, she appears in rather plain clothing and hair style, but a smile of radiance included, let a man catch her eye and he will be fascinated, and her ordinary appearance will mean very little in comparison with the beauty of her face. This is not to underestimate the value of feminine and girlish clothes, etc., but only to stress that unless radiance is added, the effect will fail to be fascinating.

DERUCHETTE, AMELIA AND DORA

The most fascinating trait of Deruchette was her ability to radiate happiness to others, to "shed joy around" and "cast light upon dark days." She had in her smile alone a "power" which was great enough to lift the spirits of others. She radiated joy to her entire household, for her presence alone brought a "light" to the household and her approach was like a cheerful warmth. As the author says, "she passes by and we are content; she stays awhile and we are happy."

Amelia was "kind, fresh and smiling, with a smiling heart." Dora had a "gay little laugh and a delightful little voice." Mrs. Woodrow Wilson also had this quality, for her husband said, "She was so radiant, so happy!" Men simply do not want or enjoy women who are glum, depressed, or even overly serious. They seek out women who are vibrant, alive and happy!

DOLLY MADISON

The longest reigning and gayest of all first ladies of the White House was Dolly Madison. During the eight years her husband presided she won the hearts of her countrymen and was known as the most popular person in the U.S. and the most loved. In Parisian turban topped with a plume, her neck and arms strung with pearls, she was the perfect hostess — bubbly and natural, tactful and gracious. Her zest for life never ran out. Without becoming ill, one day at age 82 she simply passed from a nap to death. "She sparkled," reported a friend, "up to the very verge of the grave."

Ninon de Lenclos

Ninon de Lenclos of the 17th century courts of France was another woman of special charm and radiance. Some of the greatest men of the century loved her, and she is said to have won the hearts of three generations of men in a single family, for she lived and retained her beauty and charm into her eighties. The most interesting women of France were her devoted friends. The most wonderful thing about her, everyone said, was her eager delight in everything around her. In her own words she said, "You never hear me say 'this is good or this is bad,' but a thousand times a day I say 'I enjoy, I enjoy.'"

How to Acquire Radiant Happiness

The first thing to do is to work for inner happiness, for it will be difficult to radiate happiness to others if you are unhappy at heart. But while you are working, apply radiance wherever you can. It is surprising what you can do by conscious effort. A good suggestion is the following: After you have applied your makeup, stand before the mirror for a few seconds and practice radiance. Remember, your artful makeup will do little good if you wear a glum expression. If you leave the room with a happy face your friends or family will be apt to reflect back this same expression, and your day will begin with good spirit and charm. The radiance, however, must be of the lips, the eyes and the entire countenance and not just a stiff wooden-like smile. After this good beginning, add a cheerful attitude. Try not to be skeptical or dubious about life in general. Certainly some things we must look upon with doubt, but our attitude should be one of optimism, hope and emphasis on the brighter side of life. It will be difficult to have a smile such as Deruchette, which has the "power to lift the spirits of others," unless we also maintain a bright outlook.

Radiate your happiness "to all" and not merely those who are already pleasant. Deruchette "shed joy around," which suggests that she shed it to everyone as the rain that falls on every flower in the forest, not just a select few. Radiate not only to the happy, but also to the sad, the depressed and disconsolate. The world delights in sunny people; there are more than enough of the serious ones. A bright smile does more good for the down-hearted than food for the hungry.

Then give sunshine to the frowning, sour and disagreeable also. They need it the most of all. Give whether they are deserving or not. "God maketh the rain to fall on the just and the unjust." Your smile will be even more appreciated because it is such a rare pleasure with those who frown. A soft look can soften the hardest heart, so don't underestimate the value of your happy disposition to such people. They will credit it as a mark of a womanly woman. If you thus practice radiance upon all you meet, the deserving and the undeserving, you will acquire it as a habit and it will then seem only natural to you. If you do not show it to all, but only to your men friends, your happiness may appear as "flirting" and you may be suspected of manhunting.

DEMURE

There is another word that is always upon men's lips when speaking of attractive womanhood — the word *demure*. The dictionary terms this word "affectedly modest, decorous or serious; making a show of gravity." The true meaning of the word in connection with attractive womanhood is *an air of radiant happiness mixed with playful mischievousness, yet smothered with gravity.* The perfect illustration is of a woman who is radiantly alive and playful but who puts on an act of gravity, the corners of her lips struggling to suppress a smile of mischief and her eyes dancing in an otherwise grave face. This contrivance is attractive to men.

WOMEN WHO NEVER SEEM TO SMILE, BUT WIN MEN

We have all known women who never seem to smile and yet have succeeded in winning a man who appears to adore them. Why is this so? If you could discover the real facts you would find that although she does not smile for others she does smile for him. He probably discovered by accident her ability to smile, but until he could see her smile in such a disarming fashion she had little or no attraction for him. And now, though she still never smiles for others, when he looks at her for assurance of her continued kindly attitude, her eyes smile back, though subtly, a sincere and kindly smile.

Smiling through Adversity

As with the nature of life, we all have times when we become discouraged. It is then that smiling seems much more difficult. Not only is it difficult but unnatural. However, as with all Christian and moral teachings, we are expected to do the supernatural thing. It is a mark of true character, and especially womanly character, to smile in the face of adversity. The following lines by Ella Wheeler Wilcox expresses this trait beautifully:

It is easy enough to be pleasant
When life flows by like a song.
But the one worthwhile is the one who can smile
When everything goes dead wrong.
For the test of the heart is trouble
And it always comes with the years.
And the smile that is worth the praises of earth
Is the smile that shines through tears.

When not to Smile

There are some occasions when it is best not to be radiant. For example, when you are in the presence of someone who is depressed, your happy attitude *may* suggest a lack of sympathy. In this case it will be best to be serious and show an understanding for what the other person is suffering. Try to be perceptive of these situations in which gravity and sympathy seem more appropriate. You can tell by the reaction of the person. If they seem offended by your happiness you can be sure they feel it is not in harmony with their low spirits, and they wish you would stop.

The Real Charm

Inner happiness combined with radiant happiness is an essential part of the real charm that men find fascinating in women. Inner happiness, as we have learned, brings a calm spirit and tranquility which is a peaceful beauty. It is like clear calm water in a pond. Radiant happiness is like the lily pads that add breathtaking beauty. Beneath the flowers you can see the stillness of the waters. The charm is in the overall effect.

THERE IS IN THIS WORLD NO FUNCTION MORE IMPORTANT THAN THAT OF BEING CHARMING — TO SHED JOY AROUND, TO CAST LIGHT UPON DARK DAYS, TO BE THE GOLDEN THREAD OF OUR DESTINY, AND THE VERY SPIRIT OF GRACE AND HARMONY. IS NOT THIS TO RENDER A SERVICE?

CHAPTER XV

Fresh Radiant Health

The foundation of fresh beauty is genuine good health, not only for the health itself, but for the fresh and joyous spirit health sustains in the woman's appearance, actions and attitude. How alluring are sparkling and dancing eyes, lustrous hair, clear voice, buoyancy of manner and the animation which good health brings to the face and the vivacity it communicates to the thoughts. We cannot, therefore, attach too much importance to this qualification.

We all know the importance of good health, but our trouble lies in thinking of good health in terms of not being ill. The perfection of healthy womanhood is more than merely being well. A fresh radiant appearance is a result of *health in rich abundance*. Health, like happiness, is based upon laws and comes as a result of understanding and applying them. The following are the fundamentals of good health:

1. Correct internal disorders.
2. Get enough sleep.
3. Exercise.
4. Drink plenty of water.
5. Get fresh air.
6. Eat properly.
7. Relax — at work or play.
8. Have a healthy mental attitude.
9. Control weight.

1. *Correct internal disorders:* It is impossible to attain health if there are internal disorders. Often women will go for years with such things as infected teeth, infected internal organs, disorders of the blood or glands and other malfunctions of the body which cause them to have poor health. Many of these ailments can be eliminated by proper attention.

2. *Get enough sleep:* We all know the value of sufficient sleep, but young women often neglect this essential due to a heavy

schedule of social life or even studies. If you are robbed of your sleep by too many things to do, ask yourself if your activities are more important than you or your health. Many things we do are a waste of time when it comes right down to facts, especially when they are measured against genuine good health.

3. *Exercise:* Exercise is as important as the food we eat in both preserving life and youth and in producing health. You may feel that you have enough exercise in the ordinary activities like walking, bending and reaching. These motions of the body do not bring into play all of the muscles. As a result, many women suffer from poor posture, sagging muscles, fat deposits and loss of health. If exercise seems like merely an added labor to your already busy schedule, remember that exercise can actually rest a weary person. Calling a different set of muscles into activity refreshes and stimulates the body.

4. *Drink plenty of water:* The body is made up of 66 percent water — more than two-thirds by weight and several gallons in all. If you do not drink enough water your body will be forced to use its water over and over again. Your whole system will suffer unless refreshed frequently with a new supply of water.

5. *Get fresh air:* A good air supply consists of three things. The first is having *fresh air with ample oxygen* content, the second is to *breathe deeply enough* to take the air into your lungs, and the third is to make certain that the air *is not lacking in moisture.* Oxygen is our most important food. What good food is to the stomach, oxygen is to the blood. You must therefore make sure that you have fresh air in your rooms and also that you breathe deeply enough to take it into your lungs. Poor posture and lack of exercise are responsible for shallow breathing, which leads to a shortage of oxygen in the blood. The purpose of exercise is not only the development of the muscles but also a healthy intake of air, deep into the lungs.

Most of us realize the importance of fresh air, but many do not realize the importance of moisture content, both day and night. Many modern heating systems dry the air so that even in a fairly moist climate the air in the house may be dry. This overly dry air can cause colds, sore throats and even lung irritation. The solutions are to either turn the furnace off at night and open the windows, have a moisturizer installed in the furnace, use a vaporizer, or hang a wet towel in the bedrooms at night. The same care can be taken in the daytime if the furnace is used then.

6. *Eat properly:* What is a safe guide for proper eating? Our appetite is not a safe guide, for even bad foods taste good. There are many foods and products on the market. Which are good and which ones harmful? Many of the studies concerning foods are confusing and some of them are contradictory.

Nature reveals to us the secrets of good eating. We cannot improve on an apple as it comes from a tree, or a banana, or a potato as it comes from the earth. *Eat foods as near to nature as possible* is the safest rule. There is fresh food available in every season. The summer brings its fruit, vegetables and melons; the fall brings apples, squash and potatoes which last until spring. Early spring brings the navel oranges, late spring the berries and more fresh vegetables. All of these are best when eaten fresh in the season in which they grow. Nature also produces the grains which remain fresh for several seasons.

Wholesome foods fall into five categories:

> fresh fruits
> fresh vegetables
> nuts
> grains
> meats

There are many highly processed and refined foods on the market today, many of them containing preservatives. They come in boxes, cans and packages. Some of the vital elements have been removed, and in an effort to make up for this lack, man has added his own created vitamins and minerals. Our Creator's foods have been tampered with. Can man improve upon nature?

7. *Relax:* The secret of being able to relax at work or play is essential to both health and charm, and is an ability which is fairly easy to acquire. The mind controls the body, and this control can cause either tension or relaxation. If you will merely *tell your body to relax* you will immediately feel a relief of tension. This same technique can be applied in getting to sleep when you are suffering tension.

8. *Have a healthy mental attitude:* The effect of unwholesome attitudes such as worry, fear, anxiety, pessimism, hate, resentments, impatience, envy, anger, or any other irritating mental image can have a detrimental effect upon the human body. Its destructive influence is carried through the nervous system to the entire body. For example, people have been known to die of anger. Even after the temporary emotion has left, the physical damage may remain. A healthy mental attitude comes as a result of good character. If you suffer from these unwholesome attitudes, it is a sign of weakness in your character and you need to develop your angelic side.

In contrast, wholesome attitudes, buoyant and kindly thoughts, have exactly the opposite effect. Faith, optimism, love, kindness, cheerfulness, sympathy and enthusiasm all harmonize with body function and tend to invigorate the system.

9. *Control weight:* Men will in almost every case, agree that fat is unattractive on women and that even an extra five pounds is distasteful. The five pounds alone is not what they object to. Being overweight says something else. It says that you are not careful, that you do not persist in working for the things that should be important to every girl. "If you are overweight now," they also reason, "how will your figure look after you are married and have children?" Boys shy away from girls with this problem if for no other reason than fear of the future. America has so many overweight people that the chances are quite high that a girl will be one of them later anwyay. A man just doesn't want to take the risk with a girl who already has this problem.

There are many good diet and reducing plans in the country at present — some of them very good. Often however, overweight people tend to become discouraged with their problem, feeling that it is a lifetime struggle and perhaps not worth the continual effort. They may set a goal which they never quite achieve. They may feel that to be slim means to "starve" for the rest of their lives. This is a discouraging thought that some girls feel they do not have the courage to face.

But take heart with this thought. When a girl finally reaches her normal size, or better still, just a few pounds below her normal weight, it is not the struggle it once was. The appetite at this point tends to become normal, or at least controllable with reasonable effort. You can reach the point that it is not a major problem any longer — for many women have done so to prove it. With reasonable care you can keep that figure for the rest of your life.

Before giving a few reducing suggestions, let's decide what your weight should be. Girls vary in bone structure, but there is a fairly good rule to follow in which you can determine your best weight. If you are of normal structure, write down 100 lbs. for the first 5 feet of your height. For each inch you are above 5 ft. add 5 lbs. When you reach the total, subtract 5 lbs. This is your normal weight. If your structure is a little larger or smaller than normal you can vary the weight slightly according to your build.

Here is another rule for weight control: After you reach your normal weight, make it a habit to *weigh every day!* If you gain one pound during the day, you can go on a diet the next day with only one pound to lose. This makes weight control easy. You will, however, have to be consistent about weighing each day, without exception, for this plan to work.

There are many good standard diets which will gradually take off the pounds. One is the diabetic diet, which is one of the most wholesome. This can be had from your doctor. Another is the plan followed by "Weight Watchers" which is now quite well known across the country. We will not go into these in detail here. I will only suggest a few other approaches to dieting.

One of the best rules to follow if you are inclined to gain weight is to make a determination to eliminate all sweets from the diet for the rest of your life. This would include all pie, cake, ice cream, candy, gum, soft drinks, cookies, pastries, puddings, etc., including such things as syrup on hotcakes or jam on bread, etc. If you will try this drastic elimination of sweets, you will find that in a month or two your desire for these things will lessen, if not entirely leave, and that you will also feel better due to improved health. There is no doubt that this step will do much to preserve your health, lengthen your life and also help you retain beautiful teeth for the rest of your life, as well as help you keep your figure. Certainly these incentives are strong enough to make this step possible. With this diet, you can eat almost everything else. You can eat all of the vegetables, potatoes and bread that you feel hungry for, within reason. You will have to avoid fats to some extent, but you will find that when you eliminate sweets, you also eliminate many of the foods that contain large amounts of fats.

Another diet suggestion is to not eat after 3:00 p.m. Those foods which you take in your body in the evening hours are more easily assimilated due to your being more relaxed. Before three you can eat a fairly reasonable diet that is well balanced. You will have to be firm in your determination to not eat after 3:00 p.m., however. If you break the rules for even a few mouthfuls of food, the diet will not "work." If you follow this plan "to the letter" you will lose close to a pound a day. If you do not find it convenient to eat your meals before 3:00, try eating only two meals a day. You can eliminate any one of the three, breakfast, lunch or dinner, but try not to eat late in the evening. Whatever plan you choose, remember that men dislike excess fat and that it will be more difficult for you to appear dainty, feminine, and girlish if you have a chunky figure. Take seriously, then, any excess weight you may have and work with determination to lose it.

If Health Is Beyond Your Reach

There are some who, because of permanent damage, cannot attain this ideal of abundant health. If, however, they maintain a healthy mental attitude, they may appear much more healthy than they actually are. Elizabeth Barrett Browning was an invalid, yet one of the truly charming women in history. Her husband, Robert Browning, adored her. Her physical weakness was not an added attraction, but she had an abundance of other womanly qualities which overcame the physical lack. Radiant health is only one qualification of Angela Human. If you have a healthy mental attitude you may still be a fascinating woman.

Cleanliness and Grooming

Good health is not the only essential in attaining a fresh appearance. Cleanliness and grooming are also important. The teeth, the hair, the nails, the feet, and cleanliness of the entire body are vital contributions to the effect of freshness. It would seem inconsistent with our ideal of Angela Human to expect her to be anything less than immaculate and well groomed.

Clothes

A fresh appearance in clothing is especially attractive to men. Such things as fresh starched collars, flowers (real or artificial), clean shining ribbons, polished shoes and clean, well pressed clothes contribute to a fresh look. Certain materials and colors appear fresh, while others are drab. Clean stripes, polka-dots, ginghams, daisy designs and animated prints suggest freshness.

Make-up

Men are not opposed to artificial allurements if it makes the woman appear more alive and healthy. In fact, your attention to these details only indicates to him your efforts to please him. Eye make-up and lipstick especially help to make the face appear bright and fresh, which is the reason they were created — to charm men.

CHAPTER XVI

Childlikeness

Except ye become as a little child, ye shall not enter the Kingdom of Heaven.

What is meant by the Biblical statement, "Except ye become as a little child?" This implies that little children have qualities which we would do well to copy, and this we do in childlikeness. We copy the adorable traits of little girls, their tenderness, innocence, playfulness, spunk, sauciness, trustfulness and joyfulness. This is the spice and spark of the subject which keeps the perfection of the angelic side from becoming cloysome. Men love this trait in women. It amuses them, enchants and fascinates them because, like femininity, it is such a contrast to their own superior strength and masculine abilities.

We find this trait in our study of Dora, Amelia, and Deruchette. Dora was "captivating, bright eyed and girlish." Amelia had the tender emotions of a little child, for her eyes would quickly fill with tears. Deruchette had a "childlike prattle," and "she who was one day to become a mother was for a long while a child." She had the giddiness, vivacity and teasing playfulness of a little girl. We will now devote ourselves to a study of this fascinating subject. The following are the different traits which make up childlikeness in women.

Sauciness

In our relationships with men they sometimes mistreat us. A man may, for example, be insulting, thoughtless, unkind, negligent or unfair; and if he is the mischievous type he may even tease us to the point of irritation. The usual response to this mistreatment is for the girl to take a sullen or resentful attitude and draw into her shell, or perhaps even be indifferent towards the man's actions. These reactions are unattractive to men and apt to cool a relationship, at least temporarily. Sometimes a girl may make the mistake of showing forth real anger. If she does she is likely to fall from her pedestal in the man's eyes and also destroy her femininity. None of these reactions are attractive or successful in dealing with men.

A girl needs to be forgiving, of course, to overlook small errors and occasional thoughtlessness, but if she shows no reaction to harsh or continual mistreatment, this is an indication of a lack of self-dignity. The man, you can be sure, will not be impressed with her lack of sensitivity, for he does not appreciate a woman he can walk on, push around and mistreat. He wants and admires women with spunk, who have enough pride and self-dignity to defend themselves against mistreatment.

When a girl is mistreated, it would be a serious mistake for her to set out to remake the man, to teach him that she expects to be treated better. All men need the freedom to be themselves and to act as their impulses dictate at the moment, whether their impulses happen to be right or wrong, wise or foolish. Let men *act themselves.* Our responsibilities as women is to learn how to *react.* We have already been shown the dangers of showing real anger, and also the foolishness of going into our shell with a sullen or resentful attitude, or even worse to be indifferent. The solution, however, is very simple. The way to react when a man is thoughtless is to show forth childlike sauciness.

There is no better school for learning sauciness than watching the antics of little children, especially little girls who have been spoiled by too much loving. They are so trusting, so sincere, so innocent, and yet so piquant and outspoken that they are often teased into anger. They are too innocent to feel hate, jealousy, resentment, and the uglier emotions. When such a child is teased she doesn't respond with some hideous sarcasm. Instead she stamps her foot and shakes her curls and pouts. She gets adorably angry at herself because her efforts to respond are impotent. Finally, she switches off and threatens never to speak to you again, then glances back at you over her shoulder to see if you thought she really meant it, only to stamp her foot in impatience when she sees that you are not the least bit fooled. One feels an irresistible longing to pick up such a child and hug her. We would do anything rather than to permit such an adorable little thing to suffer danger or want; to protect and care for such a delightfully human little creature would be nothing less than a delight.

This is much the same feeling that a woman inspires in a man when she is adorably angry. This extreme girlishness makes him feel in contrast, stronger, and so much more of a man. This is why women who are little spitfires, independent and saucy, are often sought after by men. This anger, however, must be the sauciness of a child, and not the intractable stubbornness of a woman well able to kill her own snakes.

How to be Saucy

The key to your childlike anger is this: Your anger, your spunk or sauciness must be mostly *pretense*. Your fiery display of emotions must be only on the surface. They are absent of the deep emotions of hate, bitterness or resentment. One thing to help you learn is to try ham acting. Pretend that you are in a play and must do a scene displaying anger. Since you are not experienced or talented enough to portray the emotions of real anger, you must do so by some outward show. This will come close to what we mean by *pretense* in childlike sauciness. Now, in learning this art, the following are some ideas which you can rely upon to help you.

1. *Some things to do:* One of the best things to do is to *pout,* or protrude the lower lip. You can easily learn this art from children. Some other things to do are to *stomp your foot, shake your head, open your eyes wide, place both hands on your hips,* or *square your shoulders* and *lift your chin high.* These are only a few of the outward signs of sauciness. You can discover many others on your own.

2. *Exaggerate:* Another thing to do is to exaggerate his treatment of you. Say, for example, "You are the most thoughtless man in town," or "So this is the way you treat a poor little helpless girl like me," or "Oh, what a dreadful thing to do!" Be sure to watch your words, that they represent a trustful feminine woman of high character and not a vulgar suspicious one. Do not, for example, use words that are crude or insulting, such as nasty, wicked, dumb, ridiculous, hateful, rude, etc. Also exaggerate your threats of punishment. For example, say, "I'll never speak to you again!" or "I won't do anything for you

anymore," or "You're going to be sorry, you just wait and see!" or, "I'll tell my mother on you!"

3. *Acquire a list of adjectives:* Have in your mind a list of adjectives which will be fitting for the occasion of sauciness and also which will compliment the man's masculinity. Some suggestions are big, tough, brute, stubborn, obstinate, unyielding, inflexible, unmanageable, determined, unruly, stiff-necked, indominatable, invincible, difficult, troublesome, and hardhearted. Be certain that your words compliment his masculinity and are not words that would crush his ego, such as little, imp, pipsqueek, insignificant, weak, simple minded, etc.

It is interesting to note that the reason children tend to exaggerate in both their expressions and their bold words, is due to their impotence, their feeling of helplessness in the presence of superior adults or even in the presence of other children. Unconsciously, in a moment of frustration, they feel they must make up for their smallness by exaggerations. Therefore, when a woman uses this same method, she gives the man the impression that she also is impotent and helpless and therefore childlike. A good illustration of childlike sauciness is found in the story of David Copperfield. In this particular situation, Dora responded to David's criticism with the charms of both exaggerations and adjectives.

Dora's Anger

David had criticized Dora because she didn't manage the hired help well and because of this one of them had stolen Dora's gold watch and fallen into further difficulty. He put the blame on Dora. The hired help was a young boy, a page, as he was called.

"I began to be afraid," said David, "that the fault is not entirely on one side, but that these people all turn out ill because we don't turn out very well ourselves."

"Oh, what an accusation," exclaimed Dora, opening her eyes wide, "*to say that you ever saw me take gold watches. Oh! Oh!* you *cruel fellow,* to compare your *affectionate wife* to a *transported page!* Why didn't you tell me your opinion of me before we were married? Why didn't you say, *you hard hearted thing,* that you were convinced that I was *worse than a transported page?* Oh, what a dreadful opinion to have of me! Oh, my goodness!"

If you will notice, she does exaggerate and she has her pet adjectives.

BECKY SHARP

Another illustration of sauciness is found in the story of *Vanity Fair,* the story in which we find the character of Amelia. Becky Sharp also succeeded in charming men throughout the story. On the occasion I shall mention Amelia's brother, Joseph, had tricked Miss Becky into eating hot peppers. "I shall take good care how I let you choose for me another time," said Rebecca as they went down to dinner. *"I didn't know men were fond of putting poor little harmless girls to pain."* "By Gad, Miss Rebecca, I wouldn't hurt you for the world" was Joseph's apology.

These three suggstions I have given — *childlike mannerisms, exaggerations,* and *masculine adjectives* — will usually succeed in making the man amused, charmed, enchanted, and hopefully bring him to some kindly words of apology, as did Joseph to Rebecca, "I would not hurt you for the world." But if not, if the man persists in his amusement, is so enchanted that he teases you into further anger, then the natural childlike response is to be angry with oneself. This is the fourth suggestion that I have to make on how to be saucy.

4. *Being angry with yourself:* In order to explain this let me refer again to the illustration of the little girl who became adorably angry with *herself* because her efforts to respond were impotent. As I have already explained, children, because of their littleness, feel they are no match for adults. In this little girl's moment of frustration, because she could not get the adult to apologize, she was probably thinking unconsciously, "how can a little girl like me get the best of a big strong adult like you!" The realization of her helplessness caused her to become angry with herself and more saucy than ever.

Women who are saucy apply this same principle in their relationships with men. When their sauciness succeeds only in arousing the man's amusement, without an apology, they respond with self anger, as much as to say, "what can a little girl like me do with a big overpowering man like you." Young girls who have retained this trait will sometimes stomp and fret and fume in the most amusing and adorable self-anger and even sometimes laugh at themselves for their inadequacy to get the best of men.

In applying this principle, one thing you can do is to lift your chin high, and swish off. Then, when you reach the doorway, do as the little girl did, peek back over your shoulder. At this point the man will probably be smiling in amusement. If so, then stomp your foot in self anger, lift your chin a little higher and swish off. There are many different variations of self-anger which you can learn by observation and also by practice.

When to be Saucy

When you have been irritated or provoked is the time to be saucy. If you feel within you the emotions of hate, bitterness or resentment, then it will be impossible for you to use childlike anger until you first rid yourself of these faults. You will have to work on your angelic character, to develop an ability to accept people, to be understanding and forgiving and patient, so that you will feel kindly towards them, even when you are offended. Then, when someone offends you, you will feel only slight emotions, such as irritation, and you will be able to respond like a little girl, and thereby express your offense and show your self-dignity and spunk.

Also, remember to react with sauciness only when *you* have been mistreated or teased, or perhaps some small child that you are watching over. Don't try to be saucy when it is someone else the man has offended or you may be in for trouble. Only respond when you have been insulted, neglected or treated unfairly, or when he has been thoughtless of *you*. Also, you cannot be saucy due to some negligence on his part that does not affect you, some mistake or error or failure that is in his world and that is really not your affair.

After you have studied the subject of sauciness until you feel that you understand it, practice it upon your family, your brothers and your father, or even your roommates. You will soon find that this charming art is a part of your feminine nature and therefore it will be natural to you. You may remember in the novel *The Cloister and the Hearth* the author said, "Girls like to be coy and tender, saucy and gentle by turns." Our nature is to be not only feminine, but also saucy. You need only recapture that which belongs to you by nature and that which you had not so long ago when you were a little girl. And when you do recapture this charming art, you will find that the men love it. They will be fascinated and captivated, to say nothing of being amused by your sauciness. This is due to the contrast again between their manly and superior strength and capabilities and your girlishness.

Teasing Playfulness

Another charming art of childlikeness is "teasing playfulness." You can use this "coquettish" trait when a man is overly serious, stern or cross with you, or when he sits you down to give you a lecture on how you need to improve, etc. A perfect illustration of this is found in the character of Babbie in the play *The Little Minister*. The dignified little minister looked with unadulterated horror upon her wild gypsy ways. But when he protested with her about her apparent irresponsibility she interrupted the serious lecture by teasingly wanting to know which was the taller, making him stand back-to-back to measure their respective heights. And then, when he was ready to burst with indignation at her lack of seriousness, she pouted adorably as if to say "you're not really going to be angry with poor little me" and flashed at him such a confiding, trustful, I-am-certain-you-like-me-too-well-to-hurt-me glance and smile that the poor man forgot his indignation completely in a struggle with himself to keep from gathering the adorable creature in his arms and telling her, "No, I wouldn't want to hurt you for all the world."

If you will notice, the first thing that Babbie did was to *change the subject* by wanting to know which was the taller. Then she *distracted his attention* away from his lecture by making him stand back-to-back with her. You can practice a similar teasing playfulness by following these same rules. First, change the subject to something playful and light, then distract his attention by such things as "adjusting his glasses," "straightening his tie," "smoothing his hair," etc. Make an effort to find ways and means to practice this charming art. Men will find it enchanting, and you will help to drive away the seriousness from life.

Teasing playfulness in women does not mean playing pranks. This trait is characteristic of little boys, not of little girls. At times pranks might be fitting for men but they are never fitting for women.

TENDERNESS OF EMOTION

Another trait men find especially attractive in women is tenderness of emotion like crying, sympathy and pity. Amelia, you may remember, "would cry over a dead canary," or "a mouse," or "the end of a novel." The tendency to cry is strong in young girls and usually carries over to adult life unless a girl has been so foolish as to suppress it. Women should not make the mistake of smothering their emotions while watching a dramatic or sad movie, or while listening to some inspiring music, or a moving story, or an incident which arouses their sympathy. Not only will they be healthier if they cry, but men will find their tender emotions attractive.

Girls who have this childlike trait of tenderness are easily excited to pity or sympathy. If a man, for example, is telling a story, or describing his experiences, the absorbedly interested girl gets into quite a state of excitement over what happens, sympathizes heartily with the characters involved, is horrified and delighted by turns, and can hardly wait for the end to find out if everyone escaped unhurt. This dainty betrayal of girlish tenderness of heart is highly entertaining and fascinating to men. They will sometimes concoct the wildest and most heart-rending tales just for the sake of stirring up her tender little heart. Not only is her eager sympathy attractive, but when she learns his story is all a product of his imagination, her childlike irritation, her air of saying "how could a big man like you deceive a little girl like me," her helpless fury at him for teasing her is even more amusing. Practice this bewitching art at every opportunity.

I have been speaking here of how a woman can show tenderness of emotion by sympathy for someone else or something else. Still another time is when *she* is hurt or disappointed. As I have already explained in this chapter, sometimes a man is thoughtless, unfair, etc. The usual charming response is sauci-ness; but occasionally his remark will be entirely too cutting to react in any other way than crying. If this is the case, she should try to adopt the adorable crying of little girls. She can, for example, quiver the lips, let a tear or two trickle down the cheeks, look with downcast eyes, twist her handkerchief, etc. Or she may, if necessary, use exaggerated sobs, with a heav-ing of the bosom.

If you feel a tendency to cry, try not to take on the manner-isms of a woman who is genuinely and deeply disturbed, for this is exceedingly frustrating to a man. When a woman's cry is full of emotional turmoil the man is often at his wit's end to know how to comfort her and in his desperation may even walk away and leave her. The only kind of cry that will arouse a man's amusement and be enchanting to him is one that is childlike.

CHILDLIKE JOY

We can also learn the art of childlike joy from watching little girls. Have you ever noticed a little girl when she has just been rewarded with a pleasant surprise or is promised some forthcoming good time? What does she do? She opens her eyes wide, claps her hands and jumps up and down. The benefactor receives so much enjoyment in the presence of such eagerness that he is apt to repeat the act again and again, just to see the sparkle in her eyes and the joyfulness of her manner. It takes very little to make children happy which is why we appreciate their joy and want so much to do things for them.

Exuberant women who get all excited over every little thing, usually have men who pamper and spoil them, showering them with gifts they don't even need. On the other hand, women who respond with a bland "thank you," or a mere "oh, how nice," or "oh, how thoughtful of you," do nothing to encourage the man's generosity and therefore rob him of the joy of giving. We should encourage men to spend money on us, since pamper-ing and spoiling us makes men love us more. Men have often "broken their necks" to cater to the whims of femininity and have loved doing it and loved the women more because of it.

We have been speaking here of eagerness shown when a man gives a woman rather modest gifts and does small favors for her. In contrast to this, if a man should give her something of unusual value, or which requires sacrifice on his part, child-like joy may be inappropriate for such a momentous occasion. A deeply expressed appreciation may be more significant and rewarding to the man.

Another thing which every woman should know about giving is that when a man gives her something that she does not par-ticularly like, or may even dislike, she should not make the unforgivable mistake of showing disappointment. A moment like this does not need to pose a problem, however, as many women would imagine. You need not force yourself to be insin-cere and act as though you like the gift if you honestly do not. The thing to do is to appreciate not the gift, but *the act of giving and the man giving it.* Even your words can be carefully chosen to show appreciation for the man, for his thoughtfulness and his generosity. The gift is of little consequence in comparison with the man, his feelings and the beautiful moment which you may remember for a long time if you handle it wisely. What-ever the gift is, be sure to use it, at least for awhile, with the deepest appreciation for the generous giver.

If a man happens to be negligent about gift giving, don't let this concern you too far. Perhaps in the past you have failed to show enough eagerness and joy in his giving, and he has lost interest in doing things for you. But whether true or not, the fact remains that men are known to be negligent about such matters. They seldom have good imaginations about selecting things for women and are not likely to remember hints. Do not, therefore, attach too much importance to this negligence or interpret it as a lack of caring for you. Also, some men have a tendency to dislike the compulsion of gift giving which has been handed us by tradition, such as birthdays and Christmas. They would rather buy something when they feel like it, rather than when tradition dictates.

OUTSPOKENNESS

One of the best methods of displaying a childlike manner is in being outspoken. I do not wish to imply that we have "unbridled tongues," or that we speak too frankly, with little concern for the feelings of others, a fault noticeable in some adults. The childlike manner I refer to is one of being *direct* in conversation, and not evasive, "beating around the bush," making excuses and failing to come to the point.

A little child who has been reared by kind and loving parents of whom he is not afraid tends to be honest and outspoken. He says such things as "I don't want to," or "oh, I forgot." For example, if you ask a little girl if she would like to go with you to visit Mrs. Grumbly down the street and the child really does not want to go, she will say "I don't want to." She does not hunt for excuses or ask to put it off until another time, etc. She is honest and direct. This is the response a man appreciates from a woman.

If you are shopping with a man and he suggests that you buy something you dislike, it is not necessary to explain your objections. Be honest and outspoken and say "I really don't think I want this one, I would rather look for something else." This comment will not only relieve the situation but will be appreciated and less likely to insult his tastes than would an elaboration of your ideas.

I knew a married girl who had this charm of outspokenness. On the occasion that I remember, her husband and several other men had just announced plans to sail down the Colorado river on a raft. The girl, thinking the trip quite extravagant, especially since she had been going without some of the things she needed, said in a very girlish manner, "But, what about me! I need some new cottons and some high heels." The man looked up at her in surprised wonder and amusement. How much better was this outspoken response than if she had tried to convince him of his selfishness, or even worse, had said nothing and held a grudge.

In some situations a woman should encourage such manly plans with eagerness and excitement, but in her case the trip was really beyond their means, and her outspoken words brought him back to reality and kept her from feeling resentful about it. Since she felt she must express herself — it was wise to do so in a girlish and outspoken manner.

How to Ask for Things

Another art of childlikeness is knowing how to ask a man for things. I refer to things you want to have, to do, someplace you want to go, or something you want done for you. Getting a man to do these things for you is an art worth knowing, and so simple you would hardly believe it. A woman should never use any other approach with men.

We copy this art again from little children. They just *ask for things*. They do not justify, explain or argue a point, for they are too dependent and incapable in the presence of adults. A little girl, when she wants something, will approach her father trustfully, realizing that he has the power to say yes or no. She will say "May I, please," or "Will you please," displaying her dependent attitude and causing her father to feel big and masculine, in the position of the leader. All soft hearted parents are bound to say yes to such childlike requests.

If you approach a man with a childlike request it gives him the feeling of superiority, and therefore manliness. Not only will he be encouraged to say "yes," but he will feel your childlike dependency, your littleness, in his superior position. He will enjoy doing things for you, catering to you and waiting upon you because of the wonderful way it makes him feel. If you do it right he will jump at the chance to do things for you and will love you more because of it. As I have said, men have often "broken their necks" to cater to the whims of spoiled femininity, just because of the wonderful way it makes them feel.

In asking a man for things, avoid these mistaken approaches:
1. *Hinting:* Men are too preoccupied with their own problems to notice hints. To them, women appear to be merely "airing whims." They seldom remember hints from one day to the next. Men prefer a more direct approach.
2. *Convincing:* This is also unsuccessful, since it places the woman on an equal plane with the man. This lack of respect for the man's position puts him in the frame of mind to say "no" just to show his authority. He may be in favor of granting her request, but says no automatically. He seldom realizes that the reason he took such a stand was just to preserve his position as a man.

If the man happens to be really opposed to her request he can usually think up some clever arguments against it. It is difficult to outwit a man in any situation. Trying to convince him of anything only invites opposition and does nothing for the man's feeling of superiority or manliness.

3. *Demanding:* This is also a failure since it usurps authority, threatens the man's superior position and therefore is naturally offensive to him. He may give in, but not with good feeling. Her stubborn attitude is distasteful, unattractive, and robs him of any feeling of manliness.

The only successful method of asking a man for things is childlikeness, since it places a man in the proper position of leadership and encourages him to say "yes." This in turn leads to a better relationship, since he feels more tender towards a woman he can serve and since he is charmed by her little girlish requests which make him feel so much like a man.

In developing this art, be simple and direct and avoid such expressions as "let's do this," or "I think it would be nice if we were to do this," or other such suggestions.

Remember, there are a few things which you should *not ask for.* Do not ask for things which are selfish, or things which he cannot afford. Do not ask for love or tenderness. These responses must be awakened in the man by the woman herself. They are only of value when they are given voluntarily and lose their value when given under obligation. Also, never ask a man for a dance or a date unless it is "girl's choice," since this is much too aggressive for a feminine woman. Also, when it *is* "girl's choice," do not ask a man who has not previously asked you.

If a man says "no" to your request, do not be alarmed. Give him a pretty pout and then ask yourself if you were selfish or imposing or if in any other way you did not have the right to ask. If your request is fair, and you are feminine and girlish, the man will be sure to grant it if within his power to do so.

Practice this art of asking for things on your father and your brothers and you will see for yourself their immediate response to your childlike request. Use this method to get them to lift a heavy bundle, or move some furniture, or take you shopping, or help you with your homework or fix the vacuum cleaner.

Not only will they willingly oblige, but you will notice a growing warmth in your relationship, for they will love you more as they do things for you. Be sure to always thank them in a most appreciative and girlish manner. Use this method on all men in your life. They will delight in catering to your whims and caprices and will not be able to resist the charms of such girlish femininity.

CHILDLIKE MANNER

The childlike manner is the motions or actions of a woman which appear in her voice, facial expressions, or any other motions of the body. Dora had a charming childlike manner. Her delightful little voice and her dear little ways were not only feminine but childlike. At times she would shake her curls and point her finger at her little dog as little girls do. David describes her childlike manner in his following observation: "By and by she made tea for us, which was so pretty to see her do, as if she was busying herself with a set of doll's things, that I was not particular about the quality of the beverage."

If you will watch little girls as they "play house" you will observe many things about the childlike manner. They do not hurry through their chores "just to get them over with" as grown women do. They play house for the sheer joy of doing it. They sweep, cook, or tend the baby in a most unhurried and happy manner. A girlish woman will copy this same childlike manner in doing her housework. She will delight in hanging up curtains, making her child a new dress, cooking a favorite recipe, cleaning out cupboards or even polishing floors. By so doing she demonstrates the inborn domestic nature found in little girls and so sadly missing in the adult woman who rushes through her work just to get it over with and heaves a sigh of relief when it is finished.

In *The Cloister and the Hearth* you will remember that Margaret tied Gerard's ribbons in this same unhurried and girlish manner. Then the author comments, "It is not natural to her sex to hurry ought that pertains to the sacred toilet."

GIRLISH TRUST

Still another trait of childlikeness is an attitude of trust. Just as a little girl respects her father as her leader and trusts

his ability to take care of her, to provide for her, to solve problems and make wise decisions, a woman can show this same
trust in a man. This does not mean that she never expresses herself in these matters or that she never warns him of difficulty
or danger that she may perceive, but it does mean that she is
extremely careful not to doubt his ability or capabilities. When
it comes to a man's world, "let him figure it out" should be
the rule.

She should not, for example, tell him what to do. There
is nothing a man dislikes more than a woman who gives him
directions or instructions in things that he is supposed to know
more about than she does. I remember being in the company
of a man and his wife who were trying to show us the city
they lived in. With every turn he made, she was there at his
elbow telling him what to do and what not to do. Never make
the mistake of telling a man where to turn unless he asks. It
is better to let him make a million mistakes than to give him
the feeling that you doubt his ability. Especially is this irritating in something as simple as finding his way around in life.

Also, never doubt a man's ability to solve a problem. For
example, do not doubt his ability to fix a stalled car by suggest-
ing that he call a repair man. Or do not doubt his ability to
find his way out of a financial problem or other perplexing
situation; or do not doubt his ability to reach difficult goals,
such as achieving a high education or advancement in a job.
To doubt his ability is to show a lack of trust.

On the other hand, if a man is trying to reach some difficult goal or solve a diffcult problem, do not give him the
impression that you expect it will be *easy*. For example, if a
man intends to go through a difficult education, do not doubt
his ability to reach his goal, but on the other hand, do not
give an indication that you expect it will be easy and thereby
rob him of his potential heroism. What a man wants is for you
to *recognize the difficulties of his goals and his problems, but
have a girlish trust that he will one way or another be victorious
and that only a superior man such as he could do it.* In this
way you recognize opportunity for heroism and do not doubt
his ability to be a hero. This is girlish trust.

CHILDLIKE APPEARANCE

The last quality of childlikeness which I will teach is that of appearance, in your clothes and grooming and also in your manner. The main thing to avoid is a matronly look. Matronly styles are usually the wrong length (out-of-style length), are often blousy through the bodice, button to the waist, and have medium length sleeves — often with cuffs. Colors are drab and designs small and insignificant. Matronly hair styles are those which are old fashioned and out of date. Young girls always keep up with current hair styles. Doing so is an indication of femininity and girlishness. Whatever you do, do not take on a matronly look in either your appearance or your manner. Older women tend to wobble from side to side and slant forward when they walk. To appear youthful, walk erect and keep from swinging from side to side.

To learn girlishness in dress, visit a shop for little girls and study their clothes. You will observe full skirts, pleated skirts, jumpers, petticoats and pantaloons. Dresses are gay and dashing or soft and feminine. You will see vivid colors, strong contrasts, checks, plaids, stripes, but you will also see dainty, delicate fabrics trimmed in satin and lace. Dresses will be trimmed with ruffles, lace, ribbons, daisies, buttons, bows, little white collars, black velvet ribbons, etc. Hats will be dainty with flowers and ribbons, or they will be sailor's with ribbons hanging down the back. Another place to look for children's clothes is in the children's section of pattern books. You need not have a girlish look to all your clothes, but do include some in your wardrobe for variety.

Girlish hair styles are long and flowing, or braids, pony tails, bangs, face curls, etc. Ribbons and flowers add girlishness to hair styles as do barrettes and bands. Men love these touches. Shoes that are the most girlish are ballet or baby doll types. High heels are feminine, but they are not girlish. It is best to have both kinds.

CHILDISHNESS

Childlikeness should not be confused with "childishness," which is a negative quality. To be *childish* is to copy the *faults* of children, whereas to be *childlike* is to copy their *virtues*. Some unattractive traits in children are self-centeredness, a lack of responsibility for their own actions, and expecting too much of ordinary human beings. Those who retain these traits in adult life tend to fret when they do not get their way, blame others for their unfortunate circumstances, fail to acknowledge their own mistakes and failures, and make unreasonable demands of their associates.

When we were young we expected much from our parents and thought they could do most anything. To project this unrealistic thought into adult life is to expect too much from our associates and therefore is childish. Childishness in a grown woman is unattractive to men and can even be offensive.

There are a few women who resist the idea of acting childlike, who consider it an insult to their good sense to expect them to stomp their feet and shake their heads and to act the part of a little girl. They insist upon believing that really sensible men, the kind of man they want, would be repulsed instead of attracted to such a childlike creature. Even when these women agree that such a woman is the most attractive, they mistakenly assume that for themselves the acting of such a part is impossible.

Be assured that we all have this trait somewhere in our nature — it is a part of being feminine. Remember that it was not long ago that you were a little girl and all of these traits came naturally. You can recapture this manner, this charm of youth, and make it a part of you. You will be more fascinating to men and will make them feel bigger and manlier in your presence. This marvelous feeling is what makes childlikeness so fascinating to men. *Remember, if you are to be loved and treated like a woman, you must make him feel like a man.*

There is a tendency when a woman matures to lose this childlike trait, especially after she gets married. She somehow feels that she must "grow up," without realizing that men never want women to grow up completely. Truly fascinating women always remain somewhat little girls, regardless of their age. They never take on the unattractive traits of matronliness, nor do they become skeptical, stubborn, cynical and overbearing as some older women do who have lost their girlishness.

SUMMARY OF ANGELA HUMAN

You now have the completed picture of what a man finds ideal in woman, the eight different qualities that make up Angela Human. There may be other traits that men find charming, but they are less important than those covered here. These are the ones that arouse his feelings of admiration and love and cause him to be fascinated, amused and enchanted and awaken in him a desire to protect and shelter.

You do not have to be all of these things at the same time. In fact, changefulness is charming in a woman. One time you should be bright and joyful, another time gentle and feminine, and another time saucy. Sometimes you will need to be serious, especially in your sympathetic understanding; but at other times have the giddiness, vivacity and teasing playfulness of a child, and occasionally an air of bewitching languor, or the kittenish or cooing quality which I described in the feminine manner.

If a man is cross, stern or overly serious, respond with teasing playfulness. If he mistreats you and you have a feeling of being walked on or treated unfairly, respond with childlike sauciness. Any one of these approaches would be tiresome to a man if it were used continuously. He needs a change, and you become more interesting and fascinating if you are unpredictable. As the author Charles Reade comments, "Girls like to be coy and tender, saucy and gentle by turns."

In your efforts to be fascinating do not neglect the Angelic side, which is just as essential as the Human in winning a man's love. Your admirable character, your ability to be a domestic goddess and your deep understanding of him and his problems balance the human side of you and make you more ideal. And remember, there is no single action as important as "accepting a man at face value" and allowing him to be himself. Other traits you may neglect and he may still be attentive, but if you do not accept him he will not love you. You cannot turn aside from this essential ingredient to love. All else will fail without it.

In trying to attain the qualities of Angela Human, make a chart similar to the one in the book and keep it in a secret place. Then take one quality at a time, study it thoroughly and apply it for a week or so. During this time, notice men's reactions to your efforts. It will be interesting to note how differently a man reacts when you concentrate on a specific quality than he does when you apply another. This is because you arouse in him a particular sentiment. Some things will amuse him, some will fascinate him and others will arouse a feeling of worship. When you have covered the subject, refer to the chart occasionally to keep on the track.

Rewards you can expect immediately. Men will notice you and be more attentive and interested. The results will probably seem unbelievable. You will be enjoying "flowers" instead of "weeds" and will never want to return to your former self again. You may back-slide occasionally, but this should not discourage you. Always be renewed and make another effort. It takes about a year to form habits of lasting value. In working for the goal of Angela Human you may have the feeling of standing astride at times, unable to reach higher goals but discontent with un-happy days of the past. But if you will keep the goal clearly in mind and try to picture yourself as the ideal woman, you *will* advance to higher goals and will eventually become Angela Human, never again to "eat the crumbs."

MAKING YOU DISTINCTLY YOU

We have just covered in these eight chapters the essentials of feminine charm, the qualities that all women should strive for if they are to be attractive to men. However, we must take into consideration the fact that each person born on the earth has within himself the potential for a unique personality. Each one of us has characteristics which set us apart from every other person, making us a distinct and different individual. To reach our highest potential in charm, we build the basic struc-ture of Angela Human and then add to it the crowning glory of our own unique personality.

One thing which will greatly interfere with the unfolding of your own personality is to make the mistake of copying others. Young girls are especially guilty of this practice. Since they have not yet discovered themselves, they look around for someone they find attractive and use her as a model to pattern after. If they copy goodness and femininity this is fine, but if they try to copy individualism, it will be like wearing a dress that does not fit.

I have had any number of young men tell me that one thing they admire in girls is genuineness and sincerity, and they are repelled by girls who try to be like someone else. Instead of wasting your time trying to copy someone else's charm, try to discover the real self you were born to be and work to polish it up to its brightest. Truly creative people look to within for their source of ideas. They never have to use other people as patterns, for they have a store of ideas and traits of their own. Begin to build your own personality by ceasing to make the mistake of copying other girls. Deliberately avoid being like someone else. After awhile you will turn inward for ideas and will soon find an unlimited supply.

There are sometimes unfortunate barriers to the unfolding of a charming personality. They come in the form of inhibitions, inferiority complexes and the lack of social ease around men. It is almost impossible to show forth the charms of Angela Human and the crowning glory of your personality if these fears are present. The next chapter will be devoted to a study of these problems and suggestions for gaining confidence with men.

CHAPTER XVII

Confidence or Social Ease Around Men

One of the keys to a charming personality is an air of confidence. If you will observe girls who are fascinating, you will notice that they are self-assured around men. They are at ease around men, and therefore men are at ease around them. Confidence is essential to feminine charm, whereas shyness is a barrier. The only exception to this rule is when a man momentarily notices an attractive woman and she discovers his admiring glances. If she is feminine, she will respond with timorousness or pretty confusion.

To be an introvert is a great disadvantage to anyone and is, in fact, a weakness in character. We cannot give life our best if we are withdrawn and shy. To get along in this world we need to "get out of our shells," overcome our fears and inhibitions and let the light of our personality shine forth. To hide behind the excuse that we were "born shy" is a mistake. Face shyness as a fault and then work to overcome it. Some fortunate people never have this problem. Their personalities bubble forth, and inhibitions are unknown to them. But shy people can overcome their problem. Human beings were meant to be social, and this means being an "extrovert" to some extent.

In learning to acquire this asset of personality, remember this: No one is quite as confident as he appears to be. Most of us have certain fears around people, especially strangers, and have to put on a false front of confidence to a degree. But by acting confident we give others a feeling of ease, and by so doing our confidence will naturally grow. Acquiring the attributes of Angela Human will also build confidence. Goodness of character, the arts of femininity, health and all of the rest will result in confidence, *providing there are not the barriers of an inferiority complex or insecurity present.* These common problems will be dealt with in this chapter and suggestions given for their elimination so that nothing will stand in your way of attaining the charm of social ease.

AVOID SITUATIONS WHICH DESTROY CONFIDENCE

Good experiences with people build confidence, whereas bad experiences tend to destroy it. For example, if you are called upon to give a speech before a group, and you give a poor talk, your confidence will be weakened. The next time you are called upon, you will hesitate, remembering the past experience. If you again give a poor talk your confidence will be further undermined; and if you repeatedly fail, you may feel so ill at ease before a group that you must refuse to accept invitations. If this has been your experience, avoid giving talks until you have learned of your mistakes, found ways to improve your speaking techniques and prepared yourself for a successful experience rather than a failure.

This same rule is true in your relationships with men. If you have an experience in which you fail to be attractive, if you are shunned, ignored or treated with indifference, it is best to avoid these situations which undermine confidence until you have learned of your mistakes and developed a degree of feminine charm. Plan for success with men, not failure. Some situations to avoid are the following:

DON'T BE A WALLFLOWER

Social affairs, especially dances in which boys and girls are invited to attend "without dates," can present the painful problem to "wallflowers." Being left on the sidelines will do nothing for a girl but weaken her confidence around men. Don't allow yourself to be placed in this humiliating, degrading position. If you should find yourself in this unfortunate situation, leave the dance and go into the corridor and walk around for awhile, then return. Do not be seen either sitting or standing on the sidelines. If you are repeatedly "left out," avoid "stag dances" until you have learned of your mistakes and developed the art of feminine charm. It is doubtful that these social events are justified, because of the damage they do to the girls on the sidelines. Social events should be planned which breed confidence and success for all young people and not just a select few.

Parties and games can also result in a few being left out. You may attend a swimming party, and if you do not swim well or do not enter into the games and activities, you may be ignored. Perhaps you are not a lively person on these occasions. You may "sparkle" more at indoor parties where you are dressed in a soft frilly dress but feel ill at ease at events where people are playing, running, dunking and laughing. If you feel awkward at such parties, and as a result "left out," either drop such events for the time being or determine to enter into the activities. Whatever your experiences with men, work for success rather than failure, and avoid things which destroy confidence.

Build an Image

Another way to self confidence is to build an image of yourself as a confident person. Notice people who have this social ease and try to imagine yourself like them. It is not wise to copy another person's unique personality, as has already been explained, but it is right to adopt the manner and bearing of a self-assured person. In this imagined picture, think of as many details as you can. Imagine yourself in attendance at certain social functions, how you would be dressed, how you would conduct yourself, your manner and graciousness, and how other people react to your charm. It is a fact that if we hold a picture in our minds of what we would like to be, we tend to become that image.

You may find, however, that you have certain enemies to this practice. Your own family and close friends may have you "typed" as a shy, withdrawn girl. They may continually make remarks about your timid nature, which make it difficult to picture yourself in any other light. If it is a family member who makes this mistake you can make an appeal to him, asking him to refrain from negative remarks, telling him that you are trying to become a more outgoing person and would appreciate his confidence and consideration during this period of effort on your part. Encourage him to make positive statements, if any at all. As you mature, if you are constantly in an environment that will not let you grow, that refuses to cooperate with your efforts and continually undermines your objectives, it may be wise to move away for awhile to a new environment, if this is possible, so that you can build an image of confidence and make progress towards becoming that image.

BUILD CONFIDENCE BY A GOOD APPEARANCE

One of the best ways to build confidence is to always look your best. Never permit yourself to appear at a disadvantage — to be handicapped by a slouchy hairdo, dowdy clothing or run-down shoes and accessories. If you are guilty of this fault, study and work until such defects have been corrected. Get books on the subject, learn to sew if necessary and learn the art of make-up and hair styles until you have achieved an appearance that will impress people favorably and build confidence in yourself. One of the advantages of a charming appearance is not so much what it does to others as what it does to the girl herself, and the social grace and confidence she acquires along with it. When she "feels pretty" she also feels confident.

OVERCOMING AN INFERIORITY COMPLEX

A feeling of inferiority around friends and associates can undermine confidence and in turn detract from feminine charm. There can be any number of things that cause this feeling of inferiority. Less money, less education, or fewer nice clothes can make a girl feel unequal. Or she may not feel as pretty, or that she has the same adequate social background. Or she may feel that other people have talents or achievements that far outshine hers. These things cause a feeling of inadequacy around people who may appear to have these advantages.

You need not have any special advantage or talent to feel "equal" to everyone you meet. In the most cultured society we meet people with the most charming personalities who have no particular accomplishments except their own selves to offer. These people will applaud the accomplishments of the orator, the financier, the artist, the poet, and geniuses of every description, yet they do not themselves think, nor does anyone else think, that they are inferior to those whom they applaud. Their own self assurance has made them appear equal to every other person. We can do the same by acquiring an "air of confidence."
1. *Lack of talents and accomplishments:* If you feel inadequate around certain people because they may have developed

some talent which outshines you, it is important that you have a proper attitude towards yourself and also towards the other person. Just because he or she has chosen to concentrate dedicated efforts in a particular direction does not mean that this person is superior. You are essentially as good. You were born with the same eyes, ears and other parts. You are a child of God, with the potentials such a concept embraces. You may not have developed your abilities and talents to the same degree, but you are essentially as brilliant and talented. You could be just as much of a shining light if you chose to work for those goals.

When you are in the presence of someone whom you think is more talented, say to yourself, "Everything she has, I can have, if only I try hard enough; everything she can do, I can do if only I try long enough to accomplish it. Just because she has done things I have not is no reason for thinking she is a better person than I am. I have not chosen to put my efforts in that direction. I am sure that if I did choose to develop my talent as she has done, and if I tried hard enough and long enough, I would prove talented also." In other words, when you meet someone with superior accomplishments, you can admire that person for having put forth sufficient effort to acquire those accomplishments. But you need not consider yourself inferior simply because you have thus far not chosen to put forth that effort.

For example, don't imagine, if you happen to meet an author, that you are inferior to him because you have never been able to write anything. If you had worked as hard as he has, burned as much midnight oil, written and destroyed as many miserable attempts at writing as he, you would very likely be able to do as well or better than he. If you have not chosen to use your time in such pursuits, that is no reason for believing that the author is any better than yourself. The same is true with anyone whose talents and accomplishments shine out brightly before you. Recognize their efforts as worthy of appreciation, but do not underestimate your own worth.

2. *Lack of money and material wealth:* If you are a person who is lacking in material possessions, and if you associate with people who have far more, you may have a feeling of inferiority in their presence. Your biggest thought, perhaps, is that your friends will depreciate you because of your lack. Although this

may be true with inferior people, there are many fine people of means who do not have this attitude at all.

If your friends are thinking about you at all, they are probably wondering why you are so backward and shy and why you do not assert yourself more, or why you do not forget your self-consciousness and do as everyone else does. They are not thinking of your lack of money, but of your lack of self assurance. It probably does not occur to them that money has anything to do with your shyness and self-consciousness. If you did not think of your poverty and thus let it affect your manner and self-assurance, the fact that you are not fortunate financially would seldom cross their minds. But even if it should, they are attracted to the fine character and sparking personality that you are and admire you even more because you have achieved it without the support of money. If, therefore, you will put aside your poverty as a thing not worth thinking about, others will do the same or more — they will admire you for winning without money.

People who are accustomed to money know that it is no indication of superiority. To have inherited it is merely good luck; to have acquired it is, in many cases, good luck also, or greater opportunity. In some cases, however, money is earned by great and dedicated effort, just as in any other notable accomplishment. If this is so, then you can admire the person for that effort which was all focused in one direction, but not for the wealth itself.

In comparing yourself with people of means, do not consider merely the possession of wealth as admirable, but the way in which it is used. That is the only way to measure values. If you meet someone who uses money in a noble, honorable, generous or artistic way, then give that person the special honor due him. But if you meet others who spend their money on comforts and pleasures, they are not deserving of praise just because they possess money. It is how the money is used that commands our respect.

3. *Lack of fine clothes:* Sometimes it is not merely the absence of wealth which causes self-consciousness, but the absence of fine clothes such as our more wealthy associates wear. In some circles cliques are formed in which it appears that fine clothes are the factors governing admission. In reality, however, what

excludes many a girl is not the inferiority of her clothing, but the air of being so acutely and painfully aware of her lack that, regardless of her clothes, she is not good company. She is so uncomfortable because of her imaginary disadvantage that she casts a damper on the spirits of her companions. She is not excluded because of her clothing, but because she seems odd, queer, or unpleasant. When girls and boys have a good time, they want a lively, interesting group; they don't want anyone who thinks only of herself and the lack of expensive apparel. If this has been your problem, forget your clothes and talk to these people as if your clothes were as good as theirs. If these people seem stiff at first, attribute it to your former actions, your withdrawn personality, rather than your clothes. They will be friendly as you let your personality and confidence shine forth.

Just because your clothes are not expensive does not mean, however, that you cannot be attractive — and just as attractive as those persons who wear costly clothing. A well qualified charm teacher explained to me that women of money are not always properly dressed, whereas other women of less means who will study and learn the art of dressing attractively, choosing clothing most becoming to them, can outshine women with money, and often do. If you cannot afford attractive clothes, you can learn to sew with skill and learn the art of copying expensive designs. In this way you can compete with any woman — even on a limited budget.

4. *Lack of education:* Most young women of today have ample opportunity for education. Take advantage of these schools of learning, both for the knowledge they bring to life and for the feeling of confidence an education brings. If you do feel inferior to your associates because you do not appear as well educated as they, then work a little harder and take advantage of the educational institutions available. Remember, however, as you go through life, that it is the *application* of knowledge that counts. Learning a few facts is of no particular value in building confidence. The application of these facts is. Remember also that education in itself will not make you fascinating to men, but the confidence that an education builds will.

5. *Lack of social prestige:* When you meet with people whom you consider highly polished, being yourself, perhaps, rather

awkward and sheepish in such company, don't let yourself believe that these polished social lights are any better than you are. If you had spent as much time in social pursuits, you may have been a far brighter social light than they. Never let yourself imagine that you are not as good as anyone else with whom you come in contact; never let yourself be deferential, or be made to feel inferior.

It is important for a girl to feel equal to her associates if she is to have the social ease necessary for real charm. It is difficult, if not impossible, for a girl to radiate charm or to be fascinating to a man she feels inferior to. Her own unique and charming personality will be smothered by her withdrawn and underconfident manner and attitude. She need not feel inferior, however, to a particular man, or to anyone. These complexes can be eliminated.

We have learned thus far that the way to social ease is to acquire an "air of confidence," to avoid situations which destroy confidence and to remove the barriers, such as inferiority complexes. Still another way to confidence is by developing the art of conversation. Those tense moments when we can't think of anything to say can make us feel ill at ease around people. Developing this art will promote confidence, making not only yourself, but everyone else feel at ease. This is not a difficult art to acquire. The following are some suggestions.

How to be a Good Conversationalist

Have you ever found yourself ill at ease in a group because you have never learned the art of conversation? The talk turns to music, art, travel or baseball, fishing or social activities, and you can't think of a single thing to say. You feel as if you were tongue-tied. The best way to overcome this feeling is to listen carefully to the conversation of the other girls. Take every remark of these girls and see if it is as wonderful as you have imagined. You will find that hardly any of their utterances were especially impressive, that you yourself could have said as much or more.

You will find, too, that few of them know more about the subject of conversation than you do, but that they talk, whether they know anything or not. If the conversation turns to a subject which is unfamiliar to them, they make an irrelevant remark and turn the discourse into another channel. The idea that you can't talk as well as other girls is simply an imaginary fear. You can get rid of this fear by making yourself a good conversationalist. It isn't hard. It is not necessary to be a conversational star; but if you think you must be one in order to be accepted socially, then this can be attained with a little effort. The following are a few suggestions for developing this ability:

BEING A CONVERSATIONAL STAR

1. *Background information:* The first thing to do is to gather a store of information that will be good conversation material. First — *read widely*. Read the daily newspaper — not just the comics, but the first page, the editorial page and the women's section. Scan through the rest if you have time. This will not take long. Also read a weekly news magazine to keep you up with world affairs, things of both national and international interest. They will cover things not in the daily newspapers. Read one provocative book a month, of a high moral level. Locate these from newspaper or library reviews. Also spend about fifteen minutes a day reading the Scriptures. Therein lie some of the most basic truths of life, truths which will make interesting conversation. There is nothing more elevating than discussing principles of divine truth which influence our daily lives and happiness. The conversation need not be kept deadly serious — it can lead to some lively discussions.

However, although it is important to read widely, ordinary conversation never requires a profound knowledge of any subject. You can pick up a music magazine, read a few personal items about music and musicians and converse interestingly even though your knowledge of music is exceedingly limited. You might speak even more interestingly than one who has devoted a lifetime to the study. Similarly, after reading a little on the subject of art, you can speak with ease on that subject — the same with literature, sports, or any other matter. To be a conversationalist requires no great amount of education, but only superficial knowledge of subjects of general interest. In addition to reading, you will need to *observe* situations and experiences in daily life. Keep your eyes and ears open and you will see a human drama in action. Be alert and interested in life and you will accumulate many stories to tell which are amusing, interesting and even amazing. Also keep your eyes open for things you hear other people *tell* — incidents, jokes and interesting topics that you can repeat to others.

One source of material will come right out of your own mind. If you will take time to think, you will get *ideas* or flashes of inspiration that perhaps no one has thought of before. Don't cast these ideas aside just because they are your own. Every noble thought comes first out of the human mind. Carry a note pad around with you to jot down any ideas or experiences that you collect.

2. *Review information:* The next thing to do is to review the experiences and observations you have in mind. A good conversationalist, the minute he hears something new, goes back over it, analyzes it, chuckles to himself over it a second time, and firmly fixes it in his mind as a precious addition to his stock of knowledge. No wonder, then, that he seems to have such an unlimited store. You cannot expect to shine as a conversationalist until you do as he does.

3. *Practice:* The minute you read or discover something of interest and have it well in mind, pass it along to this one and that one and still another. With every retelling of the same thing you will improve conversationally. All good story tellers either consciously or unconsciously do the same thing. Their memories would be as bad as yours if they merely laughed upon hearing a new story and then proceeded to throw all thought of it out of their minds. After you have read something of interest, don't turn immediately to something else. Go back over it with the intention of picking out the items which you intend telling to the first person you meet and fix them in mind. Then tell the experience to one person after another in a different way each time in order to learn which way seems the most effective.

You need not practice on your friends socially to begin with. You can talk to members of your family, adults and even little children. Old people are always willing and anxious to talk with the young and have time on their hands to do so. They are lonely and will enjoy a visit with you. They are good subjects for practice. It will not be long until you will be adept enough to converse with ease with all of your friends.

4. *Let the other person talk:* Only part of your store of information need be used in ordinary conversation. Encourage the other person to talk about himself, since this is half of the art of good conversation. Begin by making some comment or suggestion which will lead him to talk. Ask leading questions, but do not ask pointed questions, or ones that can be answered with yes or no. If the conversation lags, then you can begin drawing from your own store of ideas. Try to talk only a minute or so about yourself and give the other person a chance to make comments.

5. *Dating:* On dates be sure to carry your share of the conversation and do not expect your partner to do it all, unless he seems to want to. Double and triple dates make conversation easier, since everyone present can make a contribution and seem more at ease and usually more talkative. You can also learn the art of conversation on these double dates, by listening to your friends. Then a good idea is to arrange dates that will lead to conversation, such as symphonies, lectures, plays, movies, church activities, casual parties, etc. Most of these activities will give you food for thought and topics for conversation. Conversations at a dance are difficult unless you trade dances. After you become a conversation star, however, they will seem easier.

THINGS TO AVOID IN CONVERSATION

Don't gossip, use sarcasm, embarrass anyone, hurt or belittle anyone.

Don't brag, talk about yourself too much, or over-use the word "I."

When someone is talking don't swing the conversation to focus on you.

Don't interrupt or pry into people's private affairs.

Don't say, "I know a better one than that" and thus deflate the other person's story.

Don't swear, use profanity, slang, coarse language, or vulgar stories.

ICE BREAKERS

One of the most awkward feelings a girl can have is to be sitting or standing next to a man she has met, or is acquainted with, and not be able to think of anything to say to open a conversation. Sometimes it is while waiting for a bus, in an elevator, sitting in a classroom, or standing next to him at a party, that she finds herself in this situation. It is difficult to appear feminine and girlish if you feel awkward and quiet. It will be worth your while to spend some time thinking about these occasions and planning ahead for them. Think of some things to say to "break the ice." You may not use them in every case, but it is nice to have some on hand. Then, when you speak, do so with an air of confidence as has been explained. The most important point to remember is to say something as soon as you can. It does not matter so much what it is as that it sounds spontaneous. If silence develops, then the situation grows a little stale and your words will sound stiff. The first thing that flashes in your mind — say it. You do not have to say anything dramatic or impressive. The feeling of friendliness is all that you need convey.

You can also plan some *conversation pieces* for these situations. Wear an unusual pin, bracelet, scarf, vest, sweater, etc., which will arouse interest. This makes it easy for the young man to open the conversation by making a comment about it and giving you a chance to explain its purpose.

LOSE SELF-CENTEREDNESS

Another way to social ease is to lose your self-centeredness. Rid yourself of any tendency to think about yourself, how you look, what others are thinking of you, whether they like you or not, if they think you are pretty, etc. An over-concern about your own defects will cause you to feel ill at ease around people.

Although a good appearance is important in making a proper impression, men will certainly not notice a few flaws. They will be more interested in your radiant manner and your interest in them. Always dress carefully and groom yourself; but once you arrive in public, it is useless to continue to think of your appearance. Overcome this defect by striving to become genuinely interested in others, and train yourself to forget about yourself. In learning the way to social ease, we have covered the following essential points in this chapter:

1. Take on an "air of confidence."
2. Don't do things which destroy confidence.
3. Have a good appearance.
4. Overcome the barriers to confidence (inferiority complexes).
5. Become a good conversationalist.
6. Lose your self-centeredness.

PART II

Strategy With Men

Introduction

Do not let the word *strategy* alarm you. It is a perfectly legitimate word for our subject. Why shouldn't a girl use strategy with men? After all, her charms, her feminine wiles and ways are the only means she has of winning the attention of men, from whom she will choose her lifetime partner. The man is the aggressor, not the woman. She must wait patiently for the man to notice her and become interested in her. Isn't it right, then, that she know everything that she can about men and use every strategy possible to win their attention and interest?

Part One has been devoted to helping you become "a girl worth having," the kind of girl a man wants. You must have something to offer if you are to win the attention of worthy men. We have also covered the little feminine wiles and ways that enhance "this girl worth having" so that she becomes an enchanting and fascinating creature. If you have taken these chapters to heart and have applied them, you have no doubt gone far towards making yourself a more womanly woman, a bundle of feminine charm, girlish and tender in manner and general impression. Altogether you ought soon to be, if this progress is maintained, a girl any man might be attracted to, a girl well worth his attention and interest, and one who would make a desirable mate.

However, you do not want to win just any man, but one particular man. One day when you least expect it, you may chance to meet this special man, the one who will have everything you have ever wanted in a man. But you may find the perplexing problem of being faced with competition. He may have numerous other girl friends in whom he is equally interested, or perhaps one special girl friend. Or he may be lost in the pursuit of a career, so that although you are a fascinating girl, and meet every specification he may have in mind for a wife, he may not take you seriously. With such difficulties staring you in the face, you will need to have a thorough knowledge of men and how they may be won. You will need to have every device, tactic and strategy at your command to win this one rare gem of manhood.

You are now ready to begin the study of winning men, first in being directed to the right kind of man and second in knowing how to awaken his interest and desire and third in removing the obstacles that may stand in the way of marriage. This is the division of study upon which we will now concentrate.

CHAPTER XVIII

Where and How to Meet Men

WHERE MEN ARE MOST AVAILABLE

In our modern times the most available places to meet men are on our college campuses, which are filled to capacity with American manhood. Some colleges are predominantly male, others more nearly equal, and a few predominantly female. Obviously the better choice would be those where men predominate. Next to college campuses, the armed services provide the largest numbers of men. Their bases are scattered across the country. Here, however, you would have to be particular and selective. The army inducts men of all types and levels. But, although some would not be of your calibre, others are the very cream of America. One can take care to associate only with a worthy man. Industries also hire large numbers of young men, and these are also scattered across the country. Those industries that hire large numbers of men and only a few women would be a better choice.

One of the finest places to meet men is in church. Churches provide a friendly atmosphere, and almost always a newcomer is introduced, seldom overlooked. Churches are also interested in the welfare of young people and usually provide social activities where men and women can meet properly. To meet your men friends, and eventually your mate, from among people who have the same religious views is the most ideal selection for future happiness and harmony in the home. Perhaps you think that men don't go to church, at least the young men; but that does not mean that their mothers and their sisters and girl friends and their cousins don't. Become so well acquainted with them that you will be invited to their homes and their social events. Thus you may gain the acquaintanceship of the masculine side of the family. Churches in some cities, however, especially small cities and towns, are depleted of available men in our modern times. Many of them have gone to the larger cities to attend college or find employment or have joined the armed services.

If you are an eligible young woman and are in an environment with a limited opportunity to meet men, it may be wise to consider a change. This is not to say that you will necessarily meet your future mate from among large numbers. You may possibly meet him while traveling on the airplane, or at some small party. But your chances are less likely in a limited field. If you should meet a thousand men perhaps only five or six would appeal to you. If you should meet only fifty the probabilities are that you will miss the one who would be your particular type. It is therefore important that you widen your opportunities to meet men. Remember, meeting men and eventually your lifetime partner is the most important step, even the most important responsibility you have. Use every means, make every plan necessary to provide yourself with the widest and finest opportunity to meet men.

Your Limitations

Even when men are available in large numbers or small, and even though the girl associates with them day by day, she must find ways and means of meeting them socially and getting acquainted. Here a girl has some limitations. The man is the natural aggressor, even in modern times. She may sit next to a young man in the classroom, or work in the same office, but, if she is a truly feminine girl, she waits to be introduced or at least waits for him to open the conversation. If he does not, she is then limited, lest she take a forward step which may give him a negative impression of her. She does not want to run the risk of appearing as a forward girl.

The Best Opportunities to Meet Men

Your friends and associates provide the best opportunities to meet men. It is through them that you are invited to parties, socials, outings, or are introduced individually to many young men. Did it ever occur to you what a wide opportunity you have to meet many men through building a large circle of friends and associates? The young man you may someday marry will most likely be met through one of these friends, and perhaps through one you may least expect would do you such a favor.

Since your friends and acquaintances are to be of such importance in your strategy with men, manifestly the first thing to do is to increase the number of them. Don't be too particular in making casual friendships. Though some may not be the kind you would choose for close companions, you can at least be on easy speaking terms with them and promote a casual friendship.

GIRL FRIENDS

Girl friends will be your greatest allies. Increase your number of intimate girl friends to include as many as you possibly have time for. They will invite you to their parties and introduce you to men they know, and even to other girls. Do not stop with just your circle of intimate girl friends. Acquire also a wide number of acquaintances. You can be friendly to the girl you sit next to in class, or pass each day on the way to lunch, or see in the grocery store. The more of these you have the better.

Although you will have, as your primary incentive in making friends, the objectives of meeting men, this does not mean that your friendships will be insincere. Once you have made a friendship or acquaintance, make it a genuine one, and be a true and loyal friend. Also, strive to have two kinds of girl friends — those whom *you* need to enrich your life, and those who need *you*. Other girls need friends too, and you can be a real friend to them also and help them to increase their number of male acquaintances.

Your greatest assistance in meeting men will come from circles of attractive girls who are especially skilled in attracting men. Endeavor to introduce yourself into such a circle instead of remaining in a circle of unattractive girls. A whole circle of attractive girls is much more inviting to men than a single attractive girl in an unattractive circle. Go out of your way, then, to make friends with these attractive girls, invite them to your home and endeavor to win their friendship. Ordinarily men will flock to such a group of winning girls. They will not seek excuses to stay away from their social affairs and will even pay attention to an unattractive member of such a circle in order to gain entrance or acceptance into the group. You will find such a group of girls much more active socially, more given to parties and outings, etc., so that altogether by moving in such a set you will meet many times the number of men you would otherwise meet and will meet them more frequently.

It may sound a little heartless to use such strategy in moving into such socially acceptable circles. We feel a natural concern and sympathy for the girls who are "outside" this circle. But remember this. Every girl can be lovely and charming. It is neither physical beauty nor money nor expensive clothing that creates the illusion of fascinating charm that will win men's hearts. Every girl can acquire it. If you have such a sympathy for those girls who are not noticed by men, you need not help them by being in their circle as close friends, but rather by helping them to understand the "art of attracting men."

Don't choose unattractive girls for your close girl friends that you are often seen with. Boys will "type" you along with them, will naturally associate you with their unattractive ways. This also sounds cruel, for there are many deserving girls whom you will have to avoid because they are not attractive to men. But here again, they could be lovely and enchanting. Your duty is to teach them how to be attractive. But do not burden yourself and ruin your chances with men by being seen everywhere with these girls. You do not owe it to them to be close friends any more than you owe it to an unattractive man to be his wife just because you have a sympathy for him. In using strategy with men, be everything that a woman should be, and then choose friends and associates who will not detract from that picture but rather add to it.

Male Friends

Widen your circle of male friends just as you do your circle of girl friends, but when it comes to dating, "choose only men whom you consider 'worthy' and who would make proper mates if you should develop an interest." Remember, you will marry someone whom you date. Take care and wisdom to date only "good material."

It is not necessary, however, to date only men whom you find attractive. A man whom you think you could never possibly become interested in could nevertheless make a good escort and take you to important social occasions. Simply going out with him does not obligate you to accept him as a suitor. If the man takes pleasure in your company, that pleasure is its own reward, provided you don't lead him on with false hopes. Your friendship can be a social convenience to both of you, providing an opportunity for both to meet a wider circle of acquaintances. It is better to date a man you know you could never be interested in than to sit at home alone.

It is important, however, that you do not date men who are "odd" or who in any way have a social stigma attached to them. This, as with girl friends, will cause people to type you along with them and may injure your social reputation. This again may seem somewhat cruel, but dating is an intimate association and we do not "owe it to people for their sakes" to accept dates. They can be turned down gently and kindly. Simply say, "I'm sorry, I am going to be busy tonight." If he should lack the manners to accept such a brief refusal and asks "why," you do not owe him any special courtesy. Just repeat the original statement by saying "I have some things to do." If you do turn down a date with a young man, do not make the mistake of accepting another date for the same evening. This is not kind or socially acceptable and is also dishonest. When you refuse a date, if you do not already have one with someone else, then you have no choice but to stay home and "arrange to be busy."

OLDER FRIENDS AND CHILDREN

Do not limit your friendships to people of your own age. You can be casual friends with anyone of any age. To become friends with the older people is to enrich your life with their special experiences and contacts. Older people have many friends and contacts. Children, also, can lead you to a wide circle of boys and girls your own age.

Take the little girl next door, for instance. You may never have thought of paying any attention to her, but she may have an eligible young uncle or cousin, or her playmate may have a big brother, or either of them may have a young family physician with whom you may become acquainted some day. Similarly, with every man, woman and child you know — all of them may have relatives or friends unknown to you now, whom you may someday be desirous of meeting. The narrower your circle of friends, the fewer men you are likely to meet and the less likelihood of your meeting the right one. The broader your acquaintances, the more men you are likely to meet and the more likelihood of your meeting the one destined for you.

Nor should you neglect a friendship merely because you see no present prospect of their helping you meet others. At any time this acquaintance may have a visitor or acquire a new connection that will enable him or her to introduce you to someone who could be important in your life. It does not cost you anything to make a great number of acquaintances, and to keep on friendly terms with them does not necessarily mean that they become close friends.

Take Advantage of all Social Events Where Men Are

You do not need to depend alone upon social events to which you are invited. Of course accept every invitation to attend these parties and events that is extended to you. But you can also attend certain things which are "open to the public." In other words, if you are in college, go to the library at night — someone is sure to see you and introduce you around. Or attend the lecture series that the college offers, or the musical events and plays. You can attend these with girl friends, and men are sure to be present. You will, of course, have to study when in college. It is never intimated here that you neglect your education. But you will not get anywhere if you become a "book worm" or a scholarly student and then neglect the most important responsibility in your life — that of finding a proper mate. There is ample time in the college schedule for a girl to do both, and "social life" is sometimes used as an unjustifiable excuse for a girl who would have neglected her studies anyway. A girl can be a diligent student and also include an active social life in her schedule if she wants to and plans for it. *Do* attend every open affair you can, especially socials, for at such places introductions are at wholesale rather than retail. You can meet more men in one evening at a social or party than you would otherwise in a month.

BEING A GOOD HOSTESS

We have spoken at length and learned the value of attending all social occasions possible to increase the opportunity to meet men. You may further add to your chances by becoming a good hostess and planning some parties of your own. There is perhaps nothing that will more quickly make you popular with men and women alike than being a good hostess. If people enjoy themselves at your home and at your affairs, they will naturally avail themselves of your hospitality at every opportunity. This is particularly true with men. Sometimes girls will go to an affair which is distasteful to them merely because they are afraid of offending the hostess by not coming. Not so with men; if they don't expect to have a good time, a team of horses, as a rule, cannot drag them to such an affair.

Now, making people enjoy themselves requires a great deal of tact, work, study and judgment on the part of the hostess. She must be very careful, for example, not to invite anyone who is likely to be a "wet blanket" to the good spirits of the crowd. Invite only those who will help make everyone present enjoy themselves. There was, for example, a hostess who invited a certain girl to an outing whom she thought would be an asset to the party. Sandra was rich, well dressed, pretty and well-born. The hostess thought that her other guests would be just as much flattered at having Sandra along as she was herself. Quite the reverse. Sandra assumed so many airs, was so conscious of her superior position, that the straightforward young men of the party who were making their own way in the world against the handicaps of poverty and humble parentage felt rebuffed, while the more fortunate young men whom she considered worthy of her notice saw too plainly that she was interested in them only because of their wealth and position. Sandra, therefore, succeeded in making everyone either disgusted or miserable. The hostess made a serious mistake in having her. The way to make any occasion a huge success is to have only people who are both liked and likable.

You should never undertake to be a hostess without first studying, working and making preparations to keep everyone in fun and amusement throughout. This is by no means easy. Books, magazines, everything available with suggestions for increasing the enjoyableness of the occasion should be devoured and utilized. Some books and articles about entertaining, however, emphasize the less important things. They devote too much attention to suitable decorations, involving endless amounts of trouble, apparently with the assumption that people will be amused merely by looking at the decorations. This may be true in an old folks' party where everyone wants to sit quietly after the handshaking is done, but it will by no means do for a crowd of healthy and sane young people. They want action, games, something to do — something to keep them busy and interested. Give them these and they will be indifferent as to whether your decorations are superior or not.

You will find a few choice people who will help to give such an air to any event. As a hostess, it is your business to see that these people are present when you entertain because they lift a great load from your shoulders. As a girl and a hostess, you will find it well worth your while to devote your time and attention to acquiring the sincere and devoted friendship of such people. Seize every opportunity you can to win their friendship and include them in your parties. Study these people, and try to become as lively and friendly yourself. Be one whom others will want to invite to their parties to insure success. As a successful hostess and as an aid to other hostesses, you will find many opportunities to meet and attract the attention of men.

And last, but not least, remember the food. It is important to the men especially. Don't serve them bottled or ready prepared food. Show your domestic skills by preparing something special and home made. Cook food that has a delicious aroma during the party, that will whet their appetites.

Giving parties is perhaps the only aggressive way a girl can win the attentions of men in all propriety. By being a good hostess, she avoids all appearance of seeking men out and at the same time provides opportunities to meet them. Entertaining is socially acceptable for a young girl, and we should therefore take advantage of this method of meeting men and also other girls.

DON'T STAY AT HOME

In reviewing our subject of how and where to meet men, we have stated that we first place ourselves, if possible, in an environment where many men are present — to give ourselves the greatest opportunity of numbers. Then we arrange to meet men through friends and increase our chances by increasing our circle of friends. We also attend every social event possible and every event where men are present. And lastly, we create social events of our own by giving parties and outings, etc. One last point is this. Don't stay home unless it is absolutely necessary. Every chance you have to go out must be taken advantage of. And if you do not have the opportunity to go places, then you can create such opportunities of your own.

For example, attend church on Sunday morning. In the afternoon ask a girl friend to go for a walk with you, then find some excuse to call on another girl. You are likely to meet some new acquaintances during the day and old ones too. If you stay at home you are likely to meet nobody. On other days, as well as holidays, stay at home only long enough to eat, sleep and study. In spite of your personal inclinations, you must make yourself an outgoing "gadabout." Attend programs, fairs, exhibitions, games, sports of all kinds, parades, picnics, conventions, etc. Who knows just when and where you are going to meet the man who is to be your own? The "stay at home" girl may make good use of her time, but how impossible it is for the right man to find her.

And remember that your main method of getting acquainted with men is through other women. A dancing class, a gym class, a night school, a class of any kind of girls, gives you an opportunity to become acquainted with other girls, and through them, their brothers and cousins and friends. The girl who has no acquaintanceship among the men has only herself to blame. She simply hasn't sense enough to become acquainted with and make use of the men's sisters.

CHAPTER XIX

Choosing A Mate

The most important decision you will make in life is to choose your partner in marriage, the man who will be the father of your children and your companion for a lifetime. Choose, therefore, with care, and seek to be guided by the greatest wisdom.

There is a passage from the Bible, found in the Epistle of James, which teaches us the greatest source of wisdom. It reads: "If any of you lack wisdom, let him ask of God, that giveth to all men liberally, and upbraideth not; and it shall be given him. But let him ask in faith, nothing wavering." The most important guide you can ever have to assist you in the selection of your lifetime partner is found in prayer. Ask for guidance each and every day of your life. Pray for a mate who will be suitable, one with whom you can be joyously happy, and prepare yourself to be just as fine a companion for him. You are a child of God and are entitled to this special wisdom and guidance if you live worthy to receive it.

If you are an unworthy, selfish girl, with a disregard for things of worth, with little interest in religion, you are nevertheless one of God's children. He is interested in you and in your welfare and happiness. You can bring yourself "in tune," can acquire a more holy character worthy of having the blessings of inspiration for this important step in your life.

In addition to prayer, God will expect you to do your part. He will expect you to gain wisdom and good sound judgment, and to develop a sense of values to assist you in finding a suitable mate. The following suggestions are given for this purpose:

Set Your Goals High

Since marriage is a most important step, set your goals *high*. Your husband will be your day-in, day-out companion and the father of your children. He will set the scene which will be yours for the rest of your life, will make the major decisions and determine the policies that the family will follow. Choose wisely, and aim for a man of great and true worth. This implies, of course, that you are a girl of equal worth, or are working to become one. It would hardly be fair to expect to find a "special man" if you do not also have something special to offer as a wife.

The trouble with many girls is that they do not know what "true worth" means in a man, or which different qualities join together to make up an admirable character and personality. And, if a girl does chance to know, if she already has in mind an image of the "ideal man" for her, she may not know how to go about discovering his worthiness. Most of her friends she knows only superficially. She has always considered it improper to be inquisitive or to pry into a man's personal code. How, then, can she go about finding out if a man meets up to her specifications? Some guidelines are given in this chapter, but first, it is very important that you rid yourself of any false ideas which might lead you astray.

Try not to have preconceived ideas about a man's appearance, or outer shell, such as his color of eyes, hair, his build, how tall, etc. Although we all admire handsome men, to place this attribute as a requirement might blind us to true values. In my lifetime I have known a few girls who made this mistake. One was set on marrying a man with brown eyes. It was a very strange thing how blind this girl was due to one quirk in her thinking. She passed up at least three blue-eyed men who wanted to marry her and who would have made excellent husbands, and finally married a man with brown eyes. He turned out to be a disappointment to her and everyone else. There are certainly excellent men with every color of eyes, but to have this notion in your head when it comes to mate selection is a serious mistake.

A similar case was a girl who wanted to marry the most handsome man she could find. She told her girl friends, "When I walk down the street I want everyone to say, 'What a lucky girl!'" True to her vow, she did marry an especially handsome man, as everyone had to admit, but it was not long until he began stepping out on her and she was running home to mother. Handsome men can, of course, be as worthy as any others, but to place this feature on the list of requirements is to distort your perspective. Although beauty is a marvelous thing, we must discredit it in human relations, since it has little to do with love or happiness.

An opposite case is a girl who, instead of having a weak sense of values had about the finest standards in her estimation of manhood as can be imagined. The girl was young, beautiful and talented, but she married a man who was a cripple in a wheelchair. When she announced her plans for marriage, her parents were grieved and her friends astonished. In consoling them she explained, "This man has every quality I have ever wanted in a man. I will not let his physical handicap blind me to his true worth." Here was a girl of fine character and values. Although this case is extreme and unusual, there are some lessons to be learned from it.

Some girls make the mistake of limiting their choice to a man who is "popular" or much sought after by all the girls. These shining socialites may, or may not, make good husbands. And although we must acknowledge that a man who has a "way with women" is appreciated by us all, we must discredit his popularity as being any real advantage in being a worthy mate.

Another mistake is to give too much credit to social etiquette and propriety. Certainly these are admirable traits, but they should not be a determining factor in selecting a companion. A woman of my acquaintance confided to me that many years before she had "dropped" a young man because he did not use his butter knife during dinner. As it turned out, he was a "gem" of a man and outstanding in his field.

No, neither the handsome man, the popular socialite, nor the man of propriety are necessarily desirable as mates unless they also possess the qualities of true worth. And I might add, neither is the football hero, the "life of the party" or the man who takes the medals, the trophies or the awards. These men may or may not make excellent husbands. In any event, these outer signs are not those that count; they are not the real values. You will have to *search* for the "diamonds" in manhood. They may not be the glowing young men of the moment, but they will be the men of the future.

The men of great worth may not be easy to find or to recognize. There is an old song which expresses this viewpoint impressively:

My Ideal

(The word *girl* has been changed to "boy.")
Will I ever find the boy in my mind,
The one who is my ideal?
Will I ever see the one who might be
Just around the corner waiting for me?
Will I recognize the light in his eyes
That no other eyes reveal,
Or will I pass him by and never even know
That he is my ideal?

What to Look For

Look for traits of character in men. Look for dependability, honesty, loyalty, idealism, fairness and courage. Look for intelligence and also resourcefulness (the ability to solve problems). Then look for tenderness, thoughtfulness and kindness. An ideal man is partly steel and partly velvet. He has the strong unbendable traits of steadfastness and unyielding determination, but also the velvet traits of gentle tenderness. This makes a real man.

In addition to the traits of character, *look for his masculine traits.* Remember the role of man, that he was born to be the guide, protector and provider for his family. A worthy mate will have strong leadership ability and be planning to provide for his family adequately. He will be protective of you in times of danger or cold and will offer his masculine assistance when you are in need. For example, he will lift heavy objects for you and help you over the creekbed, etc. This, of course, is providing you are living the rules of femininity. And in speaking of masculinity, although a strong body build is admirable, and all women can't help but appreciate it, it would be a mistake to put too much emphasis upon this trait that the man happened to be born with. The masculine characteristics of aggressiveness and determination count for so much more.

You will have to get to know him if you are to discover his masculine and character traits. Spend many hours with him. Lead him into conversations which will reveal his attitudes about life's responsibilities, about family life and about his future. Find out how he feels about religion, children and money. What are his attitudes about material things? Does he tend to concentrate on material comforts and pleasures, or does he value the things of real worth? Although we should not have aims that are unrealistic and cannot expect to find a man without a flaw, we do need to be guided by true values and appreciate them when they are recognized.

Some Men to Avoid

There are definitely some men to avoid. One is a man of weak character. If you are considering a man who is inclined to be dishonest, lazy or weak, who has no moral convictions or stamina, then you are treading on dangerous ground. Also avoid men who have serious bad habits like drinking, or promiscuity with women. These, most any intelligent girl would naturally avoid, but it must be stressed, since now and then a charming and worthy girl will fall for an inferior man and end up with a tragic life. It is surprising to see women whom we would expect to choose wisely use the poorest of judgment in selecting a mate. The fact that these men can and sometimes do overcome their bad habits is not worth the risk for the girl involved. Once in awhile there will be a young man who comes from a home where loose moral standards are accepted or even taught. Such a man should be avoided entirely. It is difficult enough for a man with high moral standards to keep his virtue, but next to impossible for a man who has never been taught.

Another thing to watch for is a man with an oversized ego. This is the man who must have the conversation always focused on himself, his accomplishments, skills and abilities, etc. A tendency to this may be normal in a man, but an excess may be a sign of insecurities which may spell trouble later. This does not mean that you should not consider him as a possibility, since a woman can often successfully help a man to overcome this tendency by her understanding and confidence. Sometimes a man may be suffering from a lack of appreciation during his youth and you may be the one who can solve his problems for him. You should, however, be aware of this problem and consider it one of the disadvantages.

SOME FACTS TO FACE

As we learned in an earlier chapter, when you marry you must be willing to accept a man at face value. You cannot hope to remake him into some preconceived image you may have in mind. You will have to accept him, his faults, his weaknesses, his religion or lack of it, his ideas and standards as they are. You will be in for serious trouble if you enter marriage with the thought of changing a man to meet your specifications. Not only will your efforts be fruitless, but they may prove to be a wedge in your home life that can be disheartening. So face the fact that you must accept him as he is.

Along with this, you cannot expect to extract promises from him that he will change after marriage. This is unfair and takes away his precious freedom. Each person must retain his choice between good and evil and no other individual has a right to interfere. You cannot expect him to promise that he will drop a certain bad habit, or attend church regularly, etc. Also, you cannot expect him to promise that he will live in a particular town, or associate only with certain types of people, or promise that he will reach a certain goal. Women who extract promises from their future mates should release them from these obligations, for they are unfair. A man is happy only when he feels free. With these thoughts in mind, you can see that it pays to take serious thought of the man he is now. Can you accept him as he is? Can you be happy with him with no changes? These are things to carefully consider.

IS MY LOVE FOR HIM REASON ENOUGH FOR MARRIAGE?

Anyone who is knowledgeable on this subject will agree that the tender emotion called love is an essential requirement for marriage. Love standing alone, however, means very little. Almost without exception, everyone who marries is first in love. When one considers the many women who must admit that they did not do very well in choosing the right man, even though they certainly were in love, one must conclude that love in itself means very little as a reason for marrying a man.

Affection During the Time of Choosing a Mate

A young woman who wants a man of real worth has many factors to consider, as is plain to see. She must search for traits of character and masculine characteristics. She must also not be blind to a man's weaknesses. Add to this the tremendous importance of the decision — the outcome in the future if the choice is foolish and the rewards if the choice is wise — and one can begin to feel the responsibility involved in making this important choice.

It is wise, therefore, to not become involved in kissing and affection while these conclusions are being reached. When passions are stirred the mind is not entirely reliable. One can compare it to the effect of alcohol on the mind. We all know that when a person is "drunk" his reasoning is not dependable. A smart person would not think of making a momentous decision while under the effects of an alcoholic beverage. The same is true with affections — one would be foolish to select a lifetime partner while passions are aroused and sensibilities therefore numbed. For this reason, more than any other, it is extremely foolish to indulge in kissing and affection before these important decisions have been reached.

Still another reason to avoid affection during mate selection is that young people need many hours to get acquainted. They need time to discover each other for better or for worse. When they become passionate their time is consumed in this practice and they are robbed of the valuable time they need to really know each other.

What Chances Do I Have of Winning the Man of My Choice?

Once you have found the man who meets every specification that you feel is essential, and your heart is set upon winning him, you will likely wonder what your chances are. If you have applied all of the principles of Fascinating Womanhood, and have made considerable progress towards the goal of Angela Human, then your chances are excellent indeed. However, if the man of your choice happens to be difficult to win, there may be more required than just becoming an adorable woman. You may need to use strategy with such a man. All of the remainder of Part Two is devoted to a study of this subject and will teach you, step by step, how to plan a campaign that will bring the man to your feet.

There is one fact remaining that we must recognize. Just as you are drawn to certain types of men, even though others may be just as good and just as charming, so men will also be drawn to certain types of women, certain personalities. There is always a possibility that you will not be *his* type. This may be painful to face, but it need not make you unhappy. After all, you want a man who will appreciate your type — the woman you really are — who will adore your personality as it is. You want a man who is *sold on you*. It is heavenly to finally win a man who loves you for what you really are, and it would be misery to marry a man who could never appreciate your type. Wait; be patient until you find not only the man you can adore, but one who adores you also. If things do not work out with a particular man, in spite of all efforts, accept it as an answer to prayer and keep searching for the "right man" to come along.

CHAPTER XX

The Six Stages of Winning a Man

It was in the business world that the art of winning men was first developed as a comprehensive art. Since business is highly competitive and more highly organized than other fields of endeavor, it became important to develop skills and methods of winning the attention of men to the products of business. Sales managers and advertising men desiring to win men to their wares, their stores, and their institutions devoted their entire lives to the study of the subject. Many acquired such proficiency that they could play upon men's weaknesses and peculiarities as a violinist would upon his violin, to produce any effect desired.

Before long men of the business world discovered that to win men to their products, certain definite principles must be followed in a certain definite order. And they found that no man is ever won until each and every one of these principles has been applied in exactly that order. There were, of course, hundreds of different circumstances, but to the principles themselves and the sequence in which they were used there was no exception.

When comparisons were made, however, these principles which business men imagined they were the first to discover were found to have been known for thousands of years. Orators since the days of Cicero and Demosthenes, dramatists since the days of Sophocles, and clever women since the days of Ruth and Rebecca had resorted to them constantly. In every ancient book on oratory or the drama, they were expounded and recommended. The orator had to win his hearers, the dramatist his audience, and the woman her suitor. In every case the problem was one of winning men, and in every case the principles by which it was solved were found to be alike.

Let us now examine the methods of the salesman and the orator to see if we can determine the underlying principles of human nature involved in winning men. The first thing that we shall learn is that the salesman and the orator depend upon six principles in winning men. They are:

1. Having a worthwhile product, or subject
2. Winning *attention*
3. Gaining *interest*
4. Creating *desire*
5. Overcoming *judgment*
6. Bringing *action*

A salesman cannot win men unless he first has a worthwhile product, unless he has then attracted attention to the product, has brought the attention to interest, sees interest grow into desire, and unless his desire is sustained by judgment. Steered successfully through these five stages he is ready for the sixth stage — action, surrender to the desire that has been created.

Have you ever watched a good salesman in action? He is, of course, first sold on his product. Otherwise he would never be able to demonstrate dynamic enthusiasm that a salesman must have to sell his wares. Then he tries to draw your attention away from the thousand other things you have on your mind and to concentrate it on himself and what he is saying. Thus he gets your *attention*. He then tries to impress you with the importance *to you* of what he has to sell — insurance, for example. Thus he gets your *interest*. Next he pictures the comfort and security the family would enjoy when protected by insurance and the poverty and danger they might undergo if unprotected. Thus, he creates in you a *desire* for insurance. When you agree with him that insurance in general is a good thing, he endeavors to remove whatever doubts you may have about the policy or his company and to overcome whatever objections you may have about parting with the premiums. Thus he satisfies your *judgment*. Last of all, he points out that in another week you shall have to pay a higher rate, that if you wait, a spell of sickness may prevent your passing the medical examination, that as death comes suddenly without warning, delay is dangerous to the welfare of your family. Before you know it, he has your name on the dotted line. Thus he prompts you to *action*. It will be observed that before surrendering to the salesman's determination to sell you insurance, you were maneuvered through each of these stages. It will be observed also that if any one of the stages had been omitted, the last stage would never have been reached. The complete sale requires all six steps.

How Women Apply These Principles of Human Nature

These same principles which have always been found so effective can be used with equal success by any young lady desiring to attract men to herself. Whether you are an orator seeking to win men to your cause, a dramatist seeking to win men to your entertainment, a sales manager seeking to win men to your market, or a young lady seeking to win men to yourself makes no difference so far as the principles are concerned. They are not the principles of oratory, drama, salesmanship or of courtship. They are really principles of human nature.

In all of these fields the human nature dealt with is the same. There are, to be sure, variations in the methods of application, but just as the orator who has mastered these principles can devise suitable methods of applying them to different subjects and different classes of audiences, so can any young girl with the same mastery of underlying principles devise suitable methods for their application in her particular case.

This does not mean that all young girls who win men understand the principles involved. Nature, which always intended that men and women should fall in love and marry, sometimes impels girls to follow unconsciously the same methods that the orator and sales manager would follow consciously. Such girls, who may well be looked upon as nature's favorites, apparently need no other guidance but their impulses and instincts. They always do the right thing at the right time and are usually attractive to every man they meet. Other girls, though not so universally attractive, have their latent instincts for winning men aroused by meeting a particularly desirable man. They suddenly blossom out and show all evidence of real charm, and to the surprise of everyone, including themselves. We all know of instances of such transformations.

But, as was stated in the introduction of this book, there is a vast army of girls, many of them both lovely and lovable, who cannot depend upon instincts in the matter of attracting men. Either through a lifetime habit of indifference to these instincts, or through an artificial culture that has made the suppression of their natural instincts habitual, they have permitted their instincts to grow rusty. Even when nature does prompt them to do the right thing as far as winning men is concerned, they hold back because of typical distrust of their natural impulses or a fear of appearing childish. Business and professional women generally are especially subject to this handicap. As a result, their instincts atrophy from disuse until they must depend upon something more than mere impulse for guidance in captivating men.

But the absence of guiding instincts is no reason for discouragement. Many successful salesmen suffer in the beginning from the same handicap; yet it is universally acknowledged that the "born" salesman who depends upon instinct cannot compete with the salesman who follows established principles. Nor can the born speaker achieve the heights of oratory to which the trained speaker can attain. Just as these mastered an accomplishment for which they first seemed to have no natural aptitude, so can seemingly uninteresting girls, by learning how to apply the principles of human nature, make themselves masters of the art of captivating men, even when at first there seemed to be no natural talent. Today the trained speaker and the trained salesman are constantly stealing the lead from the born speaker or salesman. Tomorrow the trained winner of men's hearts will be constantly winning the men from pretty girls who depend upon instinct alone.

Is Such Strategy Unholy or Unfeminine?

Do not think that the strategy of winning men is in the least unrighteous. Is it not right that a young woman should become fascinating and adorable and deliberately plan to attract the attention of men? Is it not right that she should become a girl worth having and then try to create in some man's heart a desire for her? Her charm and her strategy are her only tools in winning men. Society does not assist her, other than to give her places to meet men. Parents in our culture take little responsibility. The girl stands alone, guided only by scattered knowledge, to win the man she will spend the rest of her life with. She must have some means of attracting a worthy man.

It is much more fair than the strategy used in just wars and political issues or causes, which result in the leadership of nations.

Remember, it is right that a girl marry and build a home for herself. This is all she wants, a little home of her own, a little nest to warm with her love and rule with her kindness. She wants merely to be someone's partner, to share with him his joys and sorrows, to sustain the one and comfort the other, to climb with him towards higher and holier aspirations. She wants merely an opportunity to be tender, loyal and devoted. She wants above all to avoid the lonely life of being unmarried, with no one to care for, to work for, to live for and die for. This is not unfeminine. It is the holiest design a woman can entertain. To use her charms, her feminine wiles and ways, and a plan based upon proven principles of human nature is fitting for her goals.

THE FIRST STAGE
BE A GIRL WORTH HAVING

The first part of the stages of winning men is to "be a girl worth having." Since all of Part One has been devoted to giving you a picture of such a girl, the kind of girl a man wants, we will only stress its importance here in our strategy in winning men. Let us turn again to the viewpoint of the orator and the salesman.

The orator knows that to be successful he must be enlisted in a good cause. The orator says, "I attribute at least half of my success in winning men to the fact that I am enlisted in a good cause. Without a good cause to speak for, men might applaud my cleverness, but they would never surrender to my views. Even in a good cause, it is difficult enough to stir men to action; in a bad cause it is almost impossible. I find, then, that the biggest part of my work is in finding a good cause to speak for. But, having done that, I do not do as many other sincere people do — depend entirely upon the cause to win men. I assume that the cause alone is helpless without the aid of art, and I exercise upon it all the principles of good oratory, all the diplomacy and strategy at my command."

"And I," the business genius tells us, "attribute the greater part of my success to the fact that I had an article of merit to begin with. Without such an article to offer, I might indeed have aroused their interest, but I could never have brought them to desire and action. My carefully prepared advertising and my intensive salesmanship would be defeated by the article itself. In the long run, I cannot create a desire for my article unless it is an article worth having, something men ought to want. Even then the task is difficult. I therefore devote half of my energy toward getting articles to sell that offer a real benefit to my customer."

We find, then, that without a cause worth speaking for, or an article worth having, the art of winning men cannot be successfully applied. This is equally true with a girl in winning men. Unless you are a girl worth having, one a man ought to want, one who will confer a real benefit upon the man who marries her, you might indeed attract his attention or arouse his interest, but you are little likely to create in him a desire to marry you. It is difficult enough even for a worthy girl to win a man, but for a girl not worth having, it is almost impossible.

You will, then, need to acquire all of the qualities of Angela Human if you are to be a girl worth having, for these qualities are those men admire and desire in women. Here, too, a warning must be given. Nine girls out of ten we know will skip the first part of our plan and concentrate upon the remaining five. The latter ones, the application of the principles, are naturally the most interesting and seem the most practical part of the work. You may get the impression that with the many ingenious arts and devices outlined in the next five chapters for the winning of men, the mastery of the first part is of comparative insignificance. This is entirely wrong. Unless you master the man's viewpoint as outlined in Part One, unless you apply this viewpoint in making yourself more desirable, you will be no more likely to succeed than the businessman who wastes all his shrewd advertising and masterful salesmanship upon a product that lacks merit, or the orator who exercises all his eloquence upon a cause which is known to be unworthy. If you expect to meet with success you will proceed right through this work in the order given and not jump immediately to the last part of your campaign.

CHAPTER XXI

Winning A Man's Attention

(OR, HOW TO MAKE MEN NOTICE YOU)

We have just learned that the first step in winning men is to be a girl worth having. But just as the salesman cannot depend upon his good product to sell itself, a young girl cannot rely upon her worthiness to win the notice of men. Here again, we copy the tactics from the business world. For example, what does the average commercial institution do when it has an exceptionally good article to offer the public? It advertises. It proclaims the merits of its article on billboards, on electric signs, in newspapers, in magazines, in pictures, etc. Sometimes it offers samples or gives demonstrations showing how the article is used. It sends salesmen out to the dealer and induces the latter to put in a large stock; it offers to trim the window for the dealer in an attractive manner, thus helping him to sell the article to the public. Everything possible is done to let people know that the product can be had by calling on the dealer, that it is worth having, and that it is the best article of its kind. The manufacturer knows that even the best product in the world will not be in demand unless people hear about it, read about it, see it on display and know where they can obtain it.

In many respects you are just like that manufacturer, except that you have something a hundred times better to offer — yourself, a girl worth having. *But it doesn't matter how well worth having you are unless men know it.* Therefore, you will have to follow the example of the manufacturer — use every method consistent with a feminine woman to let men know that you are alive, who you are, where you can be seen, and what you are worth. You want them to notice you and meet you and learn about you until they can appreciate you at your full value. Many girls, of course, shrink from calling attention to themselves, and in consequence never meet the men likely to be interested in them. Others are too bold, too obviously eager to get attention, and thereby cheapen themselves in men's eyes. Though the advertising campaign must be undertaken, and though you must leave no stone unturned to attract favorable attention to yourself, you must use the utmost care and discrimination in your choice of methods. So, with caution begin your campaign.

First, you must not be content to sit at home. How will men be able to find you if you do? You may be the most desirable girl in all the world but what good will it do you or anyone else if you hide yourself in your bedroom? You will have to get out in the world and circulate around men. Attend every social, sports event, church affair, cultural function, visit to the library, etc., that you have time for, as has been explained in Chapter 12. Only this time for a different purpose — to attract the notice of men to yourself.

Second, once you are in the company of men, you may be faced with another problem. *You may have to attract his attention away from a thousand-and-one other things he may be absorbed in.* He may be interested in other attractive girls, or deeply engrossed in conversation with other men, or may have a problem on his mind, or be lost in thoughts about his future. If you are to win his notice, you will have to use the method of the salesman and distract his attention away from these things and focus it upon yourself.

How to Win Attention

The method you will use to win the attention of men is as follows: Display any of the qualities of Angela Human, but particularly rely upon these three:
1. Appearance
2. Feminine or girlish manner
3. Feminine dependency or "beauty in distress" method

These will be your leaning posts in winning the notice of men. We will now give these three methods our attention.

1. The Appearance that Fascinates

Appearance is one of the keys in winning the notice of men. Turning again to the businessman, he says that "even when I have an article of great worth, I cannot afford to sit back and wait for men to come and ask for it. A great deal of study must be put upon the appearance of the product, the way in which it is wrapped or packed, so that the appearance alone will suggest its merit. For example, I sell, among other things, a high grade perfume. If I packed that perfume in a soda bottle and a cheap carton, it might be the finest perfume on earth, but people would not believe it worth having. I therefore pack that perfume in an exquisitely shaped and tinted cut glass bottle, with a satin lined case. This suggests the dainty exquisiteness of the perfume itself."

The same is true with a worthy girl. Her worth must be self evident. Just as the exquisite perfume must be exquisitely presented, so must the angelic, adorable, tender and gentle girl present herself in an appearance worthy of her true character. A woman of great worth must not be concealed under unfeminine clothes, or disguised by a slouchy appearance. To do so would be like putting the expensive perfume in a soda pop bottle.

We have already studied the appearance that men notice. Clothes that are fascinating to men are feminine or girlish, in sharp contrast with the clothes that men wear. We have also learned of the astonishing effect such an appearance has on men. If you will remember, back in the chapter on femininity I told the incident of the young woman who walked down the street in a tailored brown outfit and did not receive even so much as a single admiring glance. When the same girl dressed in a feminine blue outfit, every man she passed noticed her. I also told of the girl who went to the market time after time in an ordinary dress, and not a single man noticed her. When she went in the long, vivid purple dress, three employees asked her if she would like a job working there. Men cannot resist us when we look ravishingly feminine, but when dressed in drab clothing we simply do not make any appeal.

THE SUNDAY CHILD

You may have noticed this same contrast in the clothing of little children. For example, the appeal that a little girl of four makes in a plain soiled dress, ragged stockings, and untidy hair is quite different from the appeal which the same child makes on Sunday when dressed in lovely pink bonnet, soft organdy dress, with little pink knees dimpling above little socks and shiny slippers, and with a dainty ribbon and freshly curled hair setting off her bright little face. You might look upon the everyday child with indifference, but you cannot resist the impulse to gather up the Sunday child and press her to your heart. Now, if this same Sunday child, instead of dressing in the lovely Sunday outfit described, should be arrayed in a sleek tailored dress and severely plain dark hat, with her hair plastered down close to her head, she would hardly make any appeal whatever.

If we want to win the attention of men we will do as the salesman does and display our angelic character in an exquisite appearance that men will notice and admire. In addition to this, there are a few other points to consider. Since each one of us is different in coloring, body structure, and type of personality, it will be wise to give careful thought to this subject and to discover the type of clothing that is most becoming to you and will enhance your own unique personality. You will need to discover your best colors, best necklines, best styles, etc. There is much information on this subject, and we should not underestimate its value. It is a fact that what looks well on one person may look horrid on another. After we have discovered what looks best on us, we can return to the subject of pleasing men and include femininity and girlishness.

Perfume will also win the notice of men. Since we must win the man away from the many things that may be demanding his attention, perfume is a simple method of solving this problem. If his nose is in a book he may not notice your appearance, but what he can't see he can smell. Men have always loved perfume, and smart women for generations have relied upon it as a method of making men notice them. Most young girls of today are adept at using perfumes, but in case you are not, here are two simple rules. The best perfumes, unfortunately, are the most expensive ones, but they are worth it. You will find the best selections of the better ones at leading department stores.

We have been speaking here of winning the notice of men by means of feminine clothing and perfume, but we must remember that there are even more important elements to charm than this. The real charm that men find in women is a fresh glow of abundant health and radiance. This means smiles, bright eyes, rosy cheeks, etc. What men dislike is a glum expression. A woman can be dressed in the most expensive and feminine clothes in the world, but if she also wears a deadpan or sour expression she will fail to interest men. The man may be momentarily attracted to her lovely clothes, but he will not be attracted to the woman wearing them. Work therefore on all three features of the appearance that fascinates men: femininity, fresh health and radiant happiness.

2. THE ENCHANTING FEMININE AND GIRLISH MANNER

You can also depend upon the feminine and girlish manner to win the notice of men. When a man *sees* a feminine woman he is fascinated, but when he *sees her in action* he is also enchanted. Let us review the different traits of the feminine manner. There are all of the motions of the body such as the walk, use of hands, facial expressions, voice, etc. Then there are the traits of refinement, timorousness, fearfulness and submissiveness. There are also the girlish traits of teasing playfulness, sauciness, tenderness, joyfulness, and outspokenness that you can depend on to fascinate men.

Margaret, you will remember, won the attention of Gerard by first tying his ribbons in a feminine manner and then being timorous when she realized Gerard was noticing her. Dora won the attention of David by her "graceful, variable enchanting manner." The way she patted the horses, spanked her little dog, fixed the tea or shook her finger at him was appealing. She won his attention by femininity and girlishness of manner. Becky Sharp, Amelia and Deruchette also attracted men by their manner. Becky Sharp was timorous, Amelia was tender, and Deruchette had the vivacity and teasing playfulness of a child. In the novel *Seventeen* by Booth Tarkington is an illustration of how a young girl attracted the attention of a young man by her enchanting manner. The following describes the very first meeting between William Baxter, seventeen, and Miss Pratt.

MISS PRATT

"He saw that she was ravishingly pretty, far prettier than any girl he knew. At least it seemed so, for it is unfortunately much easier for strangers to be beautiful. Aside from the advantages of mystery the approaching vision was piquant and graceful enough to have reminded a much older boy of the spotless white kitten, for in spite of a charmingly managed demureness there was precisely that kind of playfulness somewhere expressed about her.

"When he saw how pretty the girl was, his heart, his physical heart, began to do things the like of which experienced by an elderly person would have brought the doctor in haste. In addition, his complexion altered — he broke out in fiery patches. He suffered from breathlessness, from pressure in the diaphragm."

How little we know men and what goes on inside of them. We probably have only a slight comprehension of the way in which a fascinating woman can turn a man's heart upside down. If we knew, we would exercise our feminine charms oftener.

Using the Eyes

One part of the feminine manner that you can always depend upon to win the notice of men is the eyes. This does not mean an old-fashioned fluttering of the eyes and a blush behind a fan, as was considered charming in colonial days. Nor does it mean a sexy "coy" glance. The charming manner of using the eyes is a form of timorousness, as was described in the chapter on femininity. The method is the following: When you see a man whom you want to notice you, try to get his attention by looking at him. As soon as he looks at you, when you catch his glance, look directly into his eyes for a moment. After a few seconds, lower your eyes or look to the side. A longer look is far too aggressive and can even be vulgar, but a brief look is feminine. This trick is used by women of low standards who have immoral designs on men, but do not cast it aside just because they do it. Nice women have also used it for generations.

3. Winning Attention by Feminine Dependency

The most effective way of winning the attention of men is by feminine dependency. You will remember that this quality is a sort of helplessness, or a need for masculine care and assistance. There is nothing that will cause a man to notice a woman sooner than her need for his assistance. You may remember that an old fashioned feminine trick of women a few generations ago was to drop their handkerchief in hopes that men would notice them. In that period of time, women wore corsets, and it was very difficult for them to bend over to pick up anything. Men, realizing their plight, quickly came to their assistance. There are many situations in which a woman can call on a man for help and in so doing win his attention.

In winning the attention of men by feminine dependency you will rely mostly upon the *beauty in distress* method. By inviting situations that require the assistance and protection of men, you win their attention. This is because your apparent need of help has made them feel masculine. Men cannot help but notice women who cause them to feel manly. In fact, you must awaken some sort of sensation within a man if he is to notice you as a woman. We have now covered the three most reliable methods of winning the attention of men — by a *fascinating appearance,* an *enchanting manner,* and by *feminine dependency.* We will now turn our attention to some practical applications.

Miss Charming

Miss Charming never stays home longer than absolutely necessary. She is always gadding about where she can be seen and noticed. Wherever a group of men can be found and the presence of girls can in any way be sanctioned, there will you find Miss Charming with all her charms. Not only does she advertise herself by being everywhere, but she also takes the pains to appear at her best. Her hair is always arranged in just the fashion most becoming to her, her face is made up with just the right amount of cosmetics, and her dress, which she has made herself, is always the most girlish and feminine to be found. Her shoes and hose are neat and trim and her skirt just the right length. She sees to it, whether consciously or unconsciously, that in any crowd of girls she stands out as one of the most feminine.

While other girls are discussing sports or personalities, she is making a last minute check on her appearance, fixing a stray hair, eyeing herself in the mirror. She is never unconscious that she is a woman and that men are around who might notice her. She is ever on the alert for their appreciative glances. A man might gaze a minute or two at another girl, deliberately weigh her charms, and decide whether or not he is interested, all without detection; but he cannot this calmly decide matters for himself with Miss Charming. Let him but steal a glance in her direction and he is immediately detected. She lets him catch her eye, then, after looking directly into his eyes for a brief moment, drops her eyes to the floor in pretty confusion. Can anything be better calculated to attract a man's attention? This then is the first stage.

In winning the attention of men, take care that you do not appear as a "forward" girl. This will frighten a man away. Your approach must be subtle — never aggressive.

A Stroll Through the Park

Imagine that you and a girl friend take a stroll through the park and meet two young men, one who is known to your girl friend and the other who is introduced. If you are dressed in feminine attire you may already have won their notice, and for want of something better to do they accompany you for a time. This is mere idling on their part, however, and not interpreted as paying attention to you. What can you do to win their attention?

The first thing to do is to get away from the main highway, the smooth sidewalk, where there is little opportunity for you to need their manly assistance. Begin adventuring in the rougher parts of the park, crossing brooks, stepping stones, climbing in and out of gullies, etc. You can find many occasions where you can pretend not to be able to help yourself and where the young men can have the pleasure of demonstrating their superior agility and strength. Every time one of them takes your hand to help you over this or that obstacle, he feels the contrast between your womanliness and his manhood. This is a good feeling for him to have and a feeling that is a genuine pleasure to him.

By the time the afternoon has passed, he will be impressed with the fact that you are an exceptionally womanly little creature and that, incidentally, he is a genuine man himself. Very likely he will ask for the opportunity to take you to the park or the woods again, if only for the sake of again experiencing that pleasurable sensation of strength and ability.

MAKING THE MOST OF A PICNIC

If you are on a picnic, follow the same plan as for the park. Don't sit down and expect to gain any attention by mere gossip. Don't stay in one spot and give the men no chance to help you. Get yourself into one predicament after another where you can reasonably expect a man to offer his help. Giving his manly aid and guidance is the only thing he very much enjoys with his association with women.

Collect a group to go adventuring, and then use every opportunity to let the men show their superior strength and agility and daring, and above all their ability to make light of the things that frighten you. Many a girl has attracted a man's attention to her femininity by being afraid of a cow and then letting the man show how groundless her fears are. Others have used mice for the same purpose, or dogs, or a dark night, or a storm or a rickety bridge where she could cling to the man in fright.

THE RAILROAD TRESTLE

There once was a girl so frightened when crossing a railroad trestle with a man, so afraid of falling through, that the man offered to carry her over. The modest little thing naturally became even more frightened at such a proposal; she blushed, became confused, and finally became so daintily reproachful that the man was enchanted. And when he finally persuaded her to place her confiding, trusting hand in his and throw herself upon his manly guidance, she maintained such an air of modest hesitancy, and yet faith in his superior strength and courage, that he could never forget the occasion. The contrast between this timid creature and his own confident, danger-scorning self made him feel twice the man he was before.

WHEN BEING TEASED

Men are usually fond of teasing women. This situation affords a wonderful opportunity to win attention by displaying a feminine manner. The girl who can't be teased and responds only with indifference, or boredom, or by turning the tables on the men themselves, is missing her best chance. That sort of conduct does not make the man feel superior or stronger or abler or bolder. It makes him feel futile. It might even make him feel as if he were no match for any woman. The girl who inspires this feeling is repulsive to a man, no matter how attractive she may be in appearance.

The genuinely clever girl will appear to be utterly dismayed by the teasing, will bite her lip in helplessness or rage and stamp her foot in impotence until the man takes pity on her utter helplessness. It is a case of "beauty in distress." A man will naturally try to help her, to comfort her, to repair the injury to her feelings. Everything he does brings home to him the contrast between this tender, sensitive creature and his own rude, rough and bearlike self.

Winning Notice at a Fair or Public Gathering

If you happen to meet a man at a fair or other crowded place, you can suggest to him by a word or glance that you would be interested in viewing some of the displays or exhibitions, but crowds around you make it somewhat impossible. You are a "beauty in distress" again and the man will most likely display his manhood by offering to guide you to it. After he has done so, and after your wondering eyes have indicated that you admire this big strong man who has been able to do for you something you could not do for yourself, your acquaintance begins to feel a sense of importance so enjoyable that he is likely to keep steering you around for the entire afternoon and ask to guide you on some other occasion. Thus, his attention is secured. To keep it from lagging, however, you will have to keep on requiring his aid and guidance and must never intimate that you are able to kill your own snakes. Such an intimation would take all of the joy out of your association, for he could no longer indulge in that glorious feeling of superiority.

The attractive girl makes a constant appeal for help, for guidance and for protection. Her eyes are always appealing to some man or another to help her in her difficulties. She never directly asks for help. She is so apparently helpless in every situation that not only *men* are impelled to offer aid, but even her businesslike and less attractive sisters feel impelled to offer it. The latter feel that same superiority toward her which a man feels, but they do not *enjoy* the feeling of superiority as the man does. A man never scorns the frailty and helplessnes of a woman because he enjoys too much the contrast it brings out between her weakness and his strength.

A crowded street corner or intersection is another place a woman can be in need of masculine assistance and thus succeed in winning a man's notice of her. Her timidity and confusion at the sight of the heavy traffic can bring nearby gentlemen acquaintances to her rescue.

AT THE DANCE

It is rather difficult to do anything to make a man feel particularly manlike at a dance. This is probably why so many admirable men feel uncomfortable on such occasions. It is equally difficult on these occasions for the woman to act particularly helpless or frail and to give some gallant young man the opportunity to offer his aid and guidance to a beauty in distress. This is probably why women instinctively rely upon appearance and dress on occasions of this kind.

Dress being the only thing likely to attract attention, they devote a great deal of time and effort to their entire appearance. Naturally their dress must be soft and delicate and feminine, in order to convey the impression that these are the qualities of the wearer. She offsets the lack of opportunity to show her need for masculine assistance by conveying the same impression in her delicate appearance. Although a formal dance is your least opportunity to show your feminine dependency, it is your greatest opportunity to display the ultimate in femininity of dress and appearance. Make the most of the situation by creating a dress that gives this impression. This, along with a feminine manner of voice, walk, hands, etc., will give you a good opportunity to win the notice of men present, even if you do not have the chance to act the part of beauty in distress.

STAG DANCES

Stag dances present some special problems for girls. In the first place, they are more casual affairs than formal dances, and you cannot rely upon an ultra feminine appearance to win notice. You can, however, dress as femininely or girlishly as the occasion will permit. Older girls usually attend dances only on dates, but stag dances are often planned for younger girls and boys, where girls either attend alone or with girl friends. Girls can feel pretty awkward at such events and will need some guidelines to see them through.

When you first enter the ballroom, do not run for some corner as many girls do. Instead, stand in the doorway for a moment, look around the room and look directly at some of the boys and girls, with an "air of confidence." Greet those you recognize with a smile. Some young man will likely notice you, smile back, and immediately seek your company. If not, you can converse with your girl friends briefly and then after a few moments look around the room again. Overcome any tendency to be shy or withdraw to some corner. Be "out front" and available.

If, however, you are overlooked, as I have said in Chapter 10, do not allow yourself the disadvantage of becoming a wallflower. Find something to do. If you are attending a casual dance in someone's home you can offer to help the hostess in the kitchen or converse with someone. If you are in a large hall where girls on the sidelines are more obvious, take a walk in the corridor or visit the ladies' room, then return to the dance. And if you are continually left out, do as I have already explained and avoid such social functions until you can discover your mistakes and work to correct them, so that men will readily seek your company.

The situations reviewed here are not only a few suggestions for winning the attention of men by a feminine manner and depedency. There are hundreds more. You will also be able to use the *childlike manner.* Sauciness, teasing playfulness, outspokenness, tender emotions, etc., can also win the notice of men.

How Character Can Win Attention

Although we rely upon a fascinating appearance, enchanting manner and helpless dependency to make men notice us, any of the traits of Angela Human can win a man's attention. It is possible that the very first thing he will notice is a display of character on your part. Men are looking too, you know, and high caliber men usually are wise enough to want a girl of worth. They may not be consciously on the alert to notice character, but only unconsciously doing so. They may be impressed by some noble deed, some kindness to child or an animal, or respect and obedience to parents. They may notice a girl's high standards by her refusing a drink, if this is a part of her belief. An example of a girl who won a man by holding to her beliefs is the following:

While standing on a walk talking to his girl friend, a young man noticed a group of girls come out of a nearby apartment and walk to the corner. As the girls crossed the street, one girl stood at the corner and waved good-bye to her friends and then returned to the apartment. The man asked his girl friend if she knew why the girl did not go along with her friends. "Yes," she said. "This is the Sabbath day and the girls are going to a movie. But this young lady does not believe in attending movies on Sunday, since it is against the beliefs of her religion." "What about the others?" he said. "Don't they belong to this same religion?" "Yes, but they are not as firm about it, I suppose."

It was rather a small matter to some, but it impressed the young man — not so much for the event in itself, but because here was a girl who would not be tempted away from the things she believed in. Later, when he was introduced to her, he remembered and was interested and later married her. She won his attention by her character.

WINNING A MAN'S ATTENTION
THROUGH YOUR DOMESTIC SIDE

If a man is normal he will want a girl who can cook and sew, who loves little children and knows how to keep a house neat and clean. Although he may only have these requirements in the back of his mind, any display of these feminine arts may quickly win his attention. The first time David Copperfield met Agnes, one of the first things he noticed was that "she was a staid and discreet little housekeeper."

One man told me that he was first attracted to his wife when she was sitting in a circle of girls and he happened to peek in her sewing basket and found that there were many different colors of embroidery thread, all neatly arranged. This was quite different from the sewing baskets of his sisters, whom he had always considered quite disorderly. Though this was a small trait, it was an indication to him of greater abilities. He married the girl and found out that his judgment was correct.

Another man was invited to a dinner party in which several girls prepared the meal. The girls had drawn slips for the part of the meal they were to prepare. The vegetable was considered the least opportunity to show any special domestic skill to the men, but the girl who drew this part took it to heart and did such a marvelous job of cooking broccoli with cheese sauce that all of the men present commented only upon that part of the meal. Men will especially be apt to notice the ability to cook, and fortunately it is here that we have the greatest opportunity to show our domestic skill. The cooking has to be superb, however, to make any favorable impression.

On the contrary, men will quickly notice any failures a girl may have in the feminine arts. A poor, carelessly prepared meal, dirty bra straps, untidy purses, unmended clothing, etc., are signs of slovenliness and indications of greater faults. Some girls may think they can cover the defects of disorderly bedrooms, messy closets or drawers, since the men do not see them, but men somehow have a way of detecting these faults. They can either detect outer signs, or they may have indulged in men's gossip sessions in which the girls' roommates have passed on information and these weak traits are the topic for discussion. The only safe thing to do is to correct your faults and become the domestic goddess that men admire. Strive for this goal in all phases of homemaking.

We have learned that in order to win the notice of men we must first have a *fascinating appearance,* which includes feminine clothes, radiant happiness and health. We add to this a *feminine* and *girlish manner* in our walk, voice, hands, etc., and also the charming feminine traits of timorousness, and refinement, and the girlish traits of sauciness, teasing playfulness, tenderness of emotion, joy and outspokenness. Although we have not covered these traits in any detail here, you can review them in the chapters given and discover the many ways you can attract the notice of men by the feminine or girlish manner.

To further win the attention of men we can display our *feminine dependency* or need for masculine assistance. By playing the part of "beauty in distress," we give men the wonderful experience of playing the part of the man and hero. If you review the different traits that win the notice of men, you will see that they all fall on the human side. Femininity, radiance, health and childlikeness (girlishness) are all human characteristics, and although we can win a man's attention in any of the qualities of Angela Human, the traits that we rely upon are the human characteristics.

CHAPTER XXII

Arousing a Man's Interest

We now come to the third part of our plan for winning men. We were told by the salesman that he could not depend upon his exquisite perfume, exquisitely presented, to sell itself, but that he had to resort to every trick and every art known to advertising and salesmanship to create an interest in it. Similarly, a young lady, although she is a highly desirable girl, and although she has the appearance and the manner of such a girl, cannot depend upon these factors alone. There are too many other girls with the same qualifications. In order to cause the man to select her in preference to one of the others, she too will have to exercise all the strategy and diplomacy at her command — every art and every device known to be effective in winning men. Our next step, then, is to arouse interest. Attention will quickly waver unless you do something to sustain it. How to bring about this transformation is the question with which we will now deal.

Though we are forced for the sake of clearness to divide our treatment of attention from our treatment of interest, they are not so sharply divided in actual practice. Often the very things that attract attention in the first place will arouse and maintain a permanent interest so that attracting attention and holding the interest are brought about by the same means. The two being so intimately interwoven, much that was said in the last chapter will be useful in maintaining interest.

METHOD OF AROUSING INTEREST

In arousing interest you can rely upon two basic steps to guide you. They are:

1. Get the man to confide.
2. Admire the manly in him.

A man's most central need, as you will remember, is to be admired for his masculine traits — his strength, aggressiveness, idealism, manly courage and determination; his proficiency in his field of study or work; and his masculine skills and abilities. *Admiring him fully for every manly trait that is within him will awaken his interest more than any other method.*

This task is not at all easy, due to two problems standing in the way. First, in your ordinary associations with a man, you may observe only a few of his masculine traits, only the more obvious ones. You may perceive that he has others, but they do not show enough to offer admiration. The second problem is: Even when you do observe a masculine trait and wish to offer admiration, you hesitate. To do so seems rather stiff or awkward, or many even sound too obvious. Especially are the traits of aggressiveness, determination or idealism difficult to admire unless there is some situation which invites your comments. If you can get him to confide, to tell you things in which these traits are a factor, then expressing admiration will seem natural and easy. And if you can get him to confide, he may reveal a whole store of things about himself in a very short time.

There are, of course, some times that admiration does not seem stiff or awkward. If a man has just received an honor, or won a game, or demonstrated some skill, then a compliment for his work is proper and easy. But these rare occasions are not plentiful 'enough for a girl who is trying to awaken an interest. She must seek the more frequent traits of manhood to admire and then find a subtle means of expressing it. The two reasons, then, for getting a man to confide are:

1. Finding enough things to admire
2. Finding a suitable means of expressing admiration — a means that is natural, subtle and spontaneous.

How to Get a Man to Confide

Unfortunately, the task of getting a man to confide is not at all easy. The reason for this is that in most cases there is an obstacle staring the girl in the face — the man's reserve, or his tendency to go into his shell, as we read about in Chapter Six. Although he longs to confide so that he can be admired, he seldom does because of this wall of reserve. This reserve is caused by fear — the fear that his innermost thoughts will not be appreciated, or that they may even be treated with indifference or ridicule. The man's big problem, then, is two conflicting feelings. The first is his desire to become confidential and the second is his tendency to go into his shell. To get a man to confide, you must *undermine the reserve so that it will disappear altogether.* Now, this is not an easy task for any girl, but it can be done by following certain definite steps.

The first thing to do is to find out what his interests are. You may have observed some of them yourself, or you may have heard about them in conversations with others. If not, you will have to *make a shrewd guess.* Remember that men will be interested in things that concern men. They will be interested in either sports, their studies, their work, special talents, skills, hobbies, world affairs, social conditions, religion, money, success, creative ideas, etc. Of all of these things, the man will only be interested in those *things he is involved in or excels in.* For example, he is interested in sports because he can display a certain skill and knowledge in them; he is interested in politics or religion because he has a few pet ideas on the subject; he is interested in certain fields of study because he feels he has talents for those fields or can accomplish big things in them. His interests in matters are in the way that he relates to them or contributes to them. Try, therefore, to make a shrewd guess as to just what his interests might be.

The next thing to do is to subtly make a suggestion or two about this interest, or suggest that you know something about what he is doing, or that you suspect him of having some big or daring venture up his sleeve. Most men will begin talking with such an invitation. Of course his reserve will not permit him to confide to you immediately his innermost hopes and ambitions, but he will in most cases say enough to see if there is any remote possibility of appreciation on your part.

No matter what he says, you must look for something which you can admire. If he speaks of details of his hobby or school — things that are of little interest to you, don't betray your indifference. He will otherwise assume that your indifference is to him personally, and not to what he says. If you are successful in winning his confidence on small matters, he may venture to confide some of the more important things.

Do not be satisfied with this, however. Remember, the reserve must be undermined or shattered if you are to win his confidence and thus his interest in you. This is not easy to do. Remember, the man longs for admiration, but this instinctive desire is curbed in a sensitive and cultured man by his horror of making a fool of himself. That is why he will hesitate a long time before indulging this desire, why he will first endeavor to find out whether his precious thoughts will be appreciatively received, and why he will cautiously experiment with the less important confidences in order to determine by the reception of these whether he is safe in going further.

You must, then, encourage further confidences. He must be brought to feel that when it comes to you, he need not withhold his confidences. He must be made to realize that he can confide his motives and aspirations to you without the least fear of ridicule or disrespect — that indeed you will interpret them in the most favorable way and will appreciate his character all the more because of the confidence he has placed in you.

He cannot be persuaded of this, of course, unless he first confides to you something on which you can practice your admiration. Gratified by this appreciation, he tries other confidences. These also meeting with encouragement, he finally lays his heart bare before you that you may know what manner of man he is, and that you may admire in him the sincerity, strength and determination of his manly character.

If you find it difficult to get the man to say anything at all about himself, you will have to take steps to win his confidence and break down his reserve in other ways. Go back and read the part about reserve in Chapter Three and concentrate on the steps to "breaking down the wall of reserve." *Let him know that you have a sympathetic and appreciative character* that always sees the best in everyone you meet. You do this by finding something appreciative to say about everyone you know and finding the good things to admire in everyone's character — never belittling, being critical or finding fault. Choose a person to talk about who has just been the subject of some unfair criticism. Deliberately defend the person and show what a sympathetic and trusting person you really are. This will help to reduce his fear that his ideas may be met with indifference or ridicule. You can also talk about experiences you have had, or ideas which demonstrate your understanding character.

You will have to realize at this point that if you are not in reality an angelic person, if you have a tendency to be critical or belittling, with an eye open for the faults in everyone, it will be difficult to disguise these defects in your character. And even if you are clever enough to deceive the man into marrying you under false pretenses, you will never hold his love and devotion unless you are the kind of woman he thinks you are.

Sometimes clever salesmen succeed in selling inferior products by techniques alone, but they never satisfy the customer unless they sell products of real worth. If you are in this situation, if you are in reality critical and belittling, then go back to the beginning of this book and concentrate on making yourself a girl worth having, so that you can not only win the interest and love of a man, but will hold his love for a lifetime.

The method suggested here is not one of technique alone. You are selling yourself as a girl worth having, indicating to the man that you have qualities of sympathy and love which he has never realized existed before. You are merely "letting your light shine."

Getting the man to talk about himself does not mean that you be inquisitive or ask too many questions, or that you urge him to tell you things he would shrink from telling others. Nor does it mean that your interest be too obvious. The task is best accomplished by being subtle and by asking leading questions or making suggestive comments.

When you have altogether shattered the man's reserve so that he will reveal his manly side, and when you have offered to him a sincere admiration for these traits, you have awakened in him the wonderful feeling of manliness. It is at this point that you arouse his interest. Strange as it may seem, when a man seems to be interested in a certain girl, it is not actually the girl herself that he is interested in, so much as he is interested in the pleasure, the comfort and the feeling of strength and manliness that her society gives to him. This, then, is the method of arousing interest.

Of course, femininity and girlishness can also arouse interest, as well as angelic character and domestic traits, for they all make a man feel masculine. But in the different stages of winning men, certain things are found to be more effective in a particular stage than others. Admiration is the one that is the most intensely effective in arousing interest.

While you are endeavoring to arouse interest you will have to make certain that you do not indulge in some common mistakes that drive men away, or your interest will avail you nothing. The following suggestions are given to alert you to these mistakes. Read them carefully and see if you have any of these tendencies.

Mistakes that Drive Men Away

1. *Husband hunting:* In showing a friendly interest in a man and admiring the manly things he says and does, care must be taken that you do not appear to be "husband hunting." There is nothing that will frighten a man away more quickly than to suspect that a girl is setting her cap for him. Thus, in winning a man's confidence, you must indicate by your manner that your interest is merely the interest you would have in anyone who is a real man and does manly things. You might even intimate how you admire certain other men for this or that quality — not in a way that would discourage his hope of winning admiration from you. If this is cleverly done he may feel challenged to tell you a few things about himself to prove to you that he is as worthy of admiration as others are. When he thus wins your increased admiration as a result of his own efforts, he cannot suspect you of an ulterior motive.

Often when men are interested in and enjoy the society of certain girls, they are driven away by their manifest inclination to take things seriously. Remember, then, that even though a man may show a genuine interest in you, he may want to go no further than the enjoyment of your friendship. He wants to be friends with you and likes to imagine that you want merely to be friends with him. You meet each other, in his opinion, merely as an enjoyable pastime. Men want to have a companionship of this nature with a few attractive girls, but seldom anything more. Keep your relationship on this basis and you will not frighten him away.

Most men are anxious to continue a friendship with girls who do not spoil the fun by taking matters too seriously. Such girls are hard to find. Get the man to think that he is "safe" with you, that there is no danger of anything serious, and he will not hesitate to associate with you frequently. A mere suggestion on your part that you are taking things too seriously, even when he delights in your company, can cause him to shun you altogether. Remember the nature of man. He was born with the instinct to pursue the woman — the woman to be pursued. When someone takes away this natural situation it is confusing to the man and will likely frighten him away.

2. *If you major in home economics, etc.:* Letting a man know that your field of study is home economics, child development, marriage, family relations, may give him the impression that you are husband hunting. There are so many girls who are forward with men — who do not know how to be subtle in their approach — that men are inclined to be "on guard" for these girls and are alert to little evidences of this aggressive attitude. It will therefore be wise to not deliberately indicate to a man that this is your educational interest. Men, of course, want women to be domestic, and notice little evidences of skill like cooking and sewing, but these seem less "husband hunting" if they appear to be skills learned at home rather than a carefully outlined preparation for marriage such as a home economics course. Such a course makes a girl seem to take marriage too seriously and indicates that she is not available just as a friend. If the man asks directly about your course of study, answer honestly, but with the attitude that "this is what every young woman should take, regardless of her plans for the future." Whatever you do, don't give him the impression that you are anxious to get married.

3. *Hide your feelings from him:* As you are trying to awaken a man's interest, if you find that you have a growing interest in him, you will have to take care that you do not let these feelings show. A safe rule is this: *Never give an indication that you like him more than he likes you.* Let the man lead in feeling and you follow. There is a time that he will welcome a tender look in your eyes, but this will be only after he is genuinely interested in you.

Hiding feelings is extremely difficult to do and there are few girls who master it. A young girl especially tends to make mistakes. The exuberant tone in her voice when he calls on the phone, the light in her eyes when he arrives, the way she looks at him in contrast to all the other men are all dead "give aways." Any girl, for that matter, finds it a challenge to conceal her feelings from a man she is in love with until he has a chance to be in love with her. One girl told me an interesting solution. When her boy friend was to arrive she became so excited and glowing that she was certain he would be able to detect her feelings. To solve this problem she went into the bedroom and pounded her fists on the wall to bring her feeling under control. With a little more effort on mental attitude she was able to act casual when he arrived.

4. *Hide your feelings from others:* If you are seriously interested in a man, do not make the mistake of revealing this fact to anyone, not even your best friend. Girls cannot be trusted with this information, and even though they may not be so foolish as to tell the man himself, they may tell other girls or even other boys. News such as this travels quickly by the "grapevine." Boys in dorms engage in gossip sessions, and often the subject for discussion is women. Do not rely upon extracting promises from girls either. There have been too many promises broken, too many secrets revealed, and too many men frightened away by such a disclosure.

If you could be certain that the man's feelings for you were as keen as your own, or more so, then he might delight in knowing the facts, but unless you are certain, play it safe and keep your feelings to yourself. Trust no one with the exception of your parents.

5. *Falling off your pedestal:* Another thing which can cause a man to lose interest in you is for you to fall off your pedestal by showing some weakness in character. By lowering your standards, by making some harsh or critical remark, or by a lazy or slovenly attitude in your work, his interest in you may weaken. By such a display he may feel that you are much less of a woman than he had thought.

How to Keep Him Guessing

There is nothing that will sustain a man's interest in you more than "keeping him guessing." This means, *do not give him the satisfaction of knowing just how you feel about him.* A woman is more intriguing to a man if he never quite knows where he stands with her. The way to do it is this:

Be friendly with him — but also be friendly with everyone else. In this way he will never quite detect whether your friendliness with him is just your nature or whether you really like him. If you are sullen around most people and then light up when he walks by you will be "wearing your heart on your sleeve." If, on the other hand, you light up around everyone, he never quite knows.

Then, don't be too available. Date him, but also date other fellows. If he has been seeing too much of you recently, when he calls "arrange to be busy." If you don't have a date with someone else, then you have "too much homework," or "unexpected home duties," or "have promised to spend the night with a girl friend."

One good way to keep a boy guessing is to have an absorbing interest in life, and particularly your own activities or responsibilities. If you work, let him know that you are interested in it and enjoy it. Show an interest in special hobbies, talents and other activities, and devote a certain amount of your time and energy to them. This will relieve him of any feeling that you may be bored with life and therefore hunting for a husband as an escape.

Intensifying Interest

When you have aroused a man's interest in you by winning his confidence and admiring the manly, you have made considerable progress. If you continue this treatment you will intensify his interests by one of the most powerful influences known to bring a man and woman together, *fascination of secrets shared.*

You know things about him and his aspirations that are known to no one else; you have been trusted with confidences that have not been exposed to the criticism and appreciation of another. Nor must it be forgotten that you yourself feel a difference between him and other men. You have given confidences as well as received them. This man knows about your ideals and your aspirations and difficulties. He understands and appreciates and reverences you as men who know less about you could never do. You and he are in a class by yourselves, apart from all the rest of the world in each other's estimation. When you meet your eyes flash in understanding and sympathy when others are absorbed in other matters. You encourage one another by word and look. Whether at church, a party, in the classroom or at a sporting event you cannot help singling each other out as being different and on a different footing from all mankind besides. You have secrets between you that others do not and cannot share. His interest then is intensified, which will provide a transition from interest to desire.

Let me remind you again of the utmost necessity of keeping your secrets confidential. And be sure that there is no relationship between you that is unwholesome or shameful in any way. Continue to win his confidence and offer him admiration, and thus sustain the interest until it grows into desire.

CHAPTER XXIII

Creating a Desire

Going back to the salesman again and his method of creating a desire, what does he do? He stops his tactics and strategy that he used in winning attention and creating interest and begins to sell the customers on the worthiness of the product itself and how indispensable it is to their welfare and happiness. He must do this before he can bring them to any kind of decision to buy the product — before he can create in them a desire for it. You, then, will use this same approach in creating a man's desire for you. You will not depend upon strategy and tactics. It will not be a result of what you do, *but what you are.* You will have to prove that you are a girl worth having and that you are indispensable to his happiness. These are the two steps that we will use in creating a desire:

1. Prove you are a girl worth having
2. Become indispensable to his happiness

To prove your worth, you will have to take on all of the qualities of Angela Human. It will not be necessary to go into detail here, but only to encourage you to review all of those chapters, and get well in mind all of the component parts that make up the ideal woman, and then work with all diligence to be like her. Work on character, the domestic skills, and inner happiness and all of understanding men. Concentrate again on femininity, dependency and childlikeness, as well as radiant happiness and health. This may seem like quite an undertaking but it is surprising what a girl can do when she realizes that her future happiness is at stake and that winning the man of her choice depends upon her.

Seek the Lord in prayer and ask Him to help you become the tender, angelic and fascinating woman that He designed you to be. If you have a picture in your mind of the girl you ought to be, and ask for your Heavenly Father's help, it will be surprising how miracles can work. Your understanding of the subject will broaden, and your ability to be the ideal woman will seem more like second nature to you. And once you come close enough to this ideal to win the man of your choice, if you want to hold his love for a lifetime you will have to continue to be Angela Human and strive to become more perfect day by day. When the Lord knows of your high and noble goals, not only of winning the man you want but of keeping him happy for a lifetime, He will not turn you away if the man is right for you. Keep this image of Angela Human firmly in your mind then, and constantly strive to be like her. Work with all energy of both mind and spirit.

Becoming Indispensable to Him

To be indispensable means that you have something the other person cannot get along without. Because of this you become essential to his well being and happiness. To be essential to a man we reach into one of his most vulnerable parts, his great need for understanding. By supplying him with all of the different elements of true understanding, by giving him admiration, sympathy and comfort in times of need, and by sharing with him his joys and sorrows, a woman can without a doubt be indispensable to a man.

Up to now, a man may have been pretty independent, at least since he reached manhood. He has found his own comforts, healed his own wounds and supplied his own needs. He may have relied upon close friends and relatives from time to time, but no one person has become indispensable to his welfare and happiness. But you can change all of this and make him dependent upon you so that he will rely upon you for comfort in difficulty, for sympathy and true understanding. We are dependent upon men for protection and shelter, but they can become dependent upon us for a different kind of need.

The way to become indispensable is this: First, continue to admire his masculinity, since this will intensify interest until it automatically grows to the point of desire. He will begin to feel that you are essential to him because you are the only woman who can make him feel really manly. This in itself is an indispensable feeling for a man. But even more important, you will find that if you continue to admire the manly you will further win his confidence so that he will turn more and more to you. *Then you will have the opportunity to supply his other needs that only a woman can do.* When he has some new idea or plan, he will long to discuss it with someone, but he dares not discuss it with anyone but you, for you are the only woman who could possibly understand and appreciate his ideas.

When he meets with a rebuff or criticism from others, the most natural thing for him to do is to turn to you. When the feeling comes to him, as it comes at times to every man, that he is not the man he ought to be, that he has not lived up to the best that is in him, the only person he knows who can make him feel like a man again is you. When his plans meet with discouragement he knows that he will find solace and understanding in your presence. Or, when his plans meet with glorious success, his fondest hopes seem about to be realized, where should he turn but to you, the only one who can share his joy and happiness with complete understanding.

As this feeling intensifies, he finds it more and more difficult to live without you, more and more necessary to have you with him as the life-long sharer of his joys and sorrows. This is a considerable removal from the apathy with which he began. The difference in his eyes between you and all other women assumes prodigious proportions. You have become indispensable to his well being and happiness. You were not indispensable before, but that was just because he did not know what real joy and happiness were until you inspired him with these feelings. If you have also proven you are a girl worth having, he has suddenly begun to realize that you are everything he has ever wanted in a woman — an inspiring character and yet a human bundle of girlish femininity. At this point you begin to create a desire in the man, a desire to have you for his own.

Along with desire, you awaken another feeling in his heart — his love. By becoming Angela Human you have inspired the feelings of worship, adoration, the tender desire to protect and shelter you. You have caused him to be fascinated, amused and enchanted, and have awakened all of the thrilling and consuming sensations of romantic love. You have, in addition, aroused his sex passions, which is also a natural part of love. These feelings combine to form the many-splendored feeling called love. Is anything better calculated to bring a man to the point of desire? It is the combination of these overwhelming feelings that can bring a man to make the big jump to marriage, that can cause him to sacrifice his freedom, tax his usually limited resources, undertake the heavy responsibilities of marriage and attempt the often impossible task of providing for the girl as she deserves.

Maintaining Interest While You Inspire Love

Love is sometimes slow to grow, so don't become impatient with this step of winning men. You can sustain his interest while love has time to grow into desire. Though we cannot rely upon strategems to turn interest to desire, we can rely upon them to maintain interest until desire is created. All you need to do is to use the principles of arousing interest while love grows. This means that you continue to win his confidence, that you continue to admire the manly in him, and along with this use every opportunity to give him the understanding and sympathy that every man needs. The disadvantage of most girls is that they do not maintain interest long enough to give the man's desire time to grow. You are under no such disadvantage; you can maintain the man's interest as long as is required to give his emotions time to develop into real love. Nature is aiding you and meant in the first place that men and women should love and marry. You only need a little time to let nature arouse in the man the desire to have you for himself. And while you are working on maintaining interest, you can work on all of the qualities of Angela Human. During this time it is essential that you do not undo the progress you have made by making mistakes that will drive men away. During the time of inspiring love, take care that you do not make the following mistakes:

Don't Wear Your Heart on Your Sleeve

Don't make the mistake of showing your feelings. And don't tell him that you love him until he has said that he loves you. Don't move faster than he does. The man is the pursuer, the girl the pursued. If you tell him you love him before he has made up his mind about you, you stop his pursuit and are apt to confuse him.

Don't Be Aggressive

Don't be physically aggressive, since this deprives a man of his masculinity. Don't squeeze close when he is driving; don't put your lips up to be kissed or reach for his hand during a movie, etc. This can kill a romance. Don't call him on the phone, let him call you. Don't send him notes unless they are answers to his.

Don't Fall from Your Pedestal

When the man is trying to decide about you is the time he is apt to shake your pedestal or test your character to see if you are the angelic creature you appear to be. Don't disappoint him by lowering your standards, making a sharp critical remark, or doing some unkind or selfish deed, or showing some other weakness of character.

Keep Him Guessing

Continue to keep him guessing. Be a woman of intrigue so that he will never know quite where he stands. Arrange to be busy at times when he wants to see you, and be genuinely interested in your life and plans and don't give any indication that your future has *him* in it.

Withhold Affection (Kissing and Cuddling)

During this time that love is growing is when a girl and a boy are most apt to be affectionate. Unless you are certain that the man is in love with you, and you with him, it is dangerous to engage in affection for the following reasons:

1. It will bring into play emotions that will make it difficult for true love to develop, and it may confuse both of you. Even if you are certain that you love him, it may cloud the issue for him. He may think his feelings for you are only physical. How can he really tell how he feels about you? The emotions of affection were meant to *accompany love* and not to precede it.

2. You cheapen yourself in his eyes when you can be had without love. Also, he will think, "If you give *me* affection without love, what will keep you from giving it to any other man?" By

withholding affection until you have his love, you put a special value on your affections.

3. It stirs the emotions to the greater passions of sex, which leads us to the next problem to consider.

DON'T INDULGE IN SEX BEFORE MARRIAGE

When a relationship grows from affection into a sexual experience the problems are multiplied many times. Most girls do not realize the dangers involved for them emotionally, physically and every other way. Not only is it morally wrong to have sex before marriage, but it is very foolish. Consider the following thoughts on this subject:

1. There are many references to immorality in the Bible which classify it as a sin of great gravity. Fornication has been recognized as a heinous sin through all biblical days, and in some periods was punishable by death. The punishment is no longer death, but in God's eyes the sin is just as serious.

2. When a woman becomes involved with a man sexually, she usually becomes involved with him emotionally as well. Ending the affair can be a crushing blow to her. This is not apt to be so with the man. Surveys show that eighty percent of the men who engage in premarital sex do not even like the girl. Having no emotional attachment, they are apt to "love her and leave her," free of any obligation of marriage.

3. Marriage was instituted as a protection to a woman. Marriage says, "Give me first your name, and promise to be mine, and then I will surrender to you in sex." The girl who yields before marriage removes her rightful protection as a woman.

4. Giving sex without marriage *cheapens* a girl in the man's eyes. Men insist upon placing a value on everything, including their women. If they can have you for nothing, they are seldom seriously interested. The unattainable woman arouses a man's interest; she becomes an interesting challenge.

5. The fifth thought is this: The man could possibly be testing you. First, he may be trying to find out if you can be had easily. Second, he may be testing your character, to see if you are the angelic creature he has been led to believe, to see if your virtue is as strong as all your other traits. To give in would be to fall

from your pedestal and also to disappoint him. (Refer to the chapter on character and the incident I told about the *Story of Dorian Grey.*)

6. Some girls yield because they are afraid of losing the man if they say no. Actually, just the opposite is true. If she surrenders, she may win him as a bed partner, but will not likely win him in marriage. Surveys show that only ten perecnt of men who engage in premarital sex marry the girl involved.

In returning to the subject of creating desire and winning the man's love, you will need to avoid these mistakes. Don't let your feelings show, control affection until love grows and don't yield in sex lest you drive the man away and reap only heartache and disappointment. Instead, concentrate on awakening real love in his heart by acquiring all of the qualities of Angela Human, by being a girl worth having. As you continue to give him admiration, sympathy, comfort and hope, sharing his every joy and sorrow, you will become indispensable to his true happiness. He will begin to feel that he cannot live without you.

Because of your delicate nature, he will begin to think of himself as the only one who can appreciate your womanliness, the only one who can properly protect you and provide for you as you deserve. He feels that it is imperative for him to look after you — that you are his to watch and shield and provide for. His attention has grown into interest, his interest has grown into worship, and his worship is now full-fledged desire.

In reviewing the method of creating desire, we have found that it is accomplished in two steps. The first is to prove you are a girl worth having, and the second is to make yourself indispensable to the man's happiness. Both of these goals are reached by becoming Angela Human, but the latter goal is dependent upon *understanding men.*

CHAPTER XXIV

Overcoming Judgment

REMOVING THE OBSTACLES TO MARRIAGE

If you will think back about the incident of the insurance salesman, you will remember that after he had created a desire in the mind of the customers, he then had to dispel certain doubts and fears that they might have in regard to insurance, their ability to pay the premiums, etc. — in other words, "satisfy their judgment." Only then would the customer feel confident enough to make a decision about buying insurance.

A man, too, may have certain doubts, fears and problems that present themselves as obstacles to marriage. He may wish to marry, and yet hesitate to undertake the responsibilities involved. He may have dependent relatives, or a heavy debt, or unknown obligations of many different kinds. He may be doubtful of his ability to provide for you, or too proud to ask you to share a lower standard of living than that to which you are accustomed. Or he may even be afraid that you do not return his feelings and be unwilling to risk the humiliation of a refusal. These objections must be overcome before he will act upon his desire to marry.

Not always, however, does the girl have to take the initiative to help him overcome these objections. Sometimes the man struggles with them himself, weighing out one problem against another until he overcomes these objections, without the girl doing or even knowing anything about them. But if his problems seem insurmountable, causing him to postpone the important step of marriage, the girl needs to sympathize with his problems and help him overcome these barriers.

THINGS IN YOUR FAVOR

A list of the objections a man may have to marriage is enough to dishearten any girl. So valid and so obvious are they that men seldom step into matrimony deliberately. They step into it only under stress of emotion, when cold reason and calm judgment are out of the question. In spite of this fact, however, you must not become discouraged. Though you should familiarize yourself with the objections he may have to marriage, and though you must recognize their importance, you must not forget that before you have reached this stage, you have already aroused in him the desire to be your guide and protector. He can no longer reason coldly and judge calmly; everything is colored by his desire to have you for his own. He is likely to cast discretion to the winds and, objection or no objections, ask you to be his lifetime partner. And if he does hesitate, if he does find it impossible to overlook some of the obstacles, then he is troubled to find this objection standing between him and his desire and is just as anxious to have it removed as you are. The overcoming of the objections is therefore not the tremendous task it would be if the man were not influenced by his own desires and sentiments.

The Two Barriers to Marriage

Standing between the man's desire to marry the girl and asking her consent are two classes of objections. The first class covers his objections to marrying *anyone*. The second class covers his objections to marrying a particular girl. We shall now consider the first class, objections to marrying anyone.

The Fear that He Cannot Earn Enough Money to Support a Wife

Probably the most common cause of hesitation in a young man who likes and wants to marry a girl is that he fears he cannot earn enough money to support a wife. In many cases, he not only fears it, he knows it. When this is the case, he does not frankly come out and tell the girl that he would like to marry her but that he can't afford it. The girl could easily tell him, under such circumstances, what she can do to help him out or how she is willing to wait or how marriage is more economical than he anticipates. Instead, he will often pay attention to her for months and yet give no evidence of his desire to marry. She may think he doesn't care for her at all. She may even become so discouraged about him as to drive him away.

As long, however, as the man continues to show interest in her, the girl should not lose heart. She should study him and try to guess what objection it is that is holding him back. If she imagines that the fear of being unable to support a wife is an obstacle, she must proceed to remove it. This is not to be done, of course, by boldly coming out into the open and showing him that he can. That would be far too aggressive and unfeminine. The following method is effective.

How to Banish His Fear of Inability to Support a Wife

Get the man to talk about his future, his plans, his expectations and ambitions. Try to make him forget his present humble position and live in the imaginative future. Talk about his successful and glorious future as if to you it is a certain and definite thing, as if there can be no doubt about it in your mind. Before long he will begin to talk and think the same way; he will become confident in himself. His present financial circumstances will be looked upon as only temporary. Since his successful future is an agreeable subject to him it will require no great effort on your part to bring it up at every opportunity. His superior financial status two or three years from now becomes a certainty; he looks upon himself as already made. You must build castles in the air for him and maintain that it will only be a matter of two or three years before these castles will be built upon solid ground. This attitude of mind on your part is contagious; the man too will feel that there is no doubt about what he will have to offer you two or three years hence. When a man becomes certain of his success there is no reason why he should not ask you to wait for him. And there should be no reason on your part why you should not be willing to wait.

Very few men actually do propose. They usually ask a girl to "wait" for them! This is because hardly one in ten thinks that it is possible, financially speaking, for him to marry immediately. There are always too many objections to an immediate marriage, objections which he thinks will be overcome at a later date. They therefore propose that you "wait for them." They have a horror of setting a definite date. After the engagement is set, however, the girl can speak freely about it, and can proceed to further remove his fears and objections to marrying sooner. She can begin to point out how unnecessary it is to wait until his success has already been accomplished, how willing she is to fight through on his present salary until he can do better, how she can help to economize, and how by marriage they can save money and time and work together more efficiently than before to hasten the day when his ambition will be realized. Finally, under the spell of some moonlit night when it is difficult to say goodnight, or when he anticipates leaving town on business, etc., and it is difficult to say good-bye, they decide to marry immediately, for better or for worse, and begin their partnership in earnest.

FEAR OF AN UNCERTAIN FUTURE

Sometimes, even when a man knows he is earning enough to support a wife, he still hesitates to go ahead because he is uncertain about his future. He may be earning enough now, but is he sure that he will continue to earn enough? Maybe he will have bad luck, lose his position, or he may not feel conditions will remain the same. There is the risk that he will make less in the future than now. There are thousands of these overly cautious young men.

The only thing a girl can do is to bolster his self confidence and use the "castle in the air" method in much the same manner as has already been described. This she does until he finally asks her to wait for him — to wait until he is sure that his earning ability is a permanent thing. Once engaged she can change his mind about postponing marriage, can alter his desire to wait until things are more secure.

WHEN A MAN'S DEPENDENTS STAND IN HIS WAY

Another obstacle that sometimes stands in the way of a man's getting married is the fact that he has a mother to support, or an aged father or smaller brothers and sisters. Many men who do not appear to have dependents — especially men living alone in a big city — are obliged to send a big part of their earnings home every month to contribute to the support of others. Often they will keep this secret because they do not like to admit that members of their families are victims of straitened circumstances. He may earn a comfortable salary, but because of his responsibilities he is not as free to marry as a man earning much less.

At the same time, the girl may know nothing about this quiet claim on his support and may think he holds back because he does not desire to marry her. Because of this, a man should never be judged harshly when he hesitates, and the girl should never become impatient and give up hope.

What She Should Do

If the girl will only wait patiently, the man will sooner or later tell her about the dependents. He may not admit that they are dependent, but he will say something from which she can surmise the facts. If they are not too far away, the girl should arrange to meet them and try to win their love and approval. In many cases, if she is an adorable girl, the dependents will realize that they are standing in the way of the young man's happiness and for fear that he will lose this girl whom they also love, will try to find a way by which they can ease the man's financial burdens so that he can feel free to marry.

Whether she has the chance to meet the dependents or not, the girl should let him know that she approves of his sacrifices for his dependents and admires him for it, that she would not under any circumstances expect him to do otherwise. The man begins to feel that if he were married to her she would not object to his using part of his income for the support of his other dependents. (She should sincerely support him on this.) Thus is part of the obstacle removed.

To further remove his obstacles, she should follow the plan outlined in the preceding problem of enthusiastically picturing his future until he feels certain that within two or three years he will make so much more money that he will be able to support a wife in spite of his other obligations. As before, all he dares do is to ask her to wait for him, but once they are engaged, she does not find it difficult to hasten things along. In the case of younger brothers and sisters being dependent upon the man, almost the only thing necessary to do, especially if they are very young, is to win their affection — an easy thing to do in the case of small children. The obstacle would then be removed, because it would be plain to any man that he would be better able to care for children with the aid of a wife than without that aid. If the children are older, they would not be a serious obstacle, for then it would only be a matter of a few years until they are self-supporting. It should not be difficult to get the man to ask the girl to wait for that length of time.

DEPENDENTS WHO WILL NOT YIELD

Too often, however, the man has a dependent mother or sister so selfish that she is unalterably opposed to his marriage to anyone at all. When the girl meets such dependents she not only fails to win their affection for herself, but arouses them to bitter opposition.

In other cases, these dependents look upon the son as already overburdened with responsibility, and not because of selfishness, but because of their anxiety for him, they oppose his adding the support of a wife to his other burdens. In either of these two situations, the obstacle is not easily removed, because to the man's own doubts have been added the open and confirming objections of others. He may become so discouraged that he gives up the idea of marriage altogether. He may even avoid the girl for a time, thinking to give her up.

In such a case as this, the girl should arrange to run into him by accident sometime and then act hurt and ill treated in rather a tender and childlike way so that the man will feel bound to call on her again to apologize. During such an apology the man is very apt to confess the real truth about his problem — that he desires her more than everything else but that it is impossible because of the burdens he has to carry. This, then, will open the door to a conversation in which she can explain that she has a perfect faith in him and is willing to wait until his burdens have been lifted, and that she is sure he is going to get ahead and solve his problems.

When the man has, on account of his unyielding dependents, given up the idea of marriage, but still continues to enjoy the girl's association, the problem is more difficult than when he temporarily drops her. The only thing she can do is to use the "castle in the air" method to work up his feeling of self reliance so that he will finally find the courage to ask her to wait for him.

Although the average girl does not realize it, all of this indulgence in day-dreams is necessary to make the average young man brave and self-confident enough to undertake her support. No matter what the objection that is standing in the man's way, it is only in this atmosphere of enthusiasm about the future, and self-confidence, that these objections can be overcome. The "castle in the air" method will have to be used constantly in overcoming the obstacles to marriage.

DEPENDENTS BY A FORMER MARRIAGE

In the case of alimony to a former wife and children, the man is not making a noble sacrifice but is fulfilling both a moral and legal obligation. He has no choice in matters but to pay. If he is a high principled man and loves his children he will take it in good spirit and assume his obligation as any other. His greatest fear may be that a new wife may not feel as he does. There is a tendency for women to resent obligations accrued by a former marriage.

If you show that you accept the idea and will support him in good spirit, you will greatly relieve his fears of difficulty in marriage. Such a reassurance of your generosity and understanding will encourage his proposal in marriage.

WHEN DEBTS BLOCK THE PATH

Sometimes a man appears to have no obligations toward dependent relatives, but has other obligations that are just as binding. For example he may have gone into debt to finish his college education and may not have been able to pay it back yet. He may be earning only enough to support himself and have little prospect of earning more in the immediate future. Sometimes the prospects of being able to pay back these loans are slim. enough without having a wife to support. This obstacle is practically impossible to overcome except by the "castle in the air" method, by reviving enthusiasm and self-assurance until he feels that his future success is so sure that he need not be afraid to ask the girl to wait for him.

SECRET OBLIGATIONS

It is almost impossible to enumerate the secret obligations a man may have which prevent his considering marriage. Among them, we must not overlook the possibility that he may feel obligated to another girl. Quite frequently a man in a big city may be engaged to a girl back home. The engagement may be of such long standing that neither of them has strong feelings any longer, and may not even have seen each other for some time. The engagement may have been a mistake, and now the contemplation of marriage a still greater mistake. In novels, the situation is usually relieved by the girl back home falling in love with someone else, but in real life the girl back home is seldom so accommodating. She may not properly care for the young man, but her prospects for getting another may be weak enough to delay her breaking the engagement, and the young man may be too honorable to express a desire to be released from his obligation.

Here is an obstacle that is almost insurmountable. The young man waits and waits, hoping that something will occur to release him from his obligation, and the girl he desires wonders why he never asks her the all-important question. Her disappointment, however, is nothing compared to the misery of the young man. All that she can do is to wait, and hope that the girl back home will break the engagement or that the young man will gain the courage to do so. The girl, however, must be careful not to misjudge the young man.

When the Man's Health Stands in His Way

Another obstacle that is sometimes insurmountable is ill health. Many an apparently strong man is a victim of diabetes, heart trouble or some other disorder. He may know that there is a strain of insanity in the family or some other hereditary disorder in the blood line. He therefore dares not marry for fear of bringing unhappiness upon the girl he loves. He knows that if his trouble should become acute he will not be able to earn a living for himself, much less a wife. A situation like this is tragic because there is little prospect of escape for the man, while the poor girl does not even have the satisfaction of knowing that he cares for her. When a man fails to speak out, remember that he sometimes can't do as he pleases. The only thing the girl can do is to use the "castle in the air" method for a month or two, which may cause him to at least offer an explanation. If this fails you may have to resort to the following.

LAST RESORT METHOD

When all else has failed to bring the young man to speak out and air his obstacles, or at least regard them as unimportant in comparison with having the girl he desires, it may be wise to arouse his jealousy by accepting the attentions of other men. In most cases, this will either cause him to speak out or drop out. For this reason it should be used only as a last resort, after much patience has been exercised.

If the man neither speaks out nor drops out, she can surmise that the obstacle may be insurmountable at present, but that he has hopes of getting around it later. She must be patient and wait with him. In the meantime she can remember: "On some romantic evening, or under stress of the emotions aroused by a good movie, or the beauties of nature, or some other occasion when cold reason is subdued and hope and tenderness are uppermost, he is likely to blurt out the whole story. As long as the man continues to show interest, he is likely at any minute or on any occasion to bring on the crisis. The girl therefore should continue to give him every opportunity, even if he hesitates for months.

GROUP II   OBSTACLES THAT PREVENT MARRIAGE TO A PARTICULAR GIRL

We now turn from the obstacles which would prevent his marriage to any girl and consider those which would prevent marriage to a particular girl. It often happens that when there are no impediments to marriage in general, there is a great impediment to marriage with a particular girl.

THE MAN'S FEELINGS OF INFERIORITY

The first obstacle here, in regards to marriage with one girl in particular, is when a man may feel a distrust of himself or a sense of inferiority around a particular girl. We all know of the story of John Alden and Priscilla. John thought so much of Priscilla and so little of himself that he couldn't even hope that Priscilla would care for him. He considered Miles Standish so much better a man that the thought of rivaling him in Priscilla's affections was undreamed of. So far from proposing for himself was he, that he undertook in all seriousness to carry Miles Standish's proposal to her. Poor Priscilla finally had to ask him "Why don't you speak for yourself, John."

Now this situation is not so infrequent as one might suppose. The bravest and most self-possessed man loses his bravery and self-possession when in the presence of the girl he worships. If he is of the right stuff, he can't help feeling unworthy in the presence of this angelic creature. He hesitates to put his fate to the test for fear that he will be exiled altogether. He may call on her a number of times with the intention of asking the all-important question, only to lose heart at the last moment and put it off until another time.

There is only one thing to do, and that is to take pity on him and help him along, as Priscilla did with John Alden. Half the men who marry do not propose without some help from the girl. Of course, this help cannot be given except when the girl positively knows that the man wants to speak and can't. The help must be given out of pity for his misery, and not out of boldness or impatience. Unless she knows he is in misery, she should not help him.

Too Proud to Ask

The next obstacle we shall consider is the man's pride. Perhaps he can support a wife, but only in a modest way and not at all in the way that this particular girl is accustomed. He is too proud to ask her to accept a lower standard of living just for his sake. Even when the girl comes from a modest home, pride sometimes prevents him because the man has a certain idea of the way his friends would expect him to maintain a household and he is too proud to risk their criticism by starting out on a more modest scale. This obstacle is to be overcome the way any other economic obstacle is, by using the "castle in the air" method until he asks her to wait for him.

When the Man's Family Objects to a Particular Girl

We now come to one of the most common obstacles of all, the objections of the man's family to a girl. It is unfortunately true in most families that a marriage of the daughter is expected as a matter of course, but the marriage of a son, until a very mature age, is looked upon with the most scrutinizing eye. Even when the family does not oppose marriage in general, they may oppose his marriage to a particular girl he desires. Mothers especially are prone to believe that no girl is quite good enough for their sons. They will discover a thousand faults in the poor girl and will resist his desire with every resource available.

To overcome this obstacle, the girl should first endeavor to win the affection and good will of his family. In only rare cases does this succeed, however. She must determine to win him without their good will. This is not as difficult as it appears because he usually resents the unfairness of the family's attitude toward the girl and is indignant at the poor reception given her. The active opposition of the family can, in fact, speed him to action.

If the family's opposition does not speed him to action the girl must resort to the "castle in the air" method — to enter into his plans, hopes and ambitions so thoroughly and so sympathetically that he cannot think of his bright future without her to share it, to be an inspiration and comfort to him. He begins to feel that he cannot live without her. Then his desire will sweep aside all obstacles of whatever nature.

Summary

There are innumerable other obstacles to marriage — such as ambition, fear of the humiliation of a refusal, fear of the contempt of his social circle when he marries beneath it, the possibility of marrying a girl with wealth, doubt whether the girl's liking is permanent, etc. In any case the method for removing the obstacle is pretty much the same. Either patiently increase his desire, or get him to project himself into the future and there picture success and the solution to his problems, or get him to speak out by arousing jealousy or by provoking him gently as Priscilla did.

It is rare that man says "Will you marry me?" It is usually "Will you marry me when" — his salary is raised, his debts paid, his education completed, he gets another job, his future is safely settled or his dreams come true. He never thinks he is ready to marry and he usually thinks it is wrong to marry until he is. The girl must convince him that "he will be ready" at a certain time and make him so sure of it that it is the most natural thing in the world to ask her to wait for him. After the engagement it should prove an easy matter to shorten the waiting period.

CHAPTER XXV

Securing Action

In theory, all obstacles out of the way, a man proposes. It is not always as simple as this, however. The man may find that unless he has a particular reason to hurry things along, it is easier to procrastinate the important step and keep things as they are. This may go on for months, with nothing resolved and the girl wondering all the time how serious the man's feelings are for her.

If this is the case, the girl can bring him to action in any one of three general ways. The first is by making it easy for him to speak out, the second is by making it hard for him *not* to, and the third is by making immediate action appear urgent and necessary. The following will explain these three ways to secure action.

METHOD No. 1   MAKING IT EASY FOR HIM TO ACT

You make it easy for a man to act in two general ways. The first is to *maintain an optimistic and enthusiastic atmosphere,* as we have already explained in "creating desire" and "overcoming judgment." Continue to "build castles in the air" and this will tend to minimize the responsibilities of matrimony. In fact, this optimistic attitude of projecting a man into his bright future can in some cases carry a romance from desire, through judgment, and into action. Not always, however, can we rely upon this approach. We sometimes have to resort to other methods. A second way of making it easy for him to act is to get him in a *romantic and sentimental frame of mind.*

Few men propose in a mood of cold and calculating reason. The girl should endeavor, therefore, to arouse in him the opposite moods — a feeling of warm, impulsive emotion, or of dreamy, drifting surrender to sentiment. In such a mood, reason is subdued and the impulse to speak out is unopposed. The manner of awakening these sentimental moods is accomplished by *creating romantic situations*. A number of suggestions are given here.

CREATING ROMANTIC SITUATIONS
BE ALONE

The first thing to avoid is a third person. No man ever becomes romantic while other people are around. When more than two are present the conversation and the atmosphere become entirely matter-of-fact.

DIM LIGHTS

The next thing to avoid is an atmosphere of bright or brilliant lights. In the glare of such lights reason is uppermost and not sentiment. The lights must be subdued to give an atmosphere of peace and comfort and to lull the nervous warnings of the man's judgment into a sentimental mood. A glow of pink thrown over everything has a "cozy" effect. In such a soft illumination a girl's hair can appear "halo like," making her appear soft and tender. They tend to converse on subjects that harmonize with the effects — tend to become confidential and dream together. Drifting thus, how easy it is for the man to gently take her hand, and in sublime forgetfulness of all of the obstacles in the outside world, whisper to her the most lovely dream of all. And how unlikely it would have been without this encouraging atmosphere.

A COZY WINTER EVENING

The atmosphere can be even more suggestive of sentiment if it is winter and the wind is howling outside and sleet is dashing against the window. How cozy and comforting it is for the girl and the boy, sitting before an open fire with the lights dimmed, to sit and dream. The man may feel that he would like for this to continue forever. There cannot be obstacles, he feels, when life is easy and peaceful as this. How easy for him to succumb to his desire and forget his fears.

SPRING AND SUMMER

In the spring and summer equally romantic effects can be secured. Sitting on a porch or patio, in a lawn swing, or anyplace amid the beauties of nature are romantic places. If there is a moon, so much the better. The gentle breeze stirring the leaves in the trees, the distant whistle of a train, the bark of a remote but watchful dog, make the world with its problems seem far away.

WATER: LAKES, RIVERS, THE OCEAN

Even in broad daylight, the effect of water is often spellbinding, especially upon those who may live daily in a crowded city. Night, water and romance are inseparable. Have you ever noticed how young people are inclined to spend their vacations or holidays on or near water? There is a reason. Nothing is more soothing, more calculated to subdue fears and draw a man and woman close to each other than a night scene on the water, with the moon and stars shining on the ripples, the gentle lap of waves upon a beach or against a boat, and the mysterious blackness of a distant shore line. Many men have innocently taken a girl on a boating excursion at night and returned to find themselves engaged.

PARKS AND GARDENS

A stroll through some beautiful garden, or in the hills or mountains, or in the woods, can often superinduce the atmosphere desired. There is nothing like getting back to nature to encourage a man to follow nature's impulse to take a mate for himself.

A HOMEY ATMOSPHERE

Next to the peace and quiet of nature, the most encouraging atmosphere is the coziness and comfort of a home — an ideal home where there is a spirit of peace and an absence of quarreling, worry and tension that seem a part of the outside world. If the girl has such an ideal home she can use this to good advantage.

RESTAURANTS THAT ENCOURAGE ROMANCE

In every large city there seem to be two or three restaurants which seem to be especially designed to encourage romantic young couples. Such restaurants are secluded, lights are subdued, they are not crowded with too many people. If there is music it is quiet and romantic. With the peaceful atmosphere of such soothing surroundings and with a girl across the table whose eyes are more comforting and sympathetic even than the atmosphere, the man will be reluctant to leave and will dream of a home where every meal would be like this. It is a time for mutual confidences and sharing dreams, when you are drawn closer and closer together.

Restaurants to avoid are those that are crowded. A small one may be better than a large busy one. Avoid the dazzling white restaurants, the gay and glittering kind, and the casinos. These don't suggest coziness and contentment; their atmosphere discourages all thought of home and marriage.

A picnic lunch in the woods, in a private park or by a river can be just as comfortable and cozy as a restaurant. Give the man time enough to absorb the atmosphere and time enough to let it penetrate deeply. Never hurry through a picnic in the woods.

MOVIES, PLAYS, ETC.

If you are going to a movie and you are given the opportunity to choose, always avoid the horror type, the gay and wicked kind, sex movies, or the criminal kind. War movies are also out as far as romance is concerned, if they have an abundance of fighting and a minimum of romance in the story. These movies discourage the atmosphere you are seeking to create. Instead choose a romantic play or dramatic story that works upon the sympathies and emotions. Try to find out in advance the value of current movies, even if you have to see them yourself in advance.

If, when you are leaving a romantic movie, the man has a lump in his throat, if he has a feeling that life is a lovely and beautiful thing after all, if he feels that love and character and idealism and truth are the only things that really count, then he is likely to speak out the things that weigh on his heart and forget all about money matters and other problems that have been standing in his way. The objections are not among the things that count when he is in this frame of mind. His emotions have been so wrought upon, are in such a turmoil, that any impulse is without opposition. An emotional mood such as this is an impulsive mood. And if the impulse strikes him, there are not the paralyzing fears to halt it.

There are few such soul-stirring movies today. It may require quite a search to find an appropriate movie that stirs the emotions. If you cannot find one, it will be better to depend upon other romantic situations and skip the movies, unless of course they are his idea.

MAKING PLANS FOR YOURSELF

Still another way to make it easy for a man to speak out is to make plans for your life which do not include marriage for awhile. In this way he will feel that he can safely ask you to wait for him, since you will not be available for marriage, or so it appears. Let him know that your plans for the future cover a considerable period of time — a year or two at least — and that your heart is set upon carrying out those plans and the thought of marrying in the meantime has not yet occurred to you. Speak of what you hope to do next year, and the next, etc.; or how you are saving up your money for a certain wonderful trip which you hope to take; or how you hope to qualify for some special job which takes two or three years preparation, and how disappointed you will be if anything occurs to upset your plans. Under these circumstances, the man who has been hesitating because immediate marriage seems out of the question and it seems unfair to ask the girl to wait a considerable length of time, finds it easy to speak out.

These are not the only methods of making it easy for a man to speak out. The girl must remember that although we can suggest general principles, each man is an individual personality requiring individual study. She must observe him carefully until she understands his character enough to make a guess about what makes it hard in his individual case to speak up. When this has been done, she can then use her knowledge to guide her in deciding what is needed to make action easy for this particular man. She may come to the conclusion that an entirely new method, not mentioned here, should be used in bringing him to action.

When the man fails to respond to the first method of securing action, making it easy for him to speak out, he is by no means a hopeless case. She can then proceed to the second method of getting action — making it hard for him *not to act.*

METHOD No. 2   MAKING IT HARD NOT TO ACT

It should be understood throughout this chapter that there is no use trying any of the methods of stirring a man to action unless it is fairly certain that he is ripe for action, that he is hesitating because of inward doubts and outward obstacles. Getting action is the last of the six steps to winning men. To attempt to make it the second, or the third, etc., is futile. If the man fails to respond to these methods of getting action, the girl can usually take it for granted that he is not ready for action. She must then devote her thoughts to increasing his desire or getting the obstacles out of the way. In securing action by making it hard not to act, the following are suggestions.

THE APOLOGY METHOD

One method is a result of the man's committing some offense towards the girl, as often happens in true romance. Sometimes a man is harsh or brutally frank, which will send the girl into a spell of gloom that can be disheartening. If she will take this occasion to let him know that he has wounded her tender feelings (after he has cooled off, of course) she will invite an apology from him. When the man is brought to an apology for having offended a tender and feminine woman, he has a tendency to condemn himself and do everything possible to relieve her feelings. In his attempt to make her feel happy again, he is very apt to also confide in her his tender feelings for her. If a romantic setting further makes it easy for him to speak, then his thoughtlessness at having wounded her feelings will make it difficult to withhold his innermost feeling of love and tenderness for her. In other words, it makes it hard for him not to speak out, or to act. He must be maneuvered into a position where he feels like a "brute" and must make amends, that an ordinary apology will appear to be inadequate, and that an elaborate expansion of his feelings towards the girl is required. If the man has a desire for the girl, and if the obstacles have been temporarily minimized, such an apology usually leads into a declaration of love and a proposal.

The Rescue Method

Another method of making it hard not to act, is the "rescue" method or the "beauty in distress" method. This is the method used by so many novelists. The heroine is the center of some misfortune and trouble and the man is forced to come to her rescue. This situation, however, is not nearly so frequent in real life as it is in fiction. The nearest the average girl can come to it is by the method of being sad and disconsolate because of problems of the future which seem to her unsolvable. In rare circumstances, however, misfortune and trouble do come, such as the girl being pressed to marry someone she dislikes, or her family meets with financial disaster, or the girl loses her position or sees someone get the promotion on which she had depended, etc. In these cases, if the girl will tactfully let the man know of her distress, it is exceedingly hard for him to refrain from comforting her, from trying to make it easy for her, from heroically and chivalrously relieving her of her burdens and taking them upon himself. If he really desires the girl, then he is encouraged to ask her for the privilege and right to protect and care for her. The "beauty in distress" method is effective, but circumstances seldom justify the use of this method.

Method No. 3
Making Action Appear Urgent or Necessary
A Sudden Change of Location

There are times when a girl must leave the city or town in which she lives and choose another location. This is a natural for securing action. If, through the circumstances of her life, she does not leave, the girl is sometimes justified to arrange a change of location with the sole reason of awakening the man to action. When a man has a genuine affection for the girl, the prospects of her going where he cannot watch over her is so appalling that it will usually stir him to action. If the girl will devulge the news of her approaching departure in a romantic setting, she can make it appear that if the man is ever going to speak out, or act, now is the time. The following is an illustration of such a situation.

THE STORY OF MARY AND ROBERT

A girl called Mary had just graduated from college. During the last year, however, a struggling young attorney named Robert had been paying marked attention to her and had given indications of genuine affection. Knowing that he was dissatisfied with his present earnings, Mary had used the "castle in the air" method extensively in the hope of increasing his self-confidence to the point where he would not hesitate to ask her to wait for him. But Robert seeemed to believe that it would be time enough to speak when his practice picked up. He had hopes that in a year or two he could take the important step of marriage.

Mary was living right in the city he was in and he could speak with her about the future later as well as now; and in a year from now he would be able to speak with more definiteness and would have something more worthwhile to offer her. But Mary did not know this at all. Though she knew Robert was deeply interested in her, she was by no means sure whether he desired or ever would desire to marry her. Mary was twenty-two and she had but a few years of youth left ahead. She had already lost a year by letting Robert have near-monopoly of her social life. If Robert ever wanted to marry her she wanted to know it and she wanted to know it now.

Robert knew that Mary, now that she was graduated, intended to take up the teaching profession. It has not occurred to him, however, that she may teach anywhere but in their home city. Mary decides that if she prepares to leave the city to teach, Robert, if he really cares for her, might be forced to speak out in order to prevent her leaving. Now Mary can, if she wishes, teach in the schools in her home town, but she gives Robert to understand that she can't bear to teach under the supervision of the town's disagreeable superintendent of schools. She is so determined to bring matters to a head that she is even willing, if necessary, to take a position in another city.

She waits for an opportune moment to bring on the crisis. After letting slip a few meetings when either the setting is not romantic, or Robert himself is not in the right mood, she finds just the situation and setting that is right for her purpose. They have spent an afternoon canoeing on the river and are now gently drifting down the stream towards home. Mary gently turns the conversation to Robert, who tells her for the hundredth time what his hopes and ambitions are, what victories he expects to win, what honors to achieve. Now is the time, she thinks.

She tells Robert that she wishes some advice. She has two offers for her services as a teacher and doesn't know which to take. One is from Eldorado, three hundred miles away, and the other from Mt. Pleasant, even farther. She outlines the details of the two offers. Robert, stunned at the thought, wants to know why she can't teach right here at home. She tells him her reason and refuses to listen to his protestations. She has no choice except to take one of the two offers.

Robert is naturally aroused at this prospect of Mary's leaving him. Mary sighs and admits she will be very lonesome, that she will feel almost an exile. Robert protests vigorously at her leaving the city, but cannot sway her conviction that there is no choice for her except between the two offers. She finally pouts that he is only making it harder for her to decide and begs him to help her to determine which is the better offer.

The longer he considers, the more appalling the prospect of her leaving becomes. He had always felt that Mary was sort of a fixture, that she would always be there waiting for him, that there was plenty of time in the future for Mary and him to reach an understanding. What if she should go to one of these cities and meet there some other man who would interest her? What if, without the guidance of her old time friends, it should be a man who wasn't trustworthy? She shouldn't be allowed to go away alone, not if he could help it. Nobody knows little Mary like he does — her tenderness and frailty and the ease with which she could be deceived. A girl like that ought not to be allowed to go around without a man's protection.

Unaware that Robert is seething with these disturbing thoughts, Mary persists in asking him for his opinion as to the best offer. Robert cannot bring himself to tell her the one or the other. There is nothing for him to do but to tell her the truth. "You're not going to take either of those offers," he says. "I won't stand for it. I hope to make you my wife one of these days and I want you right here where I can take care of you.

I can't stand the idea of your going away with no one to take care of you." Urgent necessity made him speak out.

CHANGE OF JOBS

Another example is a girl in an office who had received considerable attention from her employer. She came to him with an explanation that she had received a very tempting offer from another firm for her services and asked his advice regarding the acceptance of it. The man wanted to know if there was anything wrong with his treatment of her, or in the attitude of other employees towards her. Hinting that she was not free to tell him her reasons for leaving, the man was ill at ease, thinking that he had offended her in some way himself.

The girl showed a certain amount of persistence in her idea of leaving, which caused the man to find it difficult to let her go and very hard not to tell her about his desire for her to be more than an employee to him. He began to feel that the time to speak was then or never. Since he really loved the girl and was only hesitating because of an imagined obstacle, this situation made him speak out.

THE COMPETITION OF ANOTHER MAN

A last-resort method of awakening a man to action is to accept the attentions of another man. This step is wholly justified when there seems to be no other way of bringing a man to speak up. If she finds that the man particularly dislikes one of her acquaintances, that particular acquaintance is just the one in whom she should encourage an interest if she desires to stir a man to action. He may consider the intruder unworthy of the attentions of the girl, or may think she is in actual danger when associating with this acquaintance. He at least is certain that her association with him is entirely wrong. It is highly necessary, therefore, for him to do something about it, but he cannot very well do anything without first explaining to the girl that he has a right to interfere because of his desire to have her for his own. Therefore, one of the easiest methods of making it appear urgent for the man to take action is to accept the interests of another man, especially a man who is detestable to the man you are interested in. This method can force a man to speak out before he feels prepared. Men, however, are seldom wholly prepared for a proposal.

The Passions of Sex

The strongest force in life that will bring a man to action and cause him to take the step of marriage is that of having his sex passions aroused. Do not, then, make the mistake of sacrificing this tool for action by indulging in sexual relations. In other words, if the man can be relieved of his sex passions without marriage, he has also been relieved of his drive for marriage, or his urgency to marry. Every woman should most carefully consider this aspect of moral standards. From every aspect, however, indulging in sex before marriage is foolish, and the woman is always the greatest loser.

We have now given a sufficient number of examples which point out general principles involved in securing action. Any girl with a thorough understanding of these principles can adapt them to her own circumstances and her own particular man. By some method, either by those suggested here or by some other of her own devising, she must make it easy for him to act. If this is not sufficient, she must study out some way that will make it hard for him to not act, or she must place herself in such a light that action appears both urgent and necessary.

General Conclusions

We have now completed our discussions of the six stages of winning a man. We have begun with being a girl worth having — a product of Angela Human — have seen how attention is secured, how interest is aroused, how desire is created, how judgment is satisfied and how action is inspired.

Now, it is sometimes possible for a girl to win a man in marriage by merely attracting his attention and interest, in rather a superficial way. This was the case with Dora in *David Copperfield*. But, although an adorable girl such as Dora may thus win a man in marriage, she will not win his celestial love unless she is a girl worth having and is indispensable to his happiness. *We are not winning men to marriage alone, but to enduring and celestial love.*

The steps taught here will lead you to the goal of romantic love as well as marriage. To be sure, we have had space only for the underlying principles. It remains for you to apply these principles to your own circumstances and your own society. The mere reading of this book will not make you an expert in the art of winning men. Many people who understand thoroughly how the orator wins his audience cannot win audiences themselves; many people who know every aspect of salesmanship cannot sell an item worth fifty cents; many critics who are authorities on the novel cannot write one themselves. Similarly with women. Knowledge, helpful as it is, cannot take the place of practical experience. It must be put into practice. Since you will never find yourself in exactly the same circumstances as the young ladies in this book, you must learn to practice applying the same principles to other circumstances.

Remember too that the proper application of these principles requires a keen understanding of the characteristics of men. Every man has, in addition to common characteristics, some that are peculiar to him. To become an expert at the art of attracting men, a girl must practice the principles and stratagems upon as many men as possible, so that she may be familiar with the various characteristics which differ in each man. After observing the different reactions of different men to the same situation, she will acquire a subtler and more profound understanding of the men's human nature.

Don't Marry Too Young

Do not hasten into marriage before you are of age. There are many heartaches for those who take this step before they are adequately prepared to handle the responsibility. Take time to grow both mentally and emotionally and have a wide social experience with many boys and girls. It will help prepare for the years ahead and will give you greater wisdom in selecting a proper mate. There is nothing like "years" to help prepare a person for marriage. Wonderful as it is, marriage is for adults and not for children.

If your parents are not wise enough to caution you of this, then do it yourself. Determine that you will not become serious with a boy until you reach an age when you feel fully prepared for marriage. The proper age is almost impossible to state, since our maturity and experience vary so widely. Most girls of twenty-two are well prepared for marriage, at least emotionally. When a girl is under nineteen it is risky indeed. Marriage is a strain on her, and the responsibilities staggering, especially when children come. Learn about these facts of the life ahead, discuss it with others, and although we do not wish to discourage you from the true joys and completeness of marriage, we must at least help you to face it realistically. When a girl is mature it is an entirely different matter. She is ready and anxious to assume domestic responsibility, is prepared for problems ahead and has the capacity to face problems in good spirit. She has had her "fill of the joys of youth" and is now ready for the next stage — "the joys of a beautiful life with the man she loves."

The best way to avoid the temptation to marry young is to observe the following rules. First, before the age of sixteen date only double, or in groups. After sixteen date singly, but do not become affectionate. In this way you will be able to control passions until you become of age to become serious. During the time between sixteen and the age of marriage (about twenty-one) have your richest social life. Enjoy wonderful firendships with many boys and girls, but keep aloof from any serious romance. In this way you will determine the success of your future. Keep these thoughts in mind. They are for your benefit and yours alone. No one but you will suffer from a foolish mistake, and you alone will be rewarded for sound judgment in planning your life.

ANGELA HUMAN

The Ideal Woman
From a Man's Point of View

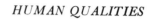

ANGELIC QUALITIES	HUMAN QUALITIES

ANGELIC QUALITIES

1. Understands Men
   Acceptance
   Admiration
   Sensitive pride
   Reserve
   Sympathetic understanding
   Desire to be superior in his
      role as man

2. Has Inner Happiness
   Happiness comes from:
      Understanding men
      Good character
      Domestic skills
      Accepting ourselves
      Ability to appreciate life

3. Has a Worthy Character
   Self mastery
   Unselfishness
   Love
   Chastity
   Honesty
   Humility
   Moral courage
   Forgiveness
   Self-dignity
   Gentle, tender quality

4. Is a Domestic Goddess
   Does job well
   Adds feminine touches
   Enjoys homemaking

HUMAN QUALITIES

1. Femininity
   In appearance
   In feminine manner
      Hands, walk, voice, laugh
      Cooing quality
      Conversation
      Refinement
      Timorousness
      Bewitching languor
   Feminine Dependency
      Need his masculine care
      Don't excel him
      Be submissive
      Be fearful

2. Radiates Happiness
      Smile, eyes
      Cheerful attitude, Demure

3. Good Health
      Correct internal disorders
      Get enough sleep
      Exercise
      Drink plenty of water
      Get fresh air
      Eat properly
      Relax at work or play
      Healthy mental attitude
      Control weight

4. Childlikeness
      Sauciness
      Teasing playfulness
      Tender emotions
      Childlike joy
      Outspokenness
      Asking for things
      Manner
      Girlish trust
      Appearance

Together He Cherishes

BOTH ARE ESENTIAL
TO HIS CELESTIAL LOVE

The Angelic arouses in man a feeling approaching worship. It brings him peace and happiness.

The Human fascinates, captivates, amuses, enchants and arouses a desire to protect and shelter.

THE SIX STAGES OF WINNING A MAN

First Stage: BE A GIRL WORTH HAVING
    How: Acquire all of the qualities of Angela Human

Second Stage: WIN HIS ATTENTION
    How: 1. By a feminine and girlish appearance
         2. By a feminine manner
         3. By feminine dependency

Third Stage: AROUSING ATTENTION
    How: 1. Get him to confide
         2. Admire the manly

Fourth Stage: CREATING DESIRE
    How: 1. Prove you are a girl worth having (by being Angela Human)
         2. Become indispensable to his happiness (applying all of Understanding Men)

Fifth Stage: OVERCOME JUDGMENT (removing obstacles)
    How: 1. By building castles in the air
         2. Other miscellaneous methods

Sixth Stage: SECURING ACTION
    How: 1. Making it easy for him to act
         2. Making it hard not to act
         3. Making action appear urgent or necessary

Remember to "aim high" — aim to be Angela Human. Don't be content to sit on the sidelines and let all of the other girls succeed in winning the desirable men. You can just as well be enjoying the "flowers of life" rather than the "weeds." You can "eat the banquet" instead of the "crumbs which fall beneath the table." Through study and effort you can become a fascinating woman, as fascinating and sought after by men as any of God's other womanly creatures.

      Life is a piece of paper, white
      On which each one of us must write
         his word or two, and then comes night.
      Greatly begin, though thou hast time
         but for a line, be that sublime
      Not failure, but low aim is crime.

ANGELIC AND THE HUMAN
DON'T

Don't try to change a man.

Don't offer suggestions, hints, etc., about how he needs to improve.

Don't use other men as shining examples.

Don't show indifference, contempt or ridicule towards his masculine abilities, achievements or ideas.

Don't try to solve his problems, but give him the courage to do so.

Don't try to excel him in anything which requires masculine strength, skill or ability.

Don't tell men what to do or where to go, or give pushy advice or suggestions.

Don't plan a career for yourself which will interfere with your success as a wonderful wife, mother and homemaker.

Avoid concentrating on material things as a means to happiness.

Don't criticize yourself for common mistakes and human errors.

Don't fall from your pedestal by lowering your standards or by being harsh or critical, etc.

Don't appear to be overly domestic, like the wholesome farm girl.

Don't appear to be too anxious to settle down to domestic life, lest you appear to be manhunting or seeking an escape or easy road.

Don't wear masculine styles, materials, accessories.

Don't act, look or think like men.

Don't use harsh, crude or vulgar words or actions.

Don't be loud or boisterous.

Don't disregard another person's "way of life."

Don't be aggressive or dominating.

Don't be capable, efficient, or competent in masculine jobs or responsibilities.

Don't "kill your own snakes."

Don't boss men around, tell them what to do, where to go, etc.

Don't be competitive with men in their own fields.

Don't excel men in anything which requires masculine strength, skill or ability.

Don't plan a career.for yourself which will make you independent.

Don't be gloomy or overly serious.

Don't wear drab clothing or fail to wear makeup, making you appear unhealthy.

Don't suppress wounded feelings.

Don't be unemotional.

Don't let men impose on you, treat you unfairly, ignore you or insult you too far.

Don't suppress the tendency to cry in sad movies or situations, or when your feelings are hurt.

Don't wear matronly styles.

Don't "beat around the bush," be evasive, or make endless explanations to men.

If you want something, don't, hint, try to convince, or demand.

Don't be a wallflower.

Don't sit at home where men cannot find you.

Do not indulge in affection during the early stages of romance.

Don't take a friendship with a man too seriously.

Don't show your feeling of love to him.

Don't show your feelings of love to others.

Don't appear to like him more than he likes you.

Don't be aggressive in romance, don't hint to be kissed, take his hand, squeeze close to him, ask him for a date, ask to marry him.

Don't indulge in sexual relations before marriage.

Don't be impatient if a man is slow to make up his mind about you.

ANGELIC AND THE HUMAN
DO

Accept him at face value.

Allow him to be himself and do the things he wants to do.

Admire the manly things about him.

Understand his masculine responsibilities and his drive for status.

Recognize his superior strength and ability in masculine things.

Need his masculine care and protection.

Respect the man's position as the leader; be a good follower.

Have a girlish trust in him, in his ability to solve problems and meet emergencies.

Accept yourself and allow for frequent mistakes.

Enjoy the simple pleasures in life.

Take a good look at your character.

Develop a character worthy of a pedestal.

Let your light shine before men.

Learn to be a Domestic Goddess:
    Enjoy homemaking.
    Do it well.
    Add feminine touches.
    Be well organized.
    Learn to handle money wisely.
    Let good homemaking become second nature to you.

Wear feminine clothes, styles and materials which make you look gentle and tender.

Wear clothes that are modest and cover underwear.

Accentuate the differences between yourself and men in your appearance, manner and actions.

Be refined, tactful, diplomatic, considerate, polite and socially well bred.

Need a man's care and protection.

If you are "stuck" with a masculine job, do it in a feminine manner.

Be dependent upon men for their care and protection.

Have the "sweet promise" somewhere in your character.

Be submissive and yield to the man's suggestions (except with your own standards and ideals — in these be firm and do not yield).

Radiate happiness and shed joy around.

Strive for abundant health.

Maintain a proper weight.

When men are thoughtless and unkind, respond with sauciness.

When a man is stern, cross, or overly serious, respond with teasing playfulness.

When a man gives you a gift or does something nice for you, respond with childlike joy.

Let men spoil you and do things for you.

Be direct and outspoken (not blunt).

If you want something, "ask for it" in a girlish manner.

Avoid situations which destroy confidence.

Overcome any tendency to an inferiority complex.

Learn to be a good conversationalist.

As often as possible attend social affairs where men are present.

Learn to be a good hostess.

Encourage a large circle of friends — girls, boys, old people and children.

In choosing a mate, look for traits of character, masculinity, and tenderness.

Avoid inferior men.

Let the man lead in romance and you follow.

Keep him guessing.

If a man is slow to make up his mind about you, create romantic situations.

If a man will not make up is mind about you, even after great patience, bring him to action by the methods taught.

NOTES